D1694333

MAKING THE HEAVENS SPEAK

Peter Sloterdijk

Making the Heavens Speak

Religion as Poetry

Translated by Robert Hughes

polity

Originally published in German as *Den Himmel zum Sprechen bringen. Über Theopoesie*
© Suhrkamp Verlag Berlin 2020.
All rights reserved by and controlled through Suhrkamp Verlag Berlin.

This English edition © Polity Press, 2023

The translation of this work was supported by a grant from the Goethe-Institut.

Polity Press
65 Bridge Street
Cambridge CB2 1UR, UK

Polity Press
111 River Street
Hoboken, NJ 07030, USA

ISBN-13: 978-1-5095-4749-4 (hardback)
ISBN-13: 978-1-5095-4750-0 (paperback)

A catalogue record for this book is available from the British Library.

Library of Congress Control Number: 2022937905

Typeset in 10.5 on 12pt Times
by Fakenham Prepress Solutions, Fakenham, Norfolk NR21 8NL
Printed and bound in the UK by TJ Books Limited

For further information on Polity, visit our website:
politybooks.com

In memory of Raimund Fellinger

Contents

Acknowledgments

The first part of this book is based on a lecture I gave on May 5, 2019, at the invitation of the Institut für soziale Gegenwartsfragen in Freiburg, as part of a lecture series entitled "After God: Lectures on Religion after its Disenchantment" at Theater Freiburg (in cooperation with Radio SWR2). I would like to thank the organizers, and Christian Matthiessen in particular, for making this opportunity possible.

When Jan Assmann celebrated his eightieth birthday in July 2018, I was invited to contribute an article to a Festschrift devoted to him in a journal of Egyptology. What I had in mind was a short essay on the subject of "theopoetry," but, since I did not finish this task on time, I promised the jubilee that I would dedicate the finished piece to him when it finally became available. The piece has now become rather longer than initially conceived and the delay has been considerable; nonetheless, my wish to dedicate this writing to him persists. However belatedly, I take the liberty here of offering it to the great scholar as a gesture beyond the occasion of the anniversary of his birth.

This context calls to mind Goethe's well-known declaration in his letter to Schiller on December 19, 1798: "As for the rest, I hate everything that merely instructs me without increasing or indirectly rousing my activity."[1] As a long-time reader of Jan Assmann's work, I can attest to its power for direct instruction – accompanied, as always, by the joy of understanding – as well as to its power for indirect stimulation, manifest in long-term effects – not least in keeping open the "Egyptian question."

The association between instruction and stimulation necessarily also calls to mind the grand master in studies of late classical and medieval philosophy, Kurt Flasch. For four decades, his work has given me ever-renewed inspiration for thought, from his work on Augustine up through his enormous new Dante translation and its lavish commentary. As a faithful reader, I owe the author more than the endnotes in this book can say, so I would like to extend my special gratitude to him here as well.

Preface

Since the title of this book might give an ambiguous impression, let me declare from the outset that what follows will treat neither the heavens of the astrologers, nor those of the astronomers, nor yet those of the astronauts. As we will find, the heavens that can be made to speak are not a possible object of visual perception. And yet, from the most ancient times, figurative ideas, attended by vocal phenomena, have imposed themselves upon the heavenward gaze: the tent buzzes with the voices of everyday life, the cave walls echo with the old magic chants, the vaulted dome resounds with cantilenas in honor of the Lord on high.

The whole of the heavens, through day and through night, has always given rise to archaic conceptions of the all-embracing. In this one figure, the monstrous, the open, and the vast could all be thought together with the protective and the domestic in a symbol of cosmic and moral integrity. On the Greenfield Papyrus (950–930 BCE), the image of Nut, the Egyptian goddess of the heavens, makes a forward-facing bridge arching over the earth. Down from antiquity, her image offers the most beautiful emblem of the protection offered by the all-encompassing. Through the figure of her likeness, the heavens are likewise present on the inside of coffins. Any of the dead, upon opening their eyes inside the coffin, would see the image of the goddess there and would thus be attended into a soothing openness.

When, in the course of secularization, the heavens lost their significance as a cosmic symbol of security, they came instead to embody cosmic caprice, in the face of which human plans and purposes must fall into eclipse. Thereafter, the silence of infinite space comes to evoke a metaphysical horror in thinkers who hearken to the void. In his verse epic, *Germany: A Winter's Tale* (1844), Heinrich Heine painted this tendency with a coat of mild irony when, with his little harp girl singing her heavenly lullaby and the old "song of renunciation," he resolved to leave heaven to the angels and birds.[1] A contrasting image is offered by "The Pot Lid," from the third edition of *The Flowers of Evil* (1868), in which Charles Baudelaire introduced a neo-Gnostic prisoner's panic in describing the heavens as the "black lid of the enormous pot where vast, amorphous Mankind boils and seethes."[2]

Given the opposed diagnoses offered by these two poets, we might consider opinions from third parties. The discussion that follows in this book will concern primarily communicative, bright heavens inviting uplift, because, in accord with the task of poetic enlightenment, the heavens constitute the common provenance of gods, verse, and the uplifting of spirits.

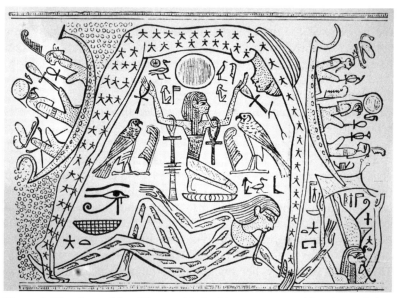

Figure 1. The sky goddess Nut, studded with stars, overarching the reclining earth god Geb and the kneeling air god Shu. An Egyptian representation of the heavens and earth, from an uncredited illustration after ancient Egyptian papyrus, in: *The Popular Science Monthly* 10 (March 1877): 546. Photo: World History Archive / Alamy Stock Photo.

I

DEUS EX MACHINA, DEUS EX CATHEDRA

Jesus told the crowds all these things in parables; without a parable he told them nothing.

Matthew 13:34

1

THE GODS IN THE THEATRE

The association between poetry and notions of the world of the gods is as old as the earliest European tradition – indeed, one finds it among the oldest written sources in civilizations the whole world over. Those who remember the eternal waves in Homer's verse will likewise recall how the poet consulted the Olympian gods with regard to the fate of the fighters on the plains before Troy. Without standing on ceremony, the poet has his heavenly ones speak – and not always with the *gravitas* one might expect from beings of such exalted rank.

Elsewhere, at the beginning of the *Odyssey*, Zeus takes the floor to deplore a wayward declaration from his daughter Athena. He strikes a majestic tone as he takes her to task: "My child, what sort of word escaped your teeth's barrier?"[1] Even the first among the dwellers of Mount Olympus cannot simply order the goddess of wisdom to be quiet. To express his displeasure, the father of the gods is driven to some rhetorical effort – to the deployment, even, of poetic formulas.

Might we claim that it was Homer, the poet, who begot the poetic gods? However one might take up such an indelicate question, it must be said that, as poets, Homer's gods would have composed only in the mode of amateurs, inasmuch as poetry is a métier requiring study – notwithstanding the common prattle one hears about one or another miracle of unskilled inspiration. Insistence upon the amateur position bears witness to Olympian aristocracy and underscores the point: no power in the world could compel a power-wielding god to learn any trade to the level of mastery.

Gods of the ancient Olympian type mostly comport themselves toward the world in the mode of detached spectators. They wade into earthly affairs no further than away-fans are wont to do; during wars, they sit in their boxes like visiting spectators backing their favorites. Entanglements are not their thing. They are like magicians, equally good at appearing and disappearing in a flash. Even if they are no longer mere embodiments of diffuse natural forces, meteorological phenomena, and the driving forces of botanical and animal fertility, even when they help to personify more abstract ethical, cognitive, and political principles, still the gods retain this lightweight character – as if the Olympian gods were something like a society of oligarchs, winking and nodding at each other as the fragrance of sacrificial fires rises to their senses.

Their choice of residence betrays them as creatures of antigravity. They have forgotten the existence, the abidance in the field of gravity, which afflicted their forebears among the generation of titanic gods. The amorphous power titans were destined to sink into darkness as the well-formed Olympian gods gained their ascendancy – excepting the mobility-impaired god Hephaestus, who never quite became socially acceptable as a blacksmith and a limping workshop rat. Since the fall of their predecessors, the gods of the second generation – the Olympian gang – have been troubled by the presentiment that the vanquished titans could eventually return. Gods at this level know that all victories are merely provisional. If the gods had an unconscious, it would bear an inscription: We are spirits of the dead who have come a long way – we owe our ascendancy to a nameless vital impulse, and nothing excludes the possibility that one day it will show us to the door.[2]

One aspect here is especially important for what follows – namely, that Homer's gods were gods who spoke. They were, as Aristotle said of human beings, living beings who "have language." And it was through poetry that they were brought within range of human hearing, even if this perhaps mostly consisted in conversations among immortals overheard by chance – as if the horses were listening in as spectators placed their bets before the race.

In the centuries after Homer, the phenomenon of speaking gods comes to be incorporated into the culture of Greek theatre. The Athenian stage set its storylines in motion before the assembled citizenry and, through the general intelligibility of the action, thereby contributed to the emotional synchronization of the public life of the city. Democracy began as affective populism, and from the outset it made use of the communicable effects of emotion. As Aristotle would later sum it up, the audience in the theatre felt "pity and fear," *éleos* and *phóbos* – or, better, a lament and a shudder, often together in the same passage of the tragedy. The emotional agitation portrayed by the actors was lived through in unison by most of the patrons, men and women alike, and they purged themselves of their tensions through an almost detached sympathy with the sufferings of the torn or dismembered figure on the stage. The Greeks had a specific verb for this effect – *synhomoiopathein*: simultaneously feeling the same suffering.[3] Likewise in the comedies that followed the tragedies: the people laughed together, as a rule, and in the same places. The decisive factor for the edifying effect of the drama was that, when contemplating the twists and turns of fate on the stage, it was precisely *together* that people arrived at the limit where one ceased to ask further questions. The veiled, the suprasensible – the numinous, one might say – filled the scene in the real present. As this effect rarely occurred and perished with the mediocre pieces of the post-classical period, the Athenian public eventually lost its interest; by the fourth century BCE, audience members who sacrificed a day for exhausted performances on the Dionysian stage were compensated with a theatre coin, an obol.

In this context, one ingenious invention of Attic theatrical art calls for discussion in greater detail. The dramaturges (the "event makers") – still largely identical with the poets – had understood that conflicts between people fighting over irreconcilables tend to come to a dead end. Because human means were powerless to resolve such moments, they were exploited by ancient theatre as pretexts for the introduction of a divine figure. But because a god could not simply appear from the wings like any old messenger, it was necessary to devise a method for making the god soar in from above. For this purpose, Athenian theatre-engineers built a machine that made it possible for gods to appear from out of the heavens. *Apò mekhanês theós*: a crane swiveled over the scene, to the boom of which was attached a platform or lectern – and, from there, the god could address the human scene below. The Athenians called this device a *theologeion*.

Those who performed on this astounding crane were, of course, not priests educated in theology – there were no such persons as of yet, and the very term had not been coined. Instead, they were actors performing behind sublime masks, and they portrayed the god or goddess as an awe-inspiring, problem-solving authority. Obviously, the dramaturges were not afraid to become "theurgically" active – they saw gods as effects that might be contrived, much as some practical Kabbalists were later convinced that they could perform theotechnical procedures by reproducing the Creator's own devisings with letters. Other Hellenic venues were content with arranging the *theologeion* as a kind of gallery, or as an elevated balcony on the rear wall of the theatre – though this, of course, would oblige them to forgo the fascinating effect of the gods' hovering entrance.

The most powerful stage epiphany comes to pass, toward the end of Aeschylus' *Eumenides* (performed 458 BCE in Athens), when the goddess Athena enters to intervene in the affair of Orestes the matricide, breaking a stalemate between the party of vengeance and the party of conciliation and supplying a congenial alternative, whereby the avenging "Furies" (the Erinyes) transform themselves into "the gracious ones" (the Eumenides). Something quite similar is staged in Sophocles' *Philoctetes* (performed 409 BCE), when the divine Heracles floats in to change the mind of the Greeks' obstinate enemy, the title character who up to that moment has persisted with his grief and bitterness, but who now finally surrenders the bow necessary for a Hellene victory in the Trojan War.

A *theologeion* is not an orator's lectern, nor a sermon pulpit, but rather a device specific to the theatre. It represents a trivial "machine" in the original sense of the word – a special effect, a trick of scenography, devised to capture the attention of the audience. Functionally, however, it is decidedly non-trivial: it shifts a god or goddess from a state of invisibility into one of visibility. Moreover, one not only sees the god or goddess hovering above the scene, one hears the deity speak and issue instructions. There is no doubt that this is mere "theatre," but that initial theatre would never have existed without the assumption that all the actors and characters, mortal and immortal, could be represented as real for the duration of the play. If the gods do not appear on their own, their advent will have to be arranged. The later Latin term *deus ex machina* deals with effects of this type and, considered in its technical dramatic sense, means simply this: only a figure who intervenes from the outside can supply the extricating slip from a hopelessly knotted conflict. That the god or goddess appears *coram publico*, in full view of the public, at the pivotal point of the action, is at first nothing more than a dramaturgical requirement; however, this appearance also signifies a moral postulate – indeed, something like a sacred task of the theatre. One might call it the "dramaturgical proof of God": to disentangle the knots of the conflict requires a divine figure, hence the god or goddess exists. It would be irreverent – but not entirely wrong – to describe them as "happy-ending providers." Indeed, the solutions we long for, in whatever the sphere, can often only be achieved with the help of higher powers, even if only by way of the good fortune of enjoying clear presence of mind. In this way, "solutions" become noteworthy as heavenly services[4] long before they come to our attention as answers to mathematical functions and business problems. Let us add the observation that a great number of eighteenth-century opera libretti would, in their aversion to tragedy, have been inconceivable without a god or goddess issuing from the *machina*.

Given this context of Greek theodramatic art, one might ask whether the more theologically elaborated "religions" had some kind of equivalent to the theatre crane or the balcony for the presentation of their own divine figures. For present purposes, we must content ourselves with the unhappy term "religion," despite it being overloaded with confusion, speculation, and imputations – especially in the years since Tertullian, with his *Apologeticum* (197 CE), inverted the expressions *superstitio* and *religio* against common Roman usage: he calls superstition the traditional *religio* of the Romans, while Christianity, he asserts, should be called "the true religion of the true God." With this, he gave Augustine the template for his epoch-making treatise *Of True Religion* (*De vera religione*, 391 CE), in which the Roman concept was definitively appropriated for Christianity. Since then, it has come to stand for all those suggestions of shadowy things and twilit matters that darken the daylight of understanding[5] – although, we might also observe that, in order to save the concept of religion,[6] much effort has also been devoted to the task of demonstrating the possible congruence of rationality and revelation. Certainly, the *theologeion* in the narrower sense of the word was devised only once – and only once so named. In a broader sense and under other names, however, devices that produce an appearance of the higher gods and make them speak are, if not ubiquitous, still discernible across a range of phenomena.

What was dramaturgically negotiated on the Attic stage, almost as if it were a surrogate on behalf of all human cultures, was nothing less than the question of whether spectators of ritual dramatic action must be content with theotechnical effects, or whether ultimately the gods themselves might manifest their presence from behind the magic of the drama. From time immemorial, shamans, priests, and theatre people have shared the sense that profounder emotion lies within the realm of the practicable. Setting aside those who succumb to the latent cynicism of their professions, these shamans, priests, and theatre people believed that whatever was deeply moving, as such, might gain an even greater intensity of presence in the course of the sacral operation. As in any "profound play," ritual acts hold forth the possibility that what is represented might awaken to life within the very thing representing it. The gods may indeed be "near and difficult to grasp,"[7] as the poet says, but such nebulousness does not preclude the seriousness of our devotion and our immersion in their atmospheric presence.[8]

Counterparts to the Hellenic stage machinery emerge when gods of varied provenance, including those of monotheistic constitution and those of powerfully exalted character, begin to comply with their obligation to make appearances – when they answer to one or another summons and deign to render themselves perceptible to human senses. In principle, the gods could have remained almost completely hidden, since their essence is latent and transcendent and escapes mundane perception. It is not without reason that the gods are referred to as the Unseen. The subterranean gods in particular were deeply reticent to reveal themselves, even if the coming of every spring brought forth a display of their power. This was re-enacted with cultic amplification among the Mediterranean peoples – for example in the Athenian phallophoria, the springtime phallic processions of the cult of Dionysus, in which the matrons of the city would carry huge phalli, sewn from red leather, and parade about in an atmosphere of adoring mockery.

For denizens of the great Beyond in ancient times, "making appearances" would have been a secondary activity at most. Epicurus hit the point when he remarked that the gods are too blessed to much interest themselves in human affairs. For his part, his predecessor Thales of Miletus is said to have held that "All things are full of gods" – though this could mean very different things: either that, of the hundreds of Greek deities, there was always one on duty at the threshold of the human world, like a heavenly on-call clinician, or else that we are always and everywhere surrounded by divinities, except that our everyday insensibility fails to mark their presence. Homer notes in passing that the gods loved to take part in human feasts and to meet lonely wanderers without being recognized[9] – or, as it may be, allowing themselves to be recognized only after the fact from their enigmatic aura.

From epiphanic episodes, however one might interpret them, there arose, over time, cultic obligations. Once the cults arrived at some state of stability, the gods were fitted into an ecosystem of evidence that circumscribed the space for their appearances. The gods are vaguenesses that are assigned their specificity by a cult. In ancient times, they were summoned (if not compelled) to "appear" almost anywhere, but they were invited especially to make their appearances in places established for this very purpose, spaces suitable for epiphanies and designated as temples (Latin: *templum*, a place cut out and reserved), and on fixed occasions called "festivals." They fulfilled their roles of appearance and revelation through the mediation of human oracles, by way of gnomic utterances and ambiguous prophecies, or through messages in scripture wreathed in an aura of holiness. Some were willing to appear in lucid dreams, in sleep temples, or on the eve of important decisions.

Their preferred disposition was the same patience bordering on indifference with which they endured the appeals made to them by mortals. One could pray to them, shame them with great sacrifices, denounce them, accuse them of injustice, question their wisdom, even swear and curse at them without risking immediate response.[10] The gods could afford to behave as if they weren't there. Thus, the crowded heavens drifted through the ages in a spirit of forbearance.

In the end, however, the gods found they could not refuse the call to appear in the form of personal embodiment: not infrequently, they felt themselves free to take possession of a host body that they might then use and abandon as they pleased – or else, "in the fullness of time," they might desublimate into a redeeming Son of man, a Messiah. The spiritual elite among the Jews became more receptive to messianic messages in 539 BCE, after Cyrus the Great, the king of Persia famous for his religious tolerance, allowed them to return to Zion after almost 60 years of captivity in Babylon. Deutero-Isaiah set the tone for this. Messianic ideas emerged from eulogies for Cyrus, the instrument of God, and remained powerful for two and a half thousand years. What Adolf von Harnack wrote about the Gospel of Marcion, announcing the doctrine of an unknown god, proves true for an entire age of the world: "*Religion is redemption* – the indicator of the history of religion in the first and second centuries points to this position; no longer can any be a god who is not also a savior."[11] The epithet "Redeemer" or "Savior" (*soter*) had already been applied to Ptolemy I Soter, who rose to rule Egypt after the death of Alexander the Great and who inaugurated the cult of the "redeeming gods." His son, Ptolemy II Philadelphus, bore the Golden Horus name to which a pharaoh was entitled: "He whose father made him appear."

Gods who made an appearance gave their clients just as much to see and hear, and occasionally to read, as seemed necessary for their loyalty, guidance, and instruction – so generally enough to uphold the "plausibility structure"[12] and, for a community informed and given shape by ritual, to thereby secure adherence to their cultic ideas (in the classical period: *hoi patrioi nomoi, mos maiorum*, respecting ancestral custom; in the Christian period: *fides*, "faithfulness in holding fast to that which holds"). Here, plausibility means the theory-free acceptance of conventionality, including those conventions that relate to otherworldly things.

The invention of the *theologeion* by the Greeks (and the mechanical device that made it possible) thus made explicit an awkward situation that all higher religioid entities had to contend with. It clarified the task of bringing into the human lifeworld some visible manifestation of the hereafter, the higher plane, the beyond – or however one wishes to refer to the space inhabited by vague powers and suspended over the world of human experience. The earliest stage of evidence from sensible–supersensible sources was manifest by the way that participants' affect was aroused from a theatrical "play," a ceremonial rite, a fascinating blood sacrifice. In order to produce such effects, early cultures made frequent recourse to mediumistic procedures and mantic practices – either of which gave great occult powers an opportunity to make their intentions known.

When given the opportunity to make an appearance, other-worldly powers would respond, as a rule, by way of trance-induced presences – sometimes following frenzies in which a host might overstep the limit of deliberate self-harm. Those transmitting from the other side seemed to have appointed their cult medium as a kind of ambassador on the threshold between the spheres. They were occasionally heard through voices resounding among the celebrants; later, the stammering of the medium was replaced by the hushed reading of passages from scripture. The gods gave instructions in the shape of a sheep's liver or in the direction of birds in flight – all of these preludes to the arts of reading signs and close reading. Mesopotamian astrology celebrated an early triumph of reading when it gained the ability to decipher the relative position of heavenly bodies as texts and as powers influencing human destinies. The zone of signs waxes in parallel with the art of interpretation.[13] That it is not accessible to everyone is explained by its semi-esoteric nature: Jesus already reproaches those who came to test him for their inability to interpret "the signs of the times" (*semaia ton kairon*).[14] He himself was certainly more than a constellation; yet, when Jesus was born, the star of Bethlehem was there as a sign in the heavens to guide the (still-popular) astrologers from the East[15] – at least, insofar as one takes this account as more than just a fantasy of the Gospel of Matthew.[16]

Ecstatic practices and mantic methods of inquiry constituted procedures for submitting questions to the great beyond that the beyond itself could not leave entirely unanswered. As a rule, interpreters would be found who could assign a practical meaning to the encrypted symbols. As recent research shows, the lore of political signs operated at a highly refined level in western antiquity – in particular, among the Greeks and Romans.[17] "Political theology" had yet to find expression in the discourse of the day, but the gods were thought to have opinions about human affairs and would take sides in them – indeed, in special cases, they would plan long-term political undertakings in which the cooperation of earthly actors was indispensable, as in the indirect founding of Rome by the Trojan prince Aeneas. The existence of such interventions was beyond any doubt for those skilled in the art of reading signs. No imperialism arises without rulers and aspirants placing interpretations of the day's heavenly constellations into the frame of current events. To which might be added counsel issuing from the underworld. Aeneas, mythical antecedent to the Roman people, hears an admonition addressed to him from the mouth of his dead father, urging him to impose a benevolent regime upon the peoples of the Earth: *Tu regere imperio populos, Romane, memento.*[18] With this imperative, the poet Virgil, who had been commissioned to transfigure his contemporary, Caesar Augustus, created the model of a "prophecy after the event," so to speak. Historians are the modern successors of the augurs; they decipher "historical signs" with great powers of understanding and dedicate themselves to the task of presenting seemingly blind successions of events as meaningful sequences of a "world history."

The inventors of the *theologeion* have the merit of having clarified the epiphanic pressure exerted upon the heavens since they were first assigned the role of supporting the emotional and symbolic (or "religious") integration of larger social units: of ethnicities, cities, empires, and supra-ethnic cult communities – whereby the latter could also assume a metapolitical – even counter-political – character, as might be shown, for example, among Christian congregations in the centuries before Constantine the Great. The early Christian communities would have disintegrated into a confusion of individual ancillary inspirations, and would have remained ungovernable, had the first dioceses not striven for a certain degree of liturgical and theological coherence and had they not borrowed, from the Roman provincial and military administrations, techniques for managing territory and personnel. The bishops (*episcopoi*: overseers) were basically something like *praefecti* (commanders, governors) decked in religious garb; their dioceses (Greek: *dioikesis*: administration) resembled the former imperial districts following the Diocletian reforms around the year 300 CE; it was not least through these that the principle of hierarchy entered into the burgeoning organization of the church. With it, came the *haute couture* of ecclesiastical vestments that had first costumed public officials.

The stage technology, or the principle of religious dramaturgy and mediology, called *apò mekhanês theós* or *deus ex machina*, was in fact already in use in some rituals of the Near East, long before the emergence of Athenian theatre. Consider the most famous example: the Ark of the Covenant (*Aron habrit*), which had been carried along on the wanderings of the Israelites and housed in the tabernacle until it found a permanent place in the inner sanctuary of Solomon's Temple, to be entered only once a year, on Yom Kippur, the post-exilic high holiday of atonement. As a technology of revelation, this appears as a classic sacred *mekhane* that brings into presence a God who is capable of speaking and writing. According to its functional purpose, the Ark was a *theologeion ante litteram*. According to reports, it contained the two tablets "written with the finger of God"[19] that Moses had received on cloudy Mount Sinai. Later, the Ark was a repository of the holy scriptures of Israel – the Torah: more precisely, the Pentateuch, the five books of Moses.

The monolatry of ancient Israel did not permit, or even grant, the possibility of any further epiphany – at the time, the law was that those who *see* God, the devastating Prince of fire and the elements of air, and see him in his real presence, would lose their lives. The presence of the god made itself felt numinously, but it could not be translated theatrically in any way. As regards making appearances, YHWH or Elohim was limited to writing and to "nature" – both understood under the sign of authorship, and both only to be grasped as the perpetually unfolding revision of what had already been written and created. The written characters reposited inside the gilded chest of acacia wood made its proximity both sacred and dangerous: those who accidentally touched the Ark of the Covenant would be killed. From this, it can be inferred that the function of taboo, observed by nineteenth-century European ethnologists in Polynesia, existed among Semitic peoples (as with many others) from time immemorial, which is to say ever since ancient cult groups came to take "sanctifying–cursing" prohibitions with the utmost degree of seriousness. The early *religio*, if one might be permitted to extend the Roman concept, has always concerned processes on the threshold of life-giving and death-bringing things. Here, as is typical of religion, the indistinct touches upon the absolutely serious.

The writings of the ancient Israelites conformed to the schema of a *deus in machina*; one of these attained new distinction in the seventeenth century, when Christian engineers were seeking a perpetual motion machine in order to demonstrate proof of God by way of mechanics. When, in the myth, the God of Israel gave over the tablets on Sinai, he fulfilled his obligation to appear. The commandments laid down on the tablets were first repeated orally; it was only much later that copying, reading, studying, and commentary entered the discussion. The God of the people of Exodus was evidently prepared, during the years of wandering in the desert, to draw his followers along at night in the form of a pillar of fire, and by day in the form of a pillar of smoke on the horizon. The wanderers were said to have been on desert paths for 40 years before the "conquest and occupation" of their promised area of settlement – this very fact expresses a portentous tarrying before the final attainment of success. The long errancy is comprehensible only as a penitential pilgrimage: the swift path to the promised land would have been manageable at a moderate pace within 40 days or a little more, presuming the logic of a purposeful trek. That cannot be assessed here – only that the whole concept of a direct path seems not to have been one of the terms of the agreement between Israel and its Lord on high.

The departure from Egypt implies an arrival into the realm of YHWH's punitive power. Way and wayward now become synonymous. God writes straight with crooked lines, according to a proverb sometimes attributed to Augustine of Hippo. The Lord, whom one cannot call by name, manifested himself in the military and domestic triumphs of his adherents, in the bounty of births in their herds, and in the brief splendor of the royal houses of David and Solomon. Very little was missing for YHWH to have become an imperial god, with secondary temples and numerous tributary peoples all around. In the actual event, it turned out rather differently, however, and this created an insoluble tension between the never-abandoned suprematist claim of the God of Israel and the permanently precarious situation of his small and (after the diaspora of 135 CE) landless, disarmed people. Needless to say, it manifested itself in his own people as defeat, pestilence, deportation, and depression. Scriptural experts interpreted the dark events *lege artis*, as well-deserved punishments visited upon a notoriously disobedient people, and in some instances as trials of the righteous. The archetypal figures of punishment and trial served the Jews in their times of suffering, contemptuous treatment, and dispersion, allowing them to cast themselves as a "boat people" upon the sea of history, however many perished nameless and sunk into unvisitable graves.

The Christianity that branched off from Judaism had to find a way to dramatize heavenly indications in its own fashion. Even in its early writings, it made an astonishing use of the schema of the *theologeion* when it equated the appearance of Jesus, as the Messiah expected by the Jews, with the "Word of God." In this way, the Christian message went decisively beyond the examples of Greek theatrical poetry for speaking gods and, at the same time, it drama- tized the idea of a Torah that transits or returns from the written word into living being. The "sources" that highlight the difference can be found above all in Jesus' I-am declarations (*ego eimy*) in the Gospel of John, and in the You-are declaration of Simon Peter reported in Matthew 16:16: "You are the Messiah, the son of the living God." The fact that these expressions were "secondary" formulations subsequently put into the mouths of Jesus and Peter does not matter for our purposes.[20] What is decisive is that they authorized the binding together of the Jewish Messiah motif with

the doctrine of Logos from Middle Platonism, something already
put into effect by John the Evangelist around the year 100 CE
(perhaps earlier). Thanks to this convergence, which later developed
into a relation of equation, the god or God wholly entered into his
human appearance and linguistic utterances. Jesus was therefore
not only a *theologeion* in his person – that is, the source of heavenly
speech on an earthly stage – he was also, at least viewed retrospectively, the speaking God himself, and not as an actor reciting the
lines of his role, but as a performer who succeeds in speaking his
text *ex tempore*. When theology began to assign Jesus authorship in
the metaphysical sense, his earthly presence would not only testify
to an appearance of God in human form – this might be considered
a standard religious event in the region stretching between the
Nile and the Ganges (even if there with a different sense) – it
aimed to represent nothing less than the descent of the absolutely
transcendent Logos into immanence, and consequently an act of
a singular ontological "condescension," in the christological sense.

The Gospels of the New Testament report a great theo-anthro-
pological event that showed itself, in the first place, in the fact
that the God-Man making his appearance had entered into this
epiphany without reserving any option for withdrawal. Jesus had
no dramaturge, no tragic poet at his side, to feed him the words that
went along with his "role." There was no mask he could remove
backstage. It was only after the fact that his poets became his poets
– i.e., when the evangelists later told his story. Their teacher's words
had resonated with them before the fatal events of his entry into
Jerusalem and they did not hesitate to let him say what he must
have said if his earthly appearance were to have its proper meaning
(because otherwise it would be material for the report of only a
failure).[21]

Almost 300 years after the death of the man his followers
venerated as the Messiah come, the First Council of Nicaea established the creed that the Lord Jesus Christ was God from God,
Light from Light, true God from true God, begotten, not made
– whatever that might mean. This is followed a few lines further
on in the Nicene Creed by the phrase *et homo factus est*: and was
made man. Only here do we find explicitly expressed the precipitous
metaphysical declivity of Jesus' coming into the world. In a singular
case, an actual man might come into being without ceasing to
be Light from Light, notwithstanding his also being human. The
Roman philosopher Seneca the Younger (4 BCE–65 CE), tutor to
the young emperor Nero[22] and later his victim when ordered to
commit suicide, was a contemporary of Jesus, and in one letter he
suggested the state of affairs implied in what ordinary language

calls "becoming human." After subtracting out the idealized exaltations, what one is left with is this: *Sine missione nascimur*[23] – in other words: We are born with an assured prospect of death.

The *missio* is a gesture begging for "dismissal" in the context of the arena – and, by raising their thumbs, the mob might, as an exception, indicate that a gladiator who had fought bravely should not have to fight his fight to the last, fatal blow.[24] The phrase *sine missione* serves to indicate that those who have been born into the world will find no reprieve from their doom through any sign granted by the fickle crowd. This is no mere triviality – a fact to which the philosopher attests, pointing to the forgetting of death in everyday life. Don't mortals behave, from the start and for the most part, so rashly and so much besotted with the ephemeral, as if they thought they might live forever? And when the end comes at last, don't they commonly cling to the belief that they will somehow get away regardless?[25] What Seneca and Jesus have in common is the conviction that it is time to grasp the seriousness of life – its finality, its oppressiveness, its brevity, and its dependence on decisions. Everyday heedlessness is a mask of the phantasm of indestructibility, removed from time. The preacher in Judea and the philosopher in Rome put aside this mask in order to testify that there is something indestructible that is not of a fantastical, frivolous nature.

The God-Man, under the influence of Persian and Jewish sources, called himself the "Son of man" – possibly a messianic epithet, but maybe just a turn of phrase for "I" – and, one might say, he was born so that he might, with his very life, attest to his teaching and imprint it with his signature. This applies likewise to philosophers such as Socrates and Seneca and to numerous witnesses (*martyroi*) of more absolute beliefs. True: since ancient times, death's testimonial signature has been vulnerable to forgery. Some rushed into it under the pretense that they suffered it for the sake of a supreme good – wasn't it the case, already in late antiquity, that bishops had to exhort their charges not to make an exhibition of themselves as imitators of the holy martyrs? In the centuries that followed, many more people suffered witness deaths without wanting to bear witness. Anyone who studies the twentieth century will discover among its signatures false and distorted martyrdoms in large numbers.

In the case of Christ, the *theologeion*-scheme is invoked in several ways. The man who had called himself the "Son of man" handed down essential elements of his message while speaking from the Cross on which he ended his life as *deus fixus ad machinam*. His narrators and theologians made this death retrospectively take on, through God, the significance of a proof of God – thereby suffusing into the image of the Most High a tendency toward a freely chosen devitalization under the figure of "substitutionary atonement."

Tellingly, in the "Third Week" program of his *Spiritual Exercises* (composed 1522–4), Ignatius of Loyola directed retreat participants to school themselves in dying at the side of the Lord; the sense was that Christians should seek the competence to convert dying from something they must do, to something they are able to do – even to something they are willing to do, with eyes fixed on the resurrection of the first conqueror of death. When Hegel outlined alternative exercises from his lectern in Berlin, he expected that those who went through to the end of the course on coming-to-oneself as spirit would also sense an "infinite *anguish* concerning themselves"[26] because, as an untenable individuality, they each have to fill a place in the dialectical process-whole – much as becoming human in the co-absolute Son was necessary for the mediation of God with himself as a spiritual individuality – otherwise God would have had to remain merely a paragon of empty sublimity and a bogey of oriental power. It seems Hegel had calculated humanity's infinite anguish much as mathematicians after Leibniz might pursue their analyses with infinitesimal calculus.

It was not only the words spoken on the Cross that lent sublimity to Jesus' message. There was also the fact that the theophanic procedure was carried out right up to the moment of the Descent from the Cross and was interrupted by no miracle, no extricating incident. This god had not made it easy for himself to appear. "Appearing," says Hegel, "is being for an other."[27] The epiphany of Jesus took upon itself more than would have been expected for a "God from above." It should be noted here that the death and resurrection of the vegetation deities of the lower sphere (such as Attis or Osiris), associated with mother goddesses (Demeter, Isis, Cybele, and many others), were fixed motifs in the mythological script depicting the course of the year; such deities are figures of vital forces or outlines for possible persons – they are not individuals. The resurrection of the crucified Christ wants to signify more than the regeneration of the vegetative world and its imperishability. The Easter morning message proclaimed that, thereafter, impermanence would no longer have the last word, even for subjects of spiritual individuality. The itinerary of the soul was to be separated from those of the animal and vegetable world, and from the cycles of things caught up in the vernal regreening of the world.

It was from the empty grave that the God-Man established, for a third time, what was distinctive or singular about his earthly appearance. There, at the mouth of the cave, with the stone moved to one side, the *theologeion* advanced to a higher level. From the stage in Jerusalem there issued a shocking claim in the very absence of a corpse where human judgment would have expected to find one.[28] What could an absent corpse signify? What does its lack go to prove? Might one say that Christianity begins as a detective novel in which the negative *corpus delicti* re-emerged in various avatars, first as a haunted ethereal body on the outskirts of Jerusalem, then as the Eucharistic host, as the Corpus Christi body, and everywhere as a crucifix?[29] Inferring resurrection from the emptiness of the grave was factually and methodically overhasty. Paul, himself a man of haste, provided its rationale: Jesus must have risen because our faith would otherwise be in vain. The apostle to the Gentiles would not be the founder of extremism if not for the fact that he looked into the abyss here: we would be the most miserable of people if we were to err on this point.[30] But, if he has risen, and if to proclaim that is the only motif for our new beginning, then we are justified in proclaiming that the old world of law, sin, and death has been turned upside down. Whatever lies between Easter morning and Ascension Day – supposing there was such a day – forms an obscure interval in the biography of Jesus, analogous to Holy Saturday. In these 40 days, the rumors, the ravings, and the excesses come in a rush.

But what is Christianity if not a hastiness that ultimately had to take more time than it initially expected? Wasn't it at first just a trail map for the uprooted and the strivers, a map that remained in use until the church succumbed to the ties binding it to the earth and, rather than clutching at the roots of heaven, preferred to settle an imperial metropolis over the graves of the apostles?[31]

2

PLATO'S CONTESTATION

The discussion in the previous chapter obliges us to speak of an event we might here call the "Platonic contestation." However one understands those stories from Judea (and their various written records) – whether as mythical inventions or as historical reports, or as a hybrid of the two – we note that the Platonic intervention preceded them by 400 years. With an analogy from art history, one might speak of a "secession" of philosophy from poetry. In current terminology, one could describe the process as the disembedding of poetry from the philosophical space of truth. Poetry retains its affinity with lifeworld thinking *cum grano salis*, notwithstanding the fact that it often brings the wondrous into play, with talking horses, living statues, flying carpets, and elephants balancing on turtles; in a further analogy, one might speak of a disembedding of philosophical and scientific-type statements from everyday locutions.

This mutual disembedding – the decoupling of fiction and truth – has long been linked in European memory with the name of Plato. He was, par excellence, the founder of a school, and he followed thinkers such as Parmenides, Heraclitus, and Xenophanes in daring to question the authority of the ancients – whether Homer or Hesiod – who wrote verses of the gods. As a classic anti-authoritarian with authoritarian inclinations, Plato aimed to inaugurate a new start in the unfolding of truth, in which what was worth preserving would retain its rights, while the unbefitting – constituting much of the old narratives – would be eliminated by way of logical and ethical argument. Plato's didactic strategy consisted of presenting the master questioner Socrates as a mischievous generator of inescapable difficulties: whatever the teacher discussed with his interlocutor, it typically resulted in aporias or failures to advance from the zero-point. Because the pupil let the teacher engage in his "deconstruction," a space came to be created for establishing the then-new doctrine of ideas. This theory should follow entirely from thought observing its own inner movement, wherein thinking proceeds through concepts like a pedestrian in the rain – stepping from stone to stone across a soggy path. Concepts provide surefootedness, as successive steps are guided along the logical implications of the content included within the concept – and this is so however treacherous the ground about may be. If all men are mortal and if Socrates is a man, then I am walking the methodical path with dry feet when I assert that Socrates must therefore be mortal. The turn of the "spirit" (*nous*) to itself gave birth to the idea of ideas, together with their intellectual-theoretical and ontological consequences.

The result of Plato's intervention was the alienation of the divine from myth, epic, and the theatre, and its new figuration as a mental (or noetic) discursive greatness or splendor, something that can ultimately be accessed only contemplatively. In Plato's view, the *polis*, to be newly founded and composed according to the guiding principles of philosophy, should be an ensemble integrable through the divine (*to theion*). A greater degree of integration, relative to previous standards, was to be allowed in the ideal community, as it aimed toward a kind of logocratic Republic of God. Transmitting the venerable contrivances of the Greek singers, the *aoidoi*, and their tales of the gods, however, was not to be suffered without some salutary censorship. Many of the old stories let the gods appear in a light more than dubious – too often, like the most primitive of mortals, the heavenly gods displayed a crude thirst for revenge, vulgar strivings for power, and erotic drives incommensurate with their exalted degree. The Olympian community, with all its corruption, could no longer be considered suitable paragons for post-Platonic youth.

Consequently, a reformed pedagogy urged that an alliance be forged with the as yet ill-defined, but already polemical, discussion of the divine. Aristotle, often otherwise at odds with his master, takes up the academic repudiation of the ancients by derisively referring to them as *theologoi* or *mythologoi* – people who spin tales of sickly reason and present the gods and heroes as if they were a bunch of out-of-control celebrities. Aristotle associated the *theologoi* with the sophists, whom Plato had denounced as propagators of powerful lies. Going forward, the authority to teach lofty matters would be granted only to the philosophers.

Such a change in the style of speaking about divine things must have been scandalous in its day. Once the fashion in philosophy spread across classes in the Greco-Roman world (if principally among the upper classes), sublimated "god-talk" became a model of success with high potential for still further diffusion. To speak plausibly of the divine before an educated audience, one's terms were to be cast in absolute comparatives: *excelsior, superior, interior* – more excellent than the excellent, higher than the high, more intimate than the inner. And, yet, the language of abstract verticality could not avoid continued reliance on the presentive power of mountains, the clouds and the birds, the sky and the sun, lightning and the stars.

Since the emergence of academic philosophy, the better *theologia*[1] was only ever to be brought forward as a doctrine of first qualities. Because being good is the first predicate of God, Plato held that consideration of the divine must therefore be conducted, throughout, on this agathological basis. What is good is what, of itself, radiates goodness: *bonum diffusum sui*. The good thus imparted invites one to join oneself to its merit – but, of course, not everything that might be imparted is good. Other authors take up divine things (*to theion*) more conventionally, anthropomorphizing them in epic form, declaiming them in a dramatic or lyric register, or metaphorizing them within the framework of popular notions of majesty and highness. Such authors may have given it the best their day had to give, and yet they failed to properly grasp the "approach" due to the Most High. From the very beginning, humanity has cast its glance upward somehow – one cannot deny the ancients the good "will to upliftment." But what "up above" might mean, exactly, is yet to be understood, and how it might interface with interior life is so far clear to no one.

The attribution of goodness exclusively to the divine would bring forth – after a long period of incubation – fatal consequences, insofar as it opened up a conceptual space for the un-good – evil – to play the main part in almost all earthly things. At first, this development was schematized as a mere corollary of the absence of the good, but, starting as an empty negativity, it developed over time into a terrifying countervailing power. How else, in the Middle Ages of the West, could the devil have risen to be "the ruler of this world" (*archon tou kosmou*), an epithet linked to phrases used sporadically by Jesus in the Gospel of John?[2] The elevation of evil to a power in its own right went back to figures of the Indo-Iranian interpretation of the world. Early theologians of Greek inspiration, including John (if one might call him a theologian), were no longer cognizant of this fact, since they moved in the tunnel of their own terminological preliminaries, at the eastern end of which only a faint light could still be seen.

The ceding of earthly territory to evil had the advantage of explaining how God could be both almighty and, at the same time, unwilling to directly forestall or counter the evils of the world. Hence the problematic "permission theory," according to which Satan was something like a licensed subcontractor of the good Creator. It remained problematic because it determined God in qualitative terms of stainlessness and lack of suffering. The outsourcing of evil drove people into the arms of the Good, All-too-Good, which, however, was not to be held responsible for the other side of its own coin. Better to place the world in the hands of the devil than to allow oneself to contemplate the idea of a defect – a degree of suffering, even – in God himself.[3]

In Plato's dialogue *Euthyphro* (dated around 388 BCE), in which Socrates encounters his interlocutor on the street near the entrance to the law courts, the term *therapeia theon* emerged to denote something that came close to the Latin concept of *religio*. Socrates uses the term to describe Euthyphro's area of supposed special expertise – "piety" (*eusebeia*) and its practical application. In fact, the divine consistently reveals itself, in considerations both older and more recent, as a question of an approach and a treatment. It referred to a matter of diligence, reserved reflection, and scrupulous adherence to the protocol one must respect in dealing with the higher powers. Once these powers had been spiritualized to the extent that the Platonic intervention required of them, the grosser transactions between hither and thither were sloughed off – the blood sacrifices, the holocausts, those sublime-frustrating burnt offerings that cremated the animal whole without permitting the cooked parts to be consumed.

As soon as more sublime claims came to be clearly articulated, it became an open question whether a worshipper aspiring to reach the spiritual domain could still seriously approach it, while at the same time wishing to remain in the presence of the object of fascination – as with the sacrifice of consecrated cattle: the slash of the throat, the gush of the blood spouting first in a high arc, then languishing. The insight of the new understanding should have made it perfectly evident that the bleeding out and cardiac arrest in a sacrificial animal (*hostia*) did not offer its witnesses the slightest thing with regard to the otherworldly sphere.

3

OF THE TRUE RELIGION

Some 750 years after Plato's intervention, we see indications of much this same tendency in the young Aurelius Augustinus of Hippo, and in his conceptualization of the *vera religio* that gave a title to his apologetic treatise *De vera religione* [*Of True Religion*] in 390 CE. At that time, he was writing in the leisure of Thagaste, still filled with neo-Platonic euphoria, and, in the Augustinian *religio*, one can hear a distant but clear echo of the Greek "therapy" – i.e., service, ministration, treatment, cult, veneration. Cicero (106–43 BCE), near the midpoint between Plato and Augustine, likewise equated *religio* with the *cultus deorum*.

It is no accident that Christian ceremonial or cult practices are broadly referred to as "church service," or in the case of Lutheran churches "Divine Service" – suggesting a supplemental cultivation, in the proper sense, of care for the adequate *therapeia theon*. Cult is what permits no deviation, no improvisation – the fact that malpractice can cost one dearly has been well appreciated ever since there have been specialists in dealing with the otherworldly and the incalculable, from the earliest sorcerers and healers to soothsayers and viziers. It is only with management consultants in the present day that one would preach of the courage to make mistakes. The adventure of Christian dogmatics which began under Greek influence transitioned from customary concerns for the correctness of ritual protocols, to assert truth claims in a broader sense – even in the most general sense that would encompass cosmological, ontological, and ethical doctrines, far beyond the conventional sense of legal validity, cult correctness, and the proper understanding of scripture.

When the early Augustine lectured on "true religion," one still found a juvenile zealot at his philosophical exercises, drilling the

notion that truth resides in the "inner man." Plainly, toward the
end of the fourth century CE, there were already enough people
who could connect some sense with the semi-esoteric expression
"inner man." This term, circulated in late antiquity by way of
Platonism and its derivatives, referred to an interiority in which
one might localize an individualized consciousness of guilt and
repentance, of hope for salvation and gratitude, but above all of
participation in the sphere of true ideas. The "true" – in "true
religion" – still predominantly retains an adjectival importance,
while the noun *religio* denotes the set of rules to be carefully
observed in any way of life that would properly respect the gods.
"True religion" thus initially means a modus vivendi in which
Christian principles come into play. Above all else, they urge
distance from the toxic realism of "this world." And this world,
for its part, is recognizable by the fact that it is constantly issuing
invitations to participate in evil.

Under the vault of Latin Christianity, the term *religio* was largely
reserved for life under monastic rule. In the Middle Ages, *entrare
in religionem* meant joining a religious order. Toward the end of
the eighteenth century, a nun might still be called *la religieuse* in
French, as in the title of Denis Diderot's short novel. In order for
the "true religion" to become practicable, it seemed to make sense
to differentiate it from faith, and to assign faith to its own special
estate. Only life in a religious order could promote early Christian
care with respect to the danger of moral wrongdoing – and do so
to the point of a complete separation from the "world"; the sum
of temptations paving the path to perdition followed from the
allegorical equivalence of world and woman. "True life" signified
an anticipation of eternal life under merely earthly conditions – in
the best case in monastic seclusion, at times in extreme enclosure, in
which a walled-up cell actively symbolized the prospect of a death
to be welcomed.[1]

As long as the face of *religio* was shaped by the monastic option
and the existence of a professional clergy as the First Estate, the
main moral problem of the bipolar world-creation of that time
could be rendered invisible: how "Christian individuals" – Luther's
Christenmenschen – should employ themselves in order to take
charge of praxis in this world. Escape from the world is good;
the shaping of conditions still better. A thousand years after
Christianity first came to power through its alliance with thrones,
retreating into the desert could hardly remain a general solution
in perpetuity. Christian monarchies of the old European type
had taken a first step into the pragmatic field; nineteenth-century
ultramontanism took a second; the *Democrazia Cristiana* of the

twentieth century accomplished a third. With all of them, it was inevitable that Christian realpolitik, as a situation-sensitive moral pretense, would tether its liaisons to the conditions of having and wielding power.

One had to wait for the end of the Middle Ages before "religion" swelled into a storm cloud towering over the Atlantic world, benighting the mental climate of the continent named "Europe" (the lands of the West and the setting sun) and darkly distinguishing itself in the wake of Columbus's voyage. It grew in extent and power as returning ships from all points of the globe came with tidings of hundreds and thousands of peoples whose bizarre ways of dealing with their gods sometimes read like caricatures of European religious life. The cloud burst in the violent storm of the European wars of religion, in which Christian factions struggled for certainty of salvation under arms. After the long sixteenth century, which lasted from 1517 to the Peace of Westphalia in 1648, there emerged the "political class" that finally succeeded in ending the wars between states defined by their religious affiliation – an event one might interpret as a first concession to the "relativism" that Rome has lamented to this day.

Around this time, it became clear what was entailed with the inexorable change in the structure and meaning of the concept of *religio*. The cloud front of "religion" not only drifted over the war-devasted landscapes of the European powers, who armed and marched against one another under Catholic and Protestant sectarian banners, it also brought into visibility countless varieties of ancestral beliefs and local alliances with otherworldly entities, reports of which had been collected from all points of the compass by European seafarers, traders, missionaries, and ethnographers. It exposed Europeans to the frightening and subversive realization that the earth was strewn with bizarre cults which, unbeknown to themselves, effectively parody one another. The concept of "religion" as such became latently ironic. In the eyes of the explorers, the planet *Terra* was not only the "ascetic planet" populated by people of the priestly–sickly type, of which Nietzsche wrote in his polemical derivation of self-tormenting ideals;[2] it appeared, even more, to be the superstitious planet where there was no fabulation that was not believed by somebody somewhere.

In certain parts of the old Holy Roman Empire, the lore was passed down that one could look into paradise if one stood under an apple tree on Christmas Eve. Old Tibetan belief has it that Tibetans descended from monkey children after they came to eat the grain that was given to them from sacred Mount Meru. The poor in Haïti still believe to this day that the Vodou *loa* Baron Samedi leaves his cemetery on All Souls' Day to roam the streets, smoking and chatting with his followers and performing obscene couplets in his androgynous nasal voice. The Dorze people of Ethiopia's Gamo Gofa Zone are said to believe that leopards have days of fasting and usually keep to them, but it is wise to remain on guard every day. There was a rite among the Blackfoot Confederacy for a warrior in distress to cut off a finger from his left hand and offer it to the Morning Star. The Barasana-speaking people in the Vaupés basin of the northwest Amazon are said to believe that the moon is made of clotted blood, and that it descends on some nights to consume the bones of men who have had sex with menstruating women. In 1615, Francis Xavier's right forearm, used as an instrument of God in the baptism of innumerable pagans in Asia, was detached by the Jesuits from his mortal remains at the Basilica of Bom Jesus, in Goa, and sent to Rome, where it was set in a reliquary of silver and exhibited in the Church of the Gesù; the missionary himself is said to have almost died after he had baptized 10,000 pearl fishermen on the coast of Goa in one month in 1544. In January 2018, believers bought a seat on board an Air Canada plane for this reliquary and escorted it for one month, from one Canadian Catholic church to the next, in the hope that proximity to the arm of salvationist power would "touch" as many people as possible.

Paul Valéry may have been on the right track when he remarked that, in their darkness, our ancestors coupled with every enigma and begat strange children.[3] He erred only insofar as it is not only our ancestors, but also our contemporaries, who embrace enigmas only to bring forth phantoms.

As for Augustine of Hippo, at first he had in mind only what was more generally in the air in his day. Augustine was effectively a participant in establishing what Adolf von Harnack called the "gradual Hellenization of Christianity,"[4] even though, for Augustine the Roman rhetorician, the Koine Greek of the New Testament remained a foreign language throughout his life. It seemed plain to Augustine why the Christian message called for translation – and clear therefore, in his view, that it should not remain restricted to the Grecophone world. Augustine little suspected that, with his troubling, theologically thought-through doctrine of predestination for salvation and damnation, he would trigger an avalanche that would bury large parts of the old and new European psychospheres for a millennium and a half – an avalanche of ontological masochism.[5] From this and its mystical extremist derivatives came the demand that one's self-will must be destroyed if God is really to be all in all. So long as I can still say "I," I am presumably one of those rebellious spirits who, out of pride and prejudice, contribute to the establishment of a world inimical to God.

By extension, the unconditional believers – those engendering the radical minority sects – sought to achieve their surrender to the sovereignty of "the Other" through a forced submission to an absolutely superior power. There are reasons to look askance at this craving for prostration as a false self-denial, indeed to decry it as a camouflaged form of suicide – but the gesture of at once suspending and uplifting the self as a whole could also be celebrated as a surrender, a total commitment, to the feeling of utter dependence in being encompassed or embedded within the perfect cosmic whole. With the founders of the Society of Jesus, Ignatius of Loyola and Francis Xavier, it became clear how the radicalized ethics of obedience and service turned into the mobilization of the will to expand. In the circle of the younger idealists, above all Johann Gottlieb Fichte and Friedrich Schleiermacher, to be permeated by the unconditioned was declared to be compatible with an upright stance. Fichte justified, in a radically offensive manner, our capacity for an upright stance and gait, when he provided anti-ontological arguments in the service of active self-realization: external reality, being merely external and presented by the ego, deserves no special status for men and women of action – those who let themselves be overimpressed by it have not understood themselves. The external remains relevant only as material that must be forced to yield in the face of a duty-driven aggression.

From time immemorial, the "religiously musical"[6] among the ontological masochists have fevered for their own effacement no less than for a final victory over themselves. They have been inclined to believe that, if God and I were to appear at the same time and in the same place, then there would be one too many of us. For the time being, the solution could only be to obliterate the self.[7] The technique of simulating death was discovered as the next step in becoming an instrument of the divine will, in accordance with the mystical maxim: "when someone wills nothing for themselves, then God must will on their behalf."[8]

With the ancient and classical Greeks, the dilemma of the coexistence of gods and men was resolved by a clear hierarchy. If a person came too close to the sphere of gods, one spoke of hubris, the malady of insolence or arrogance. It was cured by a fall. For the ancients of the Mediterranean, the world was everything that is the case after a fall from high-altitude flights. Those who stayed in the middle – or, more simply, those who remained anchored in everyday life – resisted the godless temptation to fly. In his blinded dazzlement, Icarus, test pilot of flight upward and out of the world, was Oedipus's nearest relation.

4

REPRESENTING GOD, BEING GOD:
AN EGYPTIAN SOLUTION

He flies who flies; this king Pepi flies
away from you, ye mortals. He is not of the
earth, he is of the sky.

> Pyramid text of Pepi II Neferkare (died *c.* 2184 BCE)

Allusion to high-altitude flights and antigravity expeditions hints
at the peril faced by the older theopoetries with regard to statements about the Most High and the ascent to it. Travelers should
not make the mistake of taking it for the empirical or symbolic sun
– either source of radiance will singe the wings of naive high-fliers.
And yet, be that as it may, stories of journeys carrying subjects
up, up, and away will speak to a kind of kinetic unconscious. One
perceives in them an appeal to élan vital, a vital force that pushes
forward against all opposition. Nothing seems more unnatural
to life than an excessively long rest; on the contrary, life wants
expansion and movement. To tell people of the gods and their
mighty advantages of being is to provoke an urge for imitation
among the spiritually resonant. Is there any known telling of the
deeds and sufferings of higher beings that does not play with
the fire of emulation? What is a god or goddess, if not also an
example for believers and, as an example, an outline showing the
contours of what *followers* might yet become? Who would take a
higher being seriously, if this being were thought to inhabit only
the dissimilar, the inimitable, the incomparable? To create what
is called a "relationship," there must be a minimal family resemblance. People affiliate with the divine when they consider that they
themselves are in some sense, likewise, entities who act and give.
Being a beginning and a salutation is a capacity they share – even if

their beginning is preceded by still earlier beginnings, earlier gifts, earlier salutations.

As soon as there is talk of gods, and particularly of the heavenly, the ethereal, the ever superior, of their ontological dioceses and the ecstatic frequencies on which one receives their messages, a series of questions unfailingly makes its appearance: Which god represents which power, which virtue, which general concept? Where does its sovereign domain begin and where does it end? Who appears when and to whom and in what form? Can the gods' assumptions of form be relied upon, or are there some one suspects of mere masquerade? How does one even recognize the deities? Do they really have, as is said, an aura of mystery about them? Even if they appear in the plural, is it possible that they are aspects of a single entity? How can one approach them? By what means can one gain their support and avoid their anger? Why does it show blindness or misapprehension to want to rival them? When they appear to be angry, is that due to a disapproval of human delusions of proximity or equality with the divine? Is it really true that fear and trembling are the only keys to their kingdom? Must it be true that one either believes on one's knees or else believes not at all?

It is not hard to see how the forms of ancient polytheism, which adjusted so easily to accommodate a conversion to other codes, also came to permit a first sorting of the higher powers and a differentiation in the modes of access to them. The early forums for intercultic and intercultural rapprochement emerged from comparative polytheism. Indeed, arguably, what was later called diplomacy arose in good part from negotiations between priests of analogous gods in the cult bazaars of the ancient Near East – or was at least prefigured in them. As soon as one representative of an otherworldly power could enter into conversation with delegates of analogous powers, priestly lip service paid customary tribute to fear – even as trembling itself became superfluous. Each confessed to the other that there were mysteries that only the few could understand. Seen from the outside, the mysteries were as alike as one black box will resemble another. The atmosphere of antiquity argued in favor of the convergence of various otherworldly "beyonds" long before organized monotheisms – whether formally Christian or Islamic – began their own campaigns. With astonishing foresight, the senators of Rome decreed in 173 BCE that the immortal gods were everywhere the same (*iidem ubique di immortales*): no matter which peoples were to be subjugated by the city on the Tiber, their gods were presumed to be assimilable to the Roman pantheon from the outset.[1] That there were gods everywhere could be assumed without further investigation, simply because the *consensus gentium* affirmed it to be so.

With regard to the problem of how to regulate the imitation of the gods and how to enforce the correct approach to them, the ancient Egyptian solution remains most impressive, even thousands of years later; moreover, it also provides a most suggestive answer to the question of the adequate worldly appearance of the beyond. The pharaoh is the person for whom the determination becomes irrelevant as to whether he himself *is* the god or else merely *represents* the god.[2] His "role" – or, better, his position – precedes the distinction between appearance and essence. Even before conception in his mother's womb, the god is present in him. His existence follows *ab ovo* ritual processes. From his earliest days forward, his conduct followed the script for gods who undertook the work of the sun – rising, shining, setting, traversing the night – in short, the whole theo-cosmic drama that unfolds every day. Symbolically anticipated in the figure of the pharaoh, we can see a glimpse of Hegel's ultimate thought, in which self-exposition of the absolute in a self-feeling human soul crosses the threshold to self-signification in order to later attain self-conception in actuality.

As God in person, as Horus, as Ra, as the living sun, as the chosen one of the Great Ennead, the royal self also embodies the divine physical and moral quality accorded to the first agent of Egypt, in full possession of two natures that were merged before all time. Just as the Egyptian gods existed consubstantially and interchangeably among themselves, and just as they were familiar with the logic of reciprocal substitution, so likewise the pharaoh was subsumed within an effortless logic of participation in which self-existence encompassed alterity and alternate naming practices. Amun was sometimes said to be at the same time Ra and Ptah, the three gods all taken up into a single divinity.[3] From his palatial *theologeion*, the pharaoh sent his orderly signs out into the world. Since there was no real public, in either the ancient or the modern sense of the word, the meaning of his verbal and physical actions remained restricted within the ambit of liturgical temple plausibility, palace ritual, and some large processions *coram populo*. Whatever he did was regarded in every respect as a gesture full of cosmic-imperial meaning. His "choir" consisted not of the enslaved people in the fields along the banks of the Nile; it was composed of sign-literate priests, supervising eunuchs, and palace servants, who were compelled to count their steps behind the living god. The closest circle of his adoring devotees included funerary experts, who covered the walls of his burial chamber – and the inside of his coffin – with writings, unreadable by mortal eyes, but which composed the originary words of an unworldly literature. The pharaoh had no need to rise and ascend in order to enter into the beyond; heaven came to him in the grave, in the shape of the starry furrow on the inside of the coffin lid.

In the third millennium BCE, in Egypt, under the eyes of a heaven that had been transformed into a theoscope, a theatre of singularity opened up. With regard to theoscopy, a certain conception of the sun provides the paradigm: not only does it shine upon the righteous and the unrighteous, it also makes note of what it illuminates. It forgets nothing and must make its judgments *post mortem*, concerning whatever has come within its view. For the time being, a tiny ambit of observation serves to isolate the essentials: one divine eye – or, better, the host of eyes proper to the ensemble composed of Atum, Shu and Tefnut, Geb and Nut, Isis and Osiris, Set and Nephthys – directed its gaze upon a single individual in human form. A spotlight, like a daylight in the midst of daylight, overilluminated this single being in whom existence and importance coincide. The king was flooded with the light of otherworldly attention. Being under the eye of the deity caused the aura of this one existence to radiate in exalted overexposure – even if it were the case that the prince, considered as a person, was a dull potentate. His singularity was not the achievement of a subject-related self-reflection; rather, it was the effect of an irradiation. A day in the life of the pharaoh contains within itself things that have been happening between heaven and earth since time immemorial. To begin with, it is immaterial whether most people perceive it or not – even should it be the case (as the Universal Declaration of Human Rights will aver 50 centuries later) that all human beings are born with a dignity formally equal to the pharaoh's own. People are hardly averse to putting themselves forward for such an overexposed position. At the beginning, though, what counts is that not a minute passes without the pharaoh orienting himself to his god in the utter conviction that his god, or the ensemble of the exalted Nine, the Ennead, is observing and animating the least of the pharaoh's gestures – this, according to the pharaoh's own court theologians.

In the millennia before and after the Egyptians, clans and tribes believed almost naturally that their ancestors looked upon them with a penetrating gaze from somewhere close by, judging their actions, and not always in the spirit of purest benignity. Was there ever an afterlife that was entirely free from the resentment directed by the dead against the living? High above the lands of the Nile, the heavens turned into a source of emissions and the collection point for a permanent surveillance. The god assigned to the pharaoh – or, better, the ensemble of gods that lent him his divine status – gave focus to this one self-point in the world and, by so doing, elevated it to a singularity. The man so observed gave himself over to observation by devoting each of his impulses to otherworldly witnesses. He sent his life permanently into the solar cloud.

The constellation of Horus–Pharaoh or Ra–Pharaoh (etc.) prefigured the field of "intersubjectivity" that lay many thousands of years in the future. It marked a gaze from above that could track you, wherever you might be. In his book *On the Vision of God* (1453), Nicholas of Cusa explained to the monks of Tegernsee Abbey how it was possible that the observer depicted in a picture on the wall – possibly a painting by Rogier van der Weyden – seems to be looking at all viewers of the picture at one and the same time, and seems to be following each with his eyes as each viewer moves, as if each were the only one attracting his particular attention.[4]

In the late 1920s, the philosopher Helmuth Plessner added an anthropological note to the metaphysics of being seen (and being seen through), by describing the positionality of "the human" as an "eccentric" one per se: one is always standing reflexively "beside oneself" inasmuch as one is not only able to survey one's surroundings, but, while seeing, one also perceives oneself as potentially seen.[5] Contemporary behavioral anthropologists supplement this with a simple statement: people are better behaved when they know they are under observation.

In contemporary China, the ambition implicit within Egyptian and western theoscopy is being implemented on a large scale, in terms of social technology and moral politics.[6] Every individual there is scripted into the role of an actor or actress in the drama of the Harmonious Society. Either one conforms to one's role by portraying the good national comrade, the exemplary national comrade – or else one forsakes one's role and thereby falls under suspicion. The electronic surveillance state becomes a total reviewer in that it sends every actor, every actress into the purgatory of individual assessment. Digital surveillance promises to bring to fruition what, in the past, the state security apparatus and the social technology of denunciation had sought in vain, whether in the theocratic Republic of Geneva, in the Soviet Union, or in the German Democratic Republic. China, however, is building on its own tradition of internal spying and is reviving, under paleocommunist rhetoric, methods from the time of the emperors and their mystical informants.[7]

The pharaonic way of being is the first mode that corresponds to what Robert Musil called "the utopia of motivated life,"[8] in which the risk of an insufficiency of meaning is neutralized. At the time of the Middle Kingdom, which Egyptologists consider to have been

an era of a repressive police state, the priests spread the phobocrati-
cally virulent thesis that the gods keeping watch enjoyed a surplus
capacity for attention, which they might direct to many – maybe
even to all – mortals. Thus, the god-king under watchful eye from
above becomes a first instance, the basis of a model communicating
a new doctrine to the numberless masses who live more aimlessly:
what they do and what they fail to do are less meaningless for
heavenly agencies than had been supposed by those who had
hitherto considered themselves negligible and beneath the threshold
of observation. Since God is incapable of forgetting anything, and
yet *can* still forgive – notwithstanding the existence of very powerful
grounds for punishment – mortals are forced to take greater care
with the impressions they consign to the beyond. Thenceforth,
everything depends on the distinction between the forgivable and
the unforgivable.[9] Egypt invents what would later be called *faith*
by impressing upon the many somehow present there that they are
under the eye of all-invasive intelligences who keep an open dossier
on every life. In the hereafter, each life is thus judged according to
the record of the individual case, and processed according to ritual
correctness.[10]

"Religion" (we are still provisionally using the confusing term for
want of a better one) means the abolition of carelessness – one might
equally say: a founding and consuming suspicion of spontaneity.[11]
With the late Augustine of Hippo, the charge against carelessness or
spontaneity radicalizes to become a condemnation a priori. In each
individual, it is jealousy that makes the most prominent appearance
among the impulses under suspicion,[12] followed by a defiance that
disdains to be ordered about, even by reason. In due time, the sexual
impulse comes to keep company with both. Altogether, they form
the infernal psychodynamic trio. As the evil ego-trinity, they issue
their commandment: there shall be no other gods before them. It
was the genius of monotheism to show a way to yield up the totalitarian ego to a god, opening up the wicked ego's avenues of access
to the good, decentering the ego, binding it to itself, and taking its
evil upon itself – a task solved a little more elegantly in polytheism
by distributing evil across several agencies, none of which is understood to be completely diabolical. One must guard against the
common error of supposing that Augustine was original when he
indulged his obsession with original sin – so momentous for the
western hemisphere – by emphasizing the sexually transmitted taint
of the human condition. Two thousand years before Augustine,
a scribe in the ancient Mesopotamian city of Ur imprinted these
lines onto a clay tablet: "Never has a sinless child / been born to
his mother; / The idea has not been conceived that someone among

people should have no sin, / since ancient time, (such an idea) has never existed."[13] Those who are believers feel themselves to be under surveillance. One looks up because one believes oneself to be visible from that vantage point. If someone wants to become devout – if, in Christian terms, a person "struggles" for faith – one seeks a place among those who have won the pharaonic privilege of favorable permanent observation from the most exalted vantage point. Faith is the impossibility of being insignificant. Those who consider themselves to have attained it count themselves among the flock of the good – or, later: those elected to be able to be good.

In the Egypt of the Middle Kingdom, the elect – the good mummies – were those who were allowed to return to their tombs after successfully passing the Judgment of the Dead and vindicating their life balance before the tribunal, in order to now, in turn, be granted the status of gods, to enjoy their immortality, their ability to walk unhindered through space, their sovereignty as lords of the grave, and the care of their grave site by a priesthood attentive to ritual. A plot of otherworldly estate was requisite; it allowed the eternalized to eat "the bread of the Westerners."[14]

Plato introduced a logically modified Egypticism into the European tradition. Thereafter, it would not make a significant difference whether the watcher on high were called Horus or Amun-Ra; if it were Zeus presiding, he would be recognized as an equal colleague, whether as a thinking fire or as Zygios, protector of the wedding night; for his part, Jupiter Capitolinus, alias Jove, could stand serenely next to them, since he too displays the attributes that distinguish him as the venerable God on high; diplomatic accommodations could be expected for rough double syllables like *Donar* or *Wotan*, even if the ears of the south never altogether trusted the Germanophone. Within the sphere of those living beings who "have language," names develop jointly with realities, whereas, in the sphere of the supernominal, names are sound and smoke[15] that form a starting point. It is only the penetrating vision of heaven that is important, lending existence and giving orientation to the favored ones, while, with the Judgment of the Dead, the less favored, those who fail the trial, are consigned by the heavens to nonbeing – whereupon a monster devours their hearts.

The binding together of powers of vision with creative energy would eventually follow. This is what more or less educated preachers will speak of, when they ascend the long-established western analogues of the *theologeion* – the cathedral pulpits, later the denominational professorial chairs – in order to proclaim (according to an ontologically strained craftsman's logic) that, with

God, to inspect, to discern, to generate, to love, and to preserve form a continuous fabric of divine acts.

Latter-day ambassadors of the truth from above are not, at their pulpits and lecterns, actors who play the role of god. Instead, they step forth as an elevated kind of *theologoi*, educated in Greek theory. They present themselves as proclaimers of the true word in "apostolic discipleship"; they vest themselves as messengers, warranted by the claim that they knew someone, who had met someone, who claimed that he had met the anointed one in person at the time, until contact with him was interrupted by the salvific catastrophe on Golgotha. In later times, the ever-growing temporal remoteness from the originary link of the chain ceased to be disruptive. Right from the start, the title of Apostle served to authorize the heralds – in particular Paul, who suffered a taint, preaching to non-Jews of a Christ whom he had not met during his lifetime and of whom Paul had been jealous in the time after his passing. And yet, without a chain of witnesses, however problematic its links, there can be no succession; there can be no succession without re-enacting an original encounter in which none of the later participants had been present.

In the churches of the West, in the thirteenth century, the *theologeion* of the Greeks was reconstituted *cum grano salis* in the form of sermon pulpits; thereafter, it was theologians who actually stepped forth upon them. Since the Holy Mass culminates not in the sermon but in the transubstantiation, the priest was not compelled to glide in under a mask as *deus ex machina*. The miracle happens while he is officiating at the altar with his back to the congregation. From the pulpit, the more easily comprehensible aspects of the mystery play are explained in the vernacular. As a rule, the pulpits are attached to a pillar at a little less than halfway up and are canopied with a sounding board; it is not uncommon for the peak to be adorned by a dove; or else sometimes a dragon, vanquished by saintly irony, winds itself about the canopy.

If we grant ourselves a certain allowance for conceptual play, we might understand what more recent philosophies call "subjectivity" and "personality" as a later declination of the pharaonic mode of existence, according to which *being* God and *representing* God are not effectively distinguishable from one another. Notwithstanding all the emphasis on their difference in unity, this indistinguish-ability has remained virulent for millennia, not least because of the persistent glow of Greek philosophy glimmering from under Christian cover. Paul's contemporary, Seneca the Younger, reminded his pupil Lucilius – possibly invented by himself – of the presence of the absolute observer: "God is near you, he is with you, he is within you [*intus est*].... A holy spirit [*sacer spiritus*] indwells within us, one who marks our good and bad deeds, and is our guardian [*observator et custos*].... [B]ut what god, know we not."[16]

In Johann Gottlieb Fichte's lecture "Of the Scholar as Ruler" (1805), the function of the king is defined as a kind of civil service through the divine idea. Indeed, the office-bearer should understand himself as the medium and executive organ of the divine idea; it is the *idea* that "lives in his life instead of his own personality. It alone moves him." Until the idea speaks, "he too is silent; – he has no voice but for it.... [A]nd there remains nothing either of his person and of his life that does not burn a perpetual offering before [the Idea's] altar. And thus is he the most direct manifestation of God in the world."[17] Fichte's existential mediumism interprets the existence of the ruler – to an even greater extent than that of the scholar – as a continual, practical self-demonstration of God *per reges*. "*God is*, we will say, – for they [the true kings] are, and He in them."[18]

Even the most profane ego of our day carries within itself an echo of the pharaonic, medial, both-seeing-and-seen mode of being, insofar as the modern subject is still – perhaps now more than ever – taken up with a constant being-noticeable. Perhaps never before have so many people been conscious of their being-to-be-seen – regardless of whether or not they satisfy expectations of being worthy of being seen. But there is hardly an individual left who, because of his office, is bound to believe that the rise and fall of the Nile between the summer solstice and late September will depend on his liturgically correct behavior.

5

ON THE BEST OF ALL POSSIBLE
HEAVEN DWELLERS

Platonic thought contested the value of folk narratives recounting the unworthy behavior of gods and heroes; this, however, did not at first lead to any practical consequences of note. Greek cult customs remained just as subject to the law of inertia, and, for want of better new stories, the older ones continued to circulate. Repetition is not only the proverbial mother of all learning, it also maintains the working alliances of pride and stagnation.

It was centuries later that the impact of the Platonic intervention first became perceptible – and then with fateful new accents. From a distance, and notwithstanding its qualified approval of pederastic eroticism, the slow-maturing impulses of rational theology that followed from the teachings of Plato and his successors might be compared to a Protestantism on Hellenic soil – which one might relate to the justly observed proximity of Platonism to non-Greek elements. Wherever Platonism asserted itself, it bred enclaves of disenchantment that thrust aside its previously perceptible closeness to the Eleusinian Mystery cults. In time, the tawdry world above was neutralized: the misdeeds of the gods fell under censor, their portraits were painted over in accordance with the decorum of the spotless goodness of God, or they were set aside entirely – much as, after 1520, Protestant churches in Germany came to be emptied of their saintly images and their statues of Mary. Gauging the extent of the evacuation, the sixth book of Augustine's *City of God* shows that only disenchanted phrases remained of all the fabrications of the fabulous in the state cultic and natural theologies of Greece and Rome.

The One God from the thought workshop of the Akademia was initially anything but a "normal god" for everyone – it was enveloped in the esotericism of subtle abstraction, culminating at length in the systems of Plotinus (204–70 CE) and Proclus Lycius (412–85 CE). And yet, especially with the Christian reception of Platonism, it became clear that the new rejection of polytheism by the Akademia, at first seemingly sectarian, must also amount to something more: if, up to that point, human beings had been able to exculpate themselves with Olympian analogies and Dionysian excesses, this new development implied renunciations of self-aggrandizement and of "the free-spiriting and many-spiriting of man."[1] A unitary tendency emerged and, little by little, a monarchist trait would even come to assert itself – to the advantage of the later analogy of princes and bishops. The new God and the emptiness surrounding him corresponded as intimately to each other as, formerly, pomp and extravagance had seemed to correspond to the divine essence. Logical verticalism aimed above the picturesque heights of mountain, star, and midday sun, toward the more ethereal zenith beyond.

God, the divine, came to reside in superlatives. In fact, seen in the light of thought, God could only be the One (masculine), or, better, the One (neuter) – or, best yet: that absolute X, simpler than which nothing can be thought. If it were possible to form the superlative of One, the Onemost would be the cipher of the divine. God would be the totipotent absolute point: absolute, because of its ability to generate all other points; totipotent, because from its infinite density it can activate the possibility of emerging in every direction of becoming. At the summit of his *Paradiso* vision, Dante conceived the triune God, with mathematical and ontological correctness, as a simple superradiant light, point and circle both at once – both absolute white and all colors of the spectrum. Hegel, for his part, bound the absolute to the property of pure whiteness – albeit with regard to a bad (because still quite indeterminate) absolute.[2]

Naturally, it is also the Greatest of which the late Platonist Nicholas of Cusa will say, *Maximum est unum*: the maximum is One.[3] Point and All are the extremes, one abutting emptiness, the other fullness. With the necessity of consistency, it is the most beautiful, because being, when it appears and resounds, would be unthinkable and unreal without radiance and appeal: its orderliness not only appeals to the mathematical sense, it also animates feeling for the aesthetic and moral rightness of good proportion. Accordingly, the demiurge, the architect of the world of the One, formed the cosmos as a sphere (*sphaira*) according to the law of the morphological optimum.[4] Where proportion prevails, the right and the righteous (and its superlative, the most righteous) cannot be far off: the sphere of the One is averse to violence, it orders things through rotations, symmetries, and systems of equilibrium – ideally in such a way that the joining (*harmos*) between the parts does not catch the eye in a disharmonious way. Since it must be the oldest (*presbytaton*) and, at the same time, the most recent and youngest (*neotaton*), the circling in itself is befitting, the dynamic of a good perpetuity; on the rotating line, every point above is Being that is now undergoing itself. And, finally, because the divine cannot be anything other than the wisest (*sophotaton*), the past and the future are transparent to it. Before they even come to pass, it is done with the things that happen within time. Its basic mood is one of ungrudging universal benevolence – it differs favorably from the one-sided jealous zeal of the biblical God. Before it could enter into discussion for Europeans, it first had to take its exam in Ancient Greek.[5]

After all of that, it is hardly surprising that Platonic intellectualism relegated storytelling into a secondary position. In later years, storytelling served as an aid to help the mind over residual problems in preliminary, improper, and figurative speech – the thinker remained enough of a poet to leave a respectable allowance for the alogical.

Under Plato's stimulation, a philosophical theology comes to be articulated, which outgrows mythical poetry (including its appearance in the Athenian theatre). Alongside it, the "theology" of the Hebrew Bible, from the Torah to the historical books overstuffed with massacre, will occasionally seem like a collection of sacredly overvalued crudities that take a lot of time to refine (for instance, Hosea 6:6: "For I desire steadfast love and not sacrifice"); meanwhile, that of the New Testament emerges as a supplementary endowment of very engaging, but always also very problematic, innovations – problematic to the extent that the concept of vicarious suffering had to lead to an expansion of guilt, while "God's first love"[6] paid a high price for the success of the Jesus-is-the-Messiah sect. Since the biblical God places love above benevolence, the circles of his exegetes bring out his honored and affectingly compassionate temperament – one celebrates his personal essence, and it is empha-sized that one can address him informally, whereas it is said that the god of the philosophers is one before whom one cannot sing and dance (although, which god exactly would have an interest in seeing Heidegger dance?). In praising the God of the Bible, one leaves out of consideration the facts that nothing generates disputes so readily as preferential love, and that hardly anything stokes infernal fires so intensely as the unilateral allocation of affection. Free as a poet to let the stones speak, Dante was also enough the theologian to write down the unspeakable without reservation. It is his brick gate to hell itself that confesses what cannot be avoided in the universe of a God who is too much loving and too little contemplative: "My maker was divine authority, the highest wisdom, and the primal love!"[7]

Nothing speaks against defining philosophical theology as poetry in its second stage. It found its first court of muses among the friends of ideas on the outskirts of Athens at the turn of the fifth to the fourth century BCE.[8] Its poetic character was little changed by the fact that it was poetry written in prose, logically arranged, paraphrasable, and subject to debate. Even after its crossover into abstract conceptualization, theopoetry never leaves the realm of the fabricated, the contrived, and the overstrained. It remains a tribute to the faculty of imagination down to its humblest syllable. As a poetry that derives from ultimate grounds, it pulsates between the point and the spherical universe; the creative work of the god of the philosopher resembles a computational task in spherical geometry. In terms of form, it can only be surpassed by negative theology – which indeed was quick to follow, since it was laid out in Plato's allusions to inexpressible supreme being. It unfolds from Middle Platonism on through to Plotinus, Proclus, and Pseudo-Dionysius the Areopagite, down to the thinkers of the High Middle Ages, who are sometimes subsumed under the pithy expression "mystics." As a discourse of the God without qualities, negative theology forms yet a third theopoetry. Its enthusiasts declare that it comes first in rank because, they say (rightly or wrongly), better than any cataphatic discourse – no matter how lofty – it does justice to the unspeakable. In negative theology, God is surrounded by choirs of negation. They rapturously remove him, the non-object par excellence, from the reach of affirmative statements, even as they award him the utmost eminence. To join in the litany, it is best to do so in monastic life – this allows the monk time enough to say what God is not.[9]

Overstrain of this kind exacts a price. The monarchist and suprematist tendency toward more logically sophisticated theopoetry led to a devaluation of the popular gods. This happened with the Greeks when the irony of the city was making life difficult for the Olympians. It suffices to leaf through a work like *The Clouds* (performed 423 BCE), by the comic poet Aristophanes, to understand just how far irreligious skepticism had advanced in the city of Athens. The play gives evidence that educated Athenians of the First Enlightenment could no longer accept the stories of the mythologists: the clouds themselves stepped on to the stage and declared as a chorus that they, not Zeus, caused the thunderstorms. To similar end, the character Socrates, suspended from the *theologeion* with blasphemous ease, hands down his sophist instruction from above.

The play demonstrated how the new "friends of wisdom" in their "thinkeries"[10] were exposed to ridicule by the satirical intelligentsia of the *polis*. It presented matters as if the "new philosophers," not excluding Socrates, consistently acted as advocates of the worse cause in the chronic legal disputes between citizens and could be exposed as *cattivi maestri* – teachers with a pernicious influence. This was no small reproach at a time when higher culture (and the leadership role of Athens in it) came to take an intense interest in the key problem of *paideia*, the art of forming the youth of the *polis* on their path to adulthood.

Among thinkers in the sixth century BCE, a mordant criticism of the anthropomorphism of divine figures was already under way. Xenophanes claimed that, if cattle or horses could draw the gods, they would make them look just like cattle or horses. The sentence lent itself to replication as a meme: "It has been quite correctly observed that if triangles were to make themselves a god, they would give him three sides,"[11] etc. From there, it was no great stretch to articulate an explicit theory of projection, by virtue of which one could explain how the gods arose through the superimposition of earthly attributes onto the screen of heaven – ever supplemented by the personification indispensable for poets and theologians. The twentieth century could add little more to this motif of ancient religious criticism than the derivation of projections from early childhood, including from states that are preverbal or (especially) from close to the threshold of language acquisition. Everyone in early childhood experiences what it is like, when one is halfway to speech and turning to a being of superior power who does not respond to every distress call and who can only be manipulated to a limited extent – first one is angry, later desperate, finally resigned, but then, when the good object, apparently summoned in vain, comes after all, one is comforted and grateful.

The gay science of these projections culminated in Europe, in baroque-era depictions of paradise. In his work *Merveilles de l'autre monde* [*Miracles of the Other World*] (1614), François Arnaux, the canon at Riez Cathedral, sketches an afterlife modeled in every aspect on the splendor of the court. There, Christ in person declares: "My paradise is El Escorial of the angels, the Louvre of the blessed."[12] Later depictions of paradise unselfconsciously project the joys of earthly courtliness into the manners of the saints and the blessed in their intercourse with one another; the ears of the redeemed are delighted by music, as if it were broadcast from the salons of the great ones on earth directly into the halls of the beyond. All the same, paradise would have to wait for the "ghost seer" Emanuel Swedenborg before marital privileges could be granted there; he assured readers of his private revelations that earthly copulation conveyed only the dullest presentiment of the delights of angelic coupling.[13]

The emergence of philosophical theology bore the features of a conservative enterprise. Plato can be seen as a witness attesting on behalf of the rule of prudence in times of upheaval, according to which preservation is best achieved through modernization.[14] It led to the realization that the case for God could only be won through new media. Among these, the first was what he called *philosophia* – which was initially to be understood as an autoerotically tinged, mathematically stylized, dialogically accoutred self-exploration of the intellect – or, more especially, of the thinking soul (*nous*), its action (*noesis*), and its medium (*noema, eidos, idea*); it pursued the aim of attaining the human spirit's participation in the divine *nous* – or, more precisely, of making unconscious or forgotten participation conscious and remembered. Orphic and Pythagorean inheritances became operative here, evoking an afterlife of numbers, figures, and chords.

Apart from that, we now have grounds to observe that the "discovery of the unconscious" was not a heroic epistemological feat accomplished in Vienna around 1900 (assisted by a few preludes in the post-idealist metaphysics of the nineteenth century, notably with Schelling and Schopenhauer); it appertains to one of the remoter implications of Plato's teachings, which first began to spread around 380 BCE, initially in quiet, almost hermetic, forms. These teachings were based on the thesis that humans in their everyday disposition are entities who, under postnatal conditions, have not merely forgotten the prenatally experienced intuition of essence, but have deliberately pushed it aside in favor of "mortal thoughts."

The second new medium was "the philosopher" in person. It arose from the conversion of the rhapsode (the reciter of Homer) and the iatromantis (the spiritual healer or shaman) into a lecturer who demonstrated to clients how, given the necessary patience, one might rework "problems" (from *proballein*: to raise a topic) into stable intuitions. The philosopher's rival was called the "sophist," known today as the "public intellectual" or the "expert," a communication activist who brings quick truths before the public, sometimes out of personal commitment, sometimes for a fee. Plato's thought was realistic enough to aim to eliminate precipitancy in his curriculum: those who wanted to belong to the elite (which did not then yet exist) needed to have reached the age of 50 before they would be sufficiently mature for a reliable vision of the *agathon*.[15] To behold the real truth, one must become selfless, like a dead person.

Ever since there have been doctrines of wisdom and philosophical revivals, personal and technical mediumisms have been blended together, even if often disharmoniously. The archaic allows a *channeling* of the world above, first through the conduit of a self, be that a sorcerer, a seer or singer, a poet or soothsayer; the more modern then offers the acquisition of software, so to speak, in order to introduce higher things to thinking beings. Plato promoted his teaching with the suggestion that illumination might be achieved through the combination of practice and commitment to the Logos.

6

POETRIES OF POWER

Having said that, it would seem plausible to hypothesize that "religions," wherever one encounters their rites, their myths, their doctrines, their writings, their institutions, and their personnel, are to be understood as the products of local powers of imagination. One fable grasps another. Henri Bergson called them the works of a natural faculty of fabulation, a "myth-making function."[1] Wherever this faculty of thought flourishes, the tendency to produce religion appears as a natural color in the spectrum of anthropology. Accordingly, cathedrals would be fables written in hard stone; priests would be actors absorbed in their roles; martyrs would be sorcerers' apprentices who never return from their journeys into the hereafter; theologians would be dramaturges who deal with the grammar of fables.

The notion that religion and a faculty of projective imagination are bound together has become virtually the dominant opinion among the educated class today in western civilization. One might fancy that a telephone game from ancient times, originating with thinkers like Xenophanes, Epicurus, and Lucretius, would have whispered in the ears of the modern masses, after passing through intermediate relays such as Spinoza, Hume, Diderot, Feuerbach, Bauer, Marx, Nietzsche, and Freud. In this same lineage, speculative neurologists like Pascal Boyer and Michael Shermer came to offer new perspectives for discussion. In their view, the innate preprogramming of "the human brain," a.k.a. *the believing brain*, manufactures convictions that presume supernatural agents.[2] The relevant cognitive modules include those that are preset to communicate with those who are absent – they might be activated, for example, by participation in a formal commemoration of the dead.

Once set into operation, these areas tend, through individual self-excitation, to develop an inner life *sui generis*. The sensitivity for transcendence would be an endowment of android brains intelligent enough to reckon with the existence of more highly structured intelligences. The phrase "on earth as it is in heaven" (in Greek: *os en ourano kai epi ges*; in Latin: *sicut in caelo, et in terra*)[3] belongs to the awakening powers of attentiveness from a contingent intelligence to a necessary intelligence – necessary insofar as everything encountered (i.e., Nature, everything with which one is together in being) lends itself to being grasped as an opus – that is: as the work and artifice of an intelligence capable of handling everything real.

The first intelligent conviction that grows powerful within beings opening up to "the" world – and it is not merely fabulatory – is surely that there are powers and forces in the world which are potent both within us and beyond us. To construe their potency as "signs of life" and as storylines brings the initial achievement of poetry into effect. The ur-metaphor of "action" means that everything that happens is initially understood as propensity and deed: everything is alive, everything is populated by a host of impulses, "all things are full of gods." The universal ascription of powers at work precedes the distinction between the subjective and the objective; they form a permanent concert out of energies variously envious and benevolent. In early conceptions of such powers, it was impossible to separate the worlds of physics and fairy tale; neutral and agentless events seemed unthinkable at that period. From another point of view, it was recognized early on that such powers exist in continuities and discontinuities; they are found essentially in the plural, they limit each other, they require discretion. Where rationality begins – that is, the translatability of knowledge into the ability to do things, and the translation of the ability to do things into knowing more and wanting to do more – power comes to be understood through power.

The art of asserting correlations, later known as logic, arrives on the scene as a by-product of analogical understanding. Analogies create the connective tissue among things. What is called the world is elaborated as a panopticon out of modal relationships and incidents that always occur in association with others. Those who see a long gray trunk can, as a rule, infer a whole elephant. What makes an item appear recognizable in the first place is that it looks like something else of much the same aspect. Nietzsche speculated that it might have conferred some survival advantage if, in early days, one did not linger long on the small differences, but rather concluded more promptly that something similar was effectively the same. The great surround, which phenomenologists call the "lifeworld," forms a delirium of similarities. One perceives what one remembers. "Substance" finds its consistency insofar as it is only like itself; substance is called absolute if it can be compared only to itself and to nothing else.[4] The world is initially everything that is sustained by redundancy – for the most part, it displays the face of a tediousness that is nonetheless hospitable to life. The same-as-it-ever-was protects its own against whatever is new under the sun. But association is also created by mental representations that follow closely one upon another: a fisherman in New Guinea returns from his voyage without a catch; the question arises: who was it who bewitched his nets? He raises his eyes and sees a visitor from the neighboring village. At once it strikes him that this man is the sorcerer, and, awaiting his opportunity, he attacks suddenly, killing the man.[5]

As soon as accidents, catastrophes, and their internal fallouts have to be dealt with, cults appear on the scene that try to engage with these unrestrained powers; arts arise in which the specific ability to deal with the surprising and the dreadful is developed and then handed down. Naturally, death is the most anticipated surprise. Wherever "religion" enters the picture, a kind of mastering of inability comes into play. One may not be able to master dying, strictly speaking, but one can practice preparedness for this inability. Whoever calls upon the ambivalent heavens – mainspring of both favorable circumstances and fatal interruptions – expresses the inclination to be (indeed, the urgent anticipation of being) protected, rescued, and restored from affliction. But the expectations that people place upon the heavens would be misunderstood if one failed to recognize that mortals also like to be agreeably surprised. The fact that heaven offers no guarantees either way is a tribute to its sovereignty. Once in a while, heaven seems to justify at least some of the hopes placed in it, and this fact sustains its usefulness as an address one might call upon – until such a time that the spirit of self-help and the departure into self-sought adventures relieves it or takes it out of the game.

Relatedness to what is superior is a form of affinity and proximity, and what is related and proximal can be symbolically domesticated through alliances. The art of alliance is half of culture. Superhuman powers will go through cycles of weakness and strength in their enigmatic being-in-themselves; in order to revitalize themselves, they need human partners. This is evidenced by the old tradition of worldly institutions making ritualized offerings to render assistance to weakened otherworldly powers. When (more often) mortals in their weakness seek the help of higher sources of power, they make supplicatory sacrifices that were understood (and not only in the Enlightenment) as attempts to bribe the otherworldly. In fact, such sacrifices have always obeyed a speculative logic of compensation: if one cuts off a finger, the gods may forgo taking the whole self.[6]

From here on, one could follow Hegel's schematic narrative of "religions" as they developed out of their magical beginnings: they are ascending compromises from negotiations between, on the one hand, the experience of the self and, on the other, the mind or spirit's experience of object and resistance. Through "work" – that is, through touching, speaking, writing, traveling, struggling, producing, commanding, and obeying – these form into distinct variants of complete being in the world. As soon as people come to realize that loftier goals are within their reach, they cease to comport themselves as mere feeble powers in their intercourse with superior powers. Just as the lever acts as a mechanical advantage device for moving otherwise immovable weights, the mind or spirit – first magical, then technical and political – proves to be a force amplifier for gaining power over particular natural and cultural phenomena. The subjective pole comes to be strengthened by conceptualizing gods whose cult requires increased skill and ability on the part of mortals – such as the exercise of power in princely chancelleries, or command over troops, or the performance of complicated rites in magical cults and at semi-magical masses where practitioners mostly no longer know very precisely what the particular cult elements mean. In medieval cathedrals, a highly developed "I can" confronts an infinite that has been thought through nearly to its end. The belief in the efficacy of action fulfills (albeit vaguely) the factor of being that we might call "power in general," even if one does not know exactly how one action exerts influence upon another. The French epigrammatist Antoine de Rivarol (1753–1801) was on the scent of such phenomena when he noted – as a preamble to the technical age, as it were – "The world is full of forces that are only looking for a tool in order to become power."

The prototype of *empowerment* shows itself in heroic actions, appearing paradigmatically in the labors of Hercules, of whom Hegel remarked: "He possesses human individuality, and he worked like a slave; he was in service, and by dint of this human toil he earned himself a place in heaven.... This spiritual individuality of human beings is on a higher level than that of Zeus and Apollo."[7] Their virtue lies in having accomplished real work, although not always and everywhere in a constructive sense. Robert Oppenheimer was a late Herculean subject when, after the detonation of the first plutonium nuclear device in the desert outside Socorro, New Mexico, on the early morning of July 16, 1945, he thought of verses from the *Bhagavad Gita*: "Now I am become Death, the destroyer of worlds."

By way of the heavenly realms that overarched the great civilizations of the first millennium BCE, the horizons of the humanly possible came to be expanded to a new, more extreme degree of tension. That which extends beyond whatever people can achieve – even those who have surpassed themselves as heroes, sages, and saints – is projected as deified virtues onto heavens that are understood in ways that are no longer merely cosmological. Such a heaven no longer serves as just an everlasting counterpart to the earth; it is no longer an imagined unity subsuming the vaults of day and night and staffed by astral personnel. It has become something beyond the stars themselves; it now stands as a cipher for transcendence. When faculties that appear as part of human self-experience – prudence, justice, love, vigilance, and kindness toward strangers – are projected onto something still higher than the near and middle beyond of the known spirit, divine, and elemental zones, vertical tensions arise to expose the upward-gazing individual to new kinds of excessive ego-forming demands.[8] The metaphysical virtues produced the first extremisms and addressed them to a trans-Neptunian spiritual entity.

I should be more perfectly prudent than I will ever be capable of being; this exalts to the highest heaven an idealized intelligence as the consummate form of prudence. If I were as perfectly wise as I ought to be, I would already in my own lifetime exist as the likeness of the archetypal intellect, which understands more than will ever be understood and calculates more than can ever be calculated. Moreover, because prudence is an obligation, I should be more perfectly righteous than I can ever be, trapped in my own skin as I am, espoused to my own way of looking at things. This makes perfect righteousness or perfect justice a divine principle, whether its agency is called *Ma'at* or *Dike*, *Iustitia*, *Tao*, or anything else invoking a superhuman (or really nonhuman) impartiality. Because justice is bound to overall proportion and never satisfied with the piecemeal, I should be able to approach its individual objects with love, and yet this will be bound to more than I will ever be able to perfectly love. This makes love, in the mode of *caritas*, the most divine and most arbitrary of heavenly powers. The element of righteous injustice in love becomes apparent when I am favored or neglected regardless of whether my favor or neglect is deserved.

Moreover, I should be more perfectly attentive – attentive beyond the capacity of any being who is subject to fatigue and sleep; this makes the real God an ever-wakeful, ever-watchful observer; he embodies the utopia of sleeplessness, which breaks the complicity of night and malefaction.[9] This conception finds its parallel in the modern demand for transparency. Finally, I should be capable of treating any stranger as if the stranger belonged to my own people, as one of us; in consequence of which, the world as a whole is transformed into a symbiotic shelter, populated by strangers and speakers of other languages, who ultimately cannot remain so strange to us, and to whom the individual, like it or not, always owes whatever is essential.

Since I have known myself as bound to a supramundane world demanding such an exalted degree of virtue, the starry heavens above me and the moral law within me form a sum of imperatives that generate unbearable tensions. Concepts of child-rearing typically downplay these tensions by presenting ideals of moral development in terms of aspirational values that are approximately achievable. In *Faust: Part Two*, Goethe's Manto spoke more honestly about the nature of humanistic extremism: "On the impossible he sets his heart; Such men I love."[10] A now largely forgotten tenet of Greek thought responds likewise: the person who is not overtaxed has no part in *paideia*.

7

DWELLING IN PLAUSIBILITIES

Recent anthropology in all its branchings forms the scientific balance of the activity that human beings have always pursued to explain to themselves who they are, where they come from, where they live, with whom and with what they share their existence, and what they were created for.

Humans exist as anthropopoetic entities. Whatever they do is part of their local anthropodicy. They advance their becoming-human – and their displacement from the inhuman – by assimilating to what they "pretend" to be in relation to something higher. They have long known that there is something about them that goes beyond themselves. Blaise Pascal sums up the experience of being-open-to-the-above-and-beyond in his dictum that "man infinitely transcends man."[1]

Transcendence means more than just a passive mental opening to realities that "display themselves." As an acquisition of ability and power, it can create discrete real effects. Reality as such shows itself in the steep declivity between powers at different heights of transcendence. Naturally, it is not put into full effect permanently – and never continuously in actuality. It remains mostly virtual and has typically concluded by the time that anyone takes notice of it. That there might be such a thing as transcendence is thus something that many know only second-hand. The pyramids of Egypt and Yucatán form obscure monuments of incomprehensible practices of ascent and transcendence; the medieval cathedrals in the cities of Europe stand as relics of an incomprehensible drive to scale the heights. Asia's temple cities prove the extent to which meditative immersion was compatible with the will to build a tower. In our times, we tend to traverse more horizontal landscapes, with a few high-rises erected and reckoned as totem poles of modern urban life. Pascal's thesis holds true only in conjunction with its antithesis: man also competitively undercuts man – not infinitely, to be sure, but sometimes deeply and with scant prospect of reversing the positions of the last and the first.

Relatively stable compromises between transcending and under-cutting tendencies constitute the "cultures" which until quite recently were organized predominantly in tribal and ethnic terms. Their essential achievement was to integrate their members into broadly sufficient symbolic dwellings. They provided their people with stories and routines and habits to keep anxiety at bay, with cuisines and arts, with celebrations and images of the enemy. Their achievement as a whole can be described as conferring fitness relative to the lifeworld. They placed people in a familiar space, but hemmed in by a ring of the unknown, the unsettling. Trafficking between the sphere of the known and the uncanny beyond, were amphibious figures, who as healers and seers could sense the facts of both realms and could navigate between them. Hölderlin conjured up the primary constructivism of cultures in his late poem *In lovely blueness...* :

Full of acquirements, but poetically,
man dwells on this earth.[2]

The intensity with which Martin Heidegger worked these lines is well known.[3] *The Social Construction of Reality* (1966), by the Austrian-American sociologists Peter L. Berger and Thomas Luckmann, elucidates how semi-mythological talk of "dwelling" translates into the concept of inhabiting "plausibility structures" that give shape to collective life.[4] In their elaboration, people of all times and places reside within enclosures that are defined by a particular set of expectations about the world – something that one might refer to these days as "social constructs" or "interaction systems." It would be more appropriate to call them macropoetic structures or large social bodies – although the body metaphor is maybe too weak to be appropriate for the sprawling networks, global webs of financial transactions, and semiospherical constructs that stretch across terri-tories (nations, cultures, language groups, faith communities).[5] For small- and medium-sized units of social cohesion, expressions such as "tribes" and "nations" have found acceptance, even though one term is as problematic as the other.[6]

There is a complication inherent to "poetic dwelling" or the habitation of human groups within their plausibility structures

– Berger and Luckmann also write of "provinces of meaning" – and this complication has always tarnished the quality of living in one's own space. One has to realize that "dwellings" or "structures" or "cultures" always and everywhere function as spatialized and symbolically articulated immune systems. Their interest in self-preservation anticipates typical injuries from the environment and the social world and then forms embodied preventative measures. As embodied expectations of injury, immune systems are inherent to all higher organisms and organizations that are to any extent subject to drama. Whether innate or acquired, they can never shield their bearers from all danger. The organisms, which can only ever be partially immunized, remain exposed to risks of injury, invasion, and enslavement that exceed the scope of existing protections. Such risks proceed from the existence of aggressors against whose attacks there are no available immunizations, whether a priori (innate) or a posteriori (acquired). If sheep should ever become immune to wolves, it would necessarily imply nothing less than the "abolition of species."[7] Species, like nations later, are evolving immune-system collectives. In their external relationships, species, like most nations and peoples to date, have yet to arrive at an adequate understanding with each other, and it remains uncertain that they ever will. Our attention today is captured by the extinction of species from the ecosystem of animal life; these extinctions are attributable to the circumstance that most species have no endogenous protective systems to help them to resist technically equipped human peoples – their best chance against being overwhelmed by humanity has so far lain primarily in remaining undetected.

Frictions with the plausibility structures of strong rivals produce institutionalized expectations of injury in human collectives. Historically, typically, frictional partners appear as expansionist neighboring peoples and are initially countered by adopting an analogous posture – by a mimetic escalation of armament and a broad hardening of aggressive resolve, provided that the polemical affect cannot be assigned to professional soldiers: Persians against Babylonians; Persians against Greeks; Macedonians versus Persians; Romans against Carthaginians; Sasanians against Romans; Muslims against Byzantines; Mongols versus Chinese; Turks against Europeans; French against Habsburgs; Russians against Turks; British versus Indians; Japanese versus Chinese; Germans against British, Americans against Russians; Iranians against Saudi Arabians, etc. The rivals are particularly strong when they make their appearance on the world stage accompanied by imperial claims. Overarching the military, fiscal, and sovereign pretensions enacted by expanded entities of power is a rhetoric that is universalistic and world-religious – something that is merely partial lays claim to the whole. Where priority claims coded as universalistic react to one another, mutual contempt for the pretenders – and so also the affront of blasphemy – cannot be far off. This is particularly evident in the clash of monotheistic-type empires of meaning.

The fact that Orthodox Jews have existed alongside Christians for 2,000 years and that both forms of "monotheism" (one binitarian,[8] the other trinitarian[9]) continue to assert themselves unconverted after Islam and its monopolar dynamics have taken the stage – these facts create a structural situation that is reciprocally blasphemous.[10] Assurances made in the Universal Declaration of Human Rights that "no one shall be subjected to arbitrary interference with his privacy, family, home," like assurances of an inviolable "right to freedom of thought, conscience, and religion," are, literally and metaphorically, both canceled and raised up, as soon as "poetic dwellers" feel offended by the dissidence of their neighbors, as if heterodoxy were encroaching through the walls. They perceive this, rightly or wrongly, as an offense to plausibility – in other words: as an indirect attack on their own universalistically coded, existence-governing, premises.

Trinitarian Christians who are serious about their faith can only respond with silent contempt as soon as Muslims raise the objection that God, the eternal Solitary, has no son. At the same time, self-assured Muslims understandably feel their blood pressure rise when told by Christian theologians that Islam is essentially a coarse variant of Near Eastern Christianity that has failed to understand the Trinity.

Complications of this kind, caused by proximity to those who "dwell" and write their poetry otherwise, entail consequences for poetics in general[11] and for theopoetics in particular. They bring corrosive conflict into the heart of their own respective provinces of life, signs, and meaning. Since Aristotle, poetics has been pursued primarily as a doctrine of genres – namely: the epic, the drama, and the lyric. Within the horizon of Aristotelian observation, the invention of gods does not form an independent category – it is spread across all genres. As a classical Greek, he shares in a culture that accommodates the presentability of the gods in a variety of sign systems. The philosopher of the fourth century BCE notes impassively that Homer and Hesiod begat tales of the origins and deeds of the gods, and that later poets addressed hymns to them; in the dramas, their power comes on stage to speak in a high tone. With calm irony, he can state that the power and morality of the gods were not yet differentiated in earlier times.

Before the Platonic contestation attuned people's sensibilities to the matter, it was not obviously offensive for the Greeks to involve the Olympians in their narrative of the Trojan War. Likewise, the story that a godlike titan took up a sickle and castrated his father who at the time was asleep with his mother – this was accepted as an incident from an antiquity that was itself close to chaos – the mythical account refers to an antiquity so remote that to be disgusted about it in the moral categories of the present would be inappropriate. Above all, it was not yet considered impious or imperiling to young people to unveil the power of the immortal gods on the mortal stage – as when, for example, in Sophocles' tragedy *Ajax* (performed 442 BCE), the goddess Athena blinds the great warrior with madness such that he slaughters flocks and herds of livestock, under the delusion that he is slaying the companions of Odysseus, whom he hated; or as in Euripides' *Bacchae* (performed 406 BCE), when Dionysus causes the queen, Agave, to tear her son Pentheus to pieces in the throes of maenadic intoxication, until she regains clear consciousness and (in her *anagnorisis*) realizes that, delusionally supposing she has killed a lion and carried off a trophy, she is in fact carrying her son's bloody head in her hands. At this point, the cultic aura of the theatre was still clearly capable of neutralizing scandals caused by the gods – moreover, the topical timeliness and the exemplary nature of the action were further broken up by dating the events *in illo tempore*, the indeterminate past. It was only the intervention of philosophy that called attention to the unsuitability of representing the gods in their partiality, enviousness, and cruelty. The "new sensibility" – as if through an incipient political correctness – made it explicit that egoistic and capricious gods cannot arouse awe, even if they walk in on Olympian stilts. The late Plato repudiated the old sacrificial system from the ground up: the good does not want to be bribed with gifts and swayed with "witcheries of supplication" – it wants rather to be understood through the mind or spirit.[12]

8

THE THEOPOETICAL DIFFERENCE

From very ancient times, across the most widely divergent cultures, there have been poems that addressed themselves to divine things or to the gods – later also to the one God, or to God in general, with neither definite nor indefinite article. The earliest narratives of totems, ancestors, cultural heroes, gods, and primordial powers were based on poetry, even where they were rendered without meter, rhymes, tropes, or markers of fiction. In the early beginning, they were always embedded in ritual operations understood as self-presentations by invisible agencies, or as re-enactments of original deeds and events.

Greek tragedies, for their part, were poetic works, offering new vistas on much older, mythologically formulated stories of the gods that were still then broadly well known. Such stories, in turn, posit the victory of a younger generation of more sharply defined gods over a pre-world of amorphous gods of might. Most of the more sophisticated poetic productions were subsequent versions of older speeches and plays treating the gods. The intellectual history of great civilizations thus consistently exhibits a basic structure whereby initial earlier poetries are typically accented more cosmologically, whereas subsequent, later poetries are accented more ethically in nature. From afar, the emergence of the second poetries seems to correspond to the phantom of the "breakthroughs" of the Axial Age, perceived by Karl Jaspers in the mists of eastern and western antiquity. The principle of overwriting first-level fictions with second versions, typically capable of being written, if not actually conditioned upon writing, dissolves the phantom "Axial Age," while its factual core emerges more clearly in the light of the editorial history of theopoetries.

The canonical document of Christianity is called, with emphasis duly marked, *He kaine diatheke* (the New Testament), the second version of a covenant which, in turn, refers to an earlier series of endowments already attested in writing: the covenant on Ararat, the covenant with Abraham, the covenant on Sinai. Even the covenant of the people of Israel with their God was itself an ethicized second poetry of religion, in rivalrous contention with older "pagan" or "nature-religious" fables. The formulation "poetry of the second stage" also easily encompasses all the provinces of meaning in Christian community life and its hierarchical structures, both before and after the imperial pact of the fourth century CE. The expression *religio* can probably only be made comprehensible in its Christian appropriation if one recognizes in it the kind of ethical poetry that reaches for the whole of life. It is not the meter that makes poetry, nor the lyrical moment, but the complete integration of the person within the rules and freedoms of existence under an ethico-poetic constitution. In this sense, since their ancient Iranian, Mesopotamian, and Jewish beginnings (together with their continuations in Essenic, Gnostic, Marcionite, cenobitic, Augustinian, Benedictine, and Islamic currents), the ethicized second poetries can only have been of a "totalitarian" tendency. An illuminating indication of the self-poetizing structure of the Muslim modus vivendi is provided by the legend of Muhammad's Mi'raj, at the end of which the Prophet is said to have negotiated with Allah a reduction in the number of compulsory daily prayers, from 50 down to 5. If Allah's "initial demand" had prevailed, Islam would have become a monastic religion in which believers were primarily occupied with prayer. Under sovereignty of a God who cannot forget and therefore has to choose between forgiveness and damnation, the seriousness of hell seizes upon the worldview of strict monotheists – and, with it, the perplexity of creating viable forms of totalitarianism.

The invention of purgatory in the High Middle Ages had shown the Catholic *religio* that one way to enhance the viability of their totalitarian fiction was to promise an ontologically stable possibility of purification after death. François-René de Chateaubriand rightly remarked that "purgatorial fires" surpass hell and paradise in their poetry because they introduce the light of a future into the hereafter. The fact that the poetry of purgatory reached its apex in the second part of the greatest medieval poem, Dante's *Divine Comedy* (written between 1307 and 1320), illustrates how the spirit of the second chance opened up a space for hope in the afterlife: purgatory, the in-between hell, makes sinners paradise-worthy retrospectively, by functioning as a transcendental laundromat, removing the stains of earthly life from the face of one's soul in seven cleansing steps. From the perspective of Luther and Calvin, Dante's three-tier Catholic vision of the hereafter was insufficiently totalitarian, because it weakened the coercive pressure to repent, in which the sinful person, ever in iniquity with respect to God, takes up a position on the divine either/or.[1]

Dante's *Divine Comedy* revealed in every verse that it belonged to a theologically elaborated art of poetry that was over 1,000 years old; as a second formulation of a religious poetry of the second order, it repeated its lack of interest in cosmogonical questions of beginnings and origins and instead explicated in superhuman detail its complete absorption through the three states of ethically relevant last things: eternal hell, purifying hell, and paradise. This can be read as a further indication that there are no "Axial Age breakthroughs," as Karl Jaspers thought, but only phases, staggered in time, in which a highly implicit archaic stock of symbols is made more explicit in subsequent articulations. If there had ever been such a thing as a breakthrough, it would be attested in the *Divine Comedy*, which of course represents a late venture. Dante knows that his depiction of Paradise puts into language things that had never been said before, since, before him, no one had ever been there and returned to tell the tale; only poetry could give access to the beyond: for which reason the poet, with surpassingly legitimate presumption, claimed the right to designate his *comedia* figuring Paradise as *lo sacrato poema* – the sacred poem.[2] In the centuries after Dante, this right of the poet was never forgotten in Europe and the West. John Milton's *Paradise Lost*, in the first edition of 1667, casually bore the subtitle *A Poem Written in Ten Books*. In the tradition of Dante, not a single line of Milton's would disavow its fictional constitution – even though it took as its theme the satanic beginnings of the *conditio humana*. Nor did Friedrich Gottlieb Klopstock's *Messiah* (1749– 73), comprising 20 cantos and almost 20,000 verses, deny being a sentimental–naive verse poem in the tradition of Homer and Virgil. The highest works of culture – not excluding the Passion oratorios of Johann Sebastian Bach and the solemn masses of Mozart and Beethoven – testify with every syllable and every note how second and third poetries develop out of a dynamic of overwriting primary formulations.

Epic accounts of the life of Jesus were to be found in embryonic form as early as the second century CE. The very existence of the genre gives evidence that epic poetry, with the more refined tone it had developed since the age of Homer, had a complaint to lodge with the linguistically problematic genre of the Gospels, written as they were in sub-literary Greek of the first century CE. The practice of the "biblical epic" as documented since the era of Constantine the Great (272–337 CE) testifies to the dissatisfaction of the educated classes in the Roman provinces with the plainness of Gospel discourse. The *Evangeliorum libri quattuor* (*c.* 330 CE) by Juvencus, a presbyter from Hispania, translated naive and sublime stories about Jesus into the heroic meter of Virgil – in order, on the one hand, to shape them into a continuous biographical narrative, and, on the other hand, to demonstrate that the populism of the Jesus story was amenable to aristocratic coding.[3]

From late antiquity onward, biblical poetry was a passion of the classical West that was as plausible as it was unsuccessful. In terms of religious and cultural history, it remains of symptomatic importance insofar as it represented a variant of poetry that was preceded by an earlier form of poetry – namely: the Gospels themselves. They were a testament to the emergence of an aggressive new genre concerned with the deeds and sufferings of a providential savior. The Gospel literary form, an amalgam of vita (*bios*) and collections of sayings (*ta logia*), for its part came out of the matrix of myths reported by messengers, envoys, and helpers from the other world. The death-and-renewal myths of the agro-cultural, plant-theological, and earth-based age of the world lived on in them, transformed by a theology of heaven. From the moment the first person looked up, the view was upon an indefinite openness. From out of that openness, there approached a vague something that needed to be made more distinct.

It would be vain to try to tell the story of the elementary fancies and free positings that gave shape to the indistinct. Its older parts, in particular, would hardly constitute "a history of religious ideas," such as Mircea Eliade has advanced,[4] but rather a report on the ethnogenic rituals and ego-technical practices that, for groups and individuals alike, impart sufficient self-similarity to get through the day and the year and, good spirits so permitting, to be handed down to one's children and grandchildren.

Franco Ferrucci's novel *The Life of God* (1986) ascribes autobiographical ambitions to the biblical God – hence the subtitle given to its translated editions: *(as Told by Himself)* – and makes the matter quite clear: as soon as we see expanded horizons in the freedom of formulation, we move very promptly into the field of explicit *theological fiction*; inevitably, the bumbling author supplies a parody of Gnostic teachings from late antiquity. Something comparable can be said about Pierre Gripari's subversive tale "Le petit Jéhovah," which in a few pages lays bare the theo-psychiatric constitution of Christianity as a cleverly launched epidemic of guilt feelings – a brief *opusculum* that outweighs a whole bookshelf of literature on religious psychology. The masterwork in the field of parareligious fiction is provided by J. R. R. Tolkien's monumental, crypto-Catholic novel *The Lord of the Rings* (1954–5), which unleashed a flood of productions in *fantasy fiction* and *fantasy religion*, and, within a short time, generated a sprawling genre in film and popular iconography. After opera and the novel, film proved itself to be the ideal medium for portraying the wondrous made manifest.

What works of this type have in common, technically speaking, is the tendency to liberate the representational (and evocative) function of language, as it emerges in hymns and prayers and, under suitable circumstances, turns into self-sufficient lyric – that is, into sung invocation or into the song form of self-expression. One can read Augustine's *Confessions* as exemplary of this hybrid generic mixture of hymnal prayer and descriptive treatise: formally, it presents a prayer in the service of self-disclosure to God and the public. These confessions present the attempt – which is also hybrid in the ethical sense – to force oneself into the history of salvation through therapeutic self-exposure.

It is characteristic of theopoetry of this type that it is no longer intended for recitation within a communal cult performance. Works like this anticipate private or semi-private reading – they have quite unmistakably left behind the sphere of sacred operations. Even when they deal with "higher things," they dissociate themselves from ritual performance, and most especially from sacrificial practices, which since archaic times had provoked "numinous," fascinating, shuddering moods of participation in the serious instance of a death happening before one's eyes in the here and now – something subtly repeated in the sacrifice of Catholic Mass as transubstantial "change."

With such literary products, authors from middle and late antiquity vied for clients in the limited market for the attention of the educated class, among whom the Christian *literati* made names for themselves as disputatious confessors, promoters, and apologists. Tertullian was already writing apologetic literature for the Roman worldview. Even Augustine of Hippo was initially little more than an aesthetic rhetor, remarkable for his extreme productivity; only later did he veer onto the path of seriousness with the new order of love in heaven – *sero te amavi*: too late have I loved you.[5] Also, religious speech, whether Christian or otherwise, was in those days poetry in verse and prose, emerging from the continuing ferment of primary fables and their symbols. The well of the past is deep indeed, but so too is the form-demanding openness of the basic terms. Too much has always been said about expressions such as birth, separation, reunification, light, dark, fertility, desert, forest, world, path, field, river, rupture, and others – too much, but never enough.

When Hildegard of Bingen wrote down one of her visions, in which the angels walked along in silk robes and white shoes, she had no thought of spawning addenda to the Catholic cult – she had no other intention than to use literary means to keep her spiritual advisors and her sisters informed of her unusual condition. It was honest rhetoric, with figures of light metaphysical straining, when Thomas Aquinas made the claim that the glorified bodies of the saints in God's kingdom would shine seven times more brightly than the sun.[6] Colleagues of the *doctor angelicus* may have read it as an indication of how faintly the highest level of learning will check the temptation to juvenile grandiloquence. And when John Calvin presented the finding that metals would no longer rust in the restored paradise, that was an accessory to the revelation received from his otherwise not very fanciful pen.[7]

In community-forming structurally conservative ritual cults, whether old or new, what was said (*legomenon*) always stayed closely related to what was done (*dromenon*) and what was shown (*deiknymenon*), whereas, outside of ritual, in theopoetries, what was said appeared increasingly autonomous: often it presented itself painted in rich detail and enhanced by hyperbole, crisscrossed by subplots, accented with interiorizing shades, autobiographically enriched, interspersed with learned arguments.

With *Legenda aurea – Golden Legend*, the widely copied and reprinted collection of Christian hagiographies compiled by Jacobus de Varagine around 1264 – the frontiers of spiritual entertainment literature had already been reached. There can be no doubt about its edification, but it covered more than half the distance decoupling reading from ritual, in order to give the literate and curious of the era access to a kind of entertainment piety *alla cattolica*. These stories, naive but varied, summon up incidents in the lives of more than 150 saints who had lived in the 1,000 years since the appearance of Christ. Who, after all, would want to live among the pious if they didn't also have a story to tell?

It would take just a century more before the devotional legend was replaced by the curious and colorful early modern novella. When one considers how Jacobus de Varagine tells his tales and then how Giovanni Boccaccio composes his stories, one sees clearly the change of epoch and the shift in the focus of meaning when relaying worldly incidents. The privilege of the novella becomes apparent in the lifting of the ban on curiosity. All of a sudden, the life of the pious and the life of the impious both appear sufficiently remarkable and similarly apt to be depicted through a distanced observation – that is, "literarily" – in the sharp and prosaic contours that come with heightened detachment and closer inspection. Here, with Boccaccio, the sainted and the sanctimonious enter the picture for the first time without an aureole – painting, for its part, will take some centuries longer to shed its halos. The spirit of the novella was more akin to that of the incipient historical criticism, which sought to remove itself from the hazy cloud of credulity.

The de facto beginning of the European Enlightenment is to be found in the fourteenth century with the nominalism, anticlericalism, and feminism of Giovanni Boccaccio's book of ten tales told each day over ten days. The philosophically acute author of *Il Decamerone* (1353)[8] was hardly the first to discover hypocrisy as the close sibling of religion; he can, however, be regarded as the first phenomenologist of religious hypocrisy. Hypocrisy, in La Rochefoucauld's *bon mot*, may be the tribute that vice pays to virtue, but it also promotes the dissociation of what is done from what is said – in cult life, in politics, in private, and in public life. Common talk and the novella keep us current on disjunctions both concealed and publicly manifest. In a world ruled by pious lies on the religious side and by false accolades on the political side, novellas form the beachhead of a language of truth.

It is part and parcel of the program of the novelistic Enlightenment that the first story of the *Decameron* is about the canonization of a villain who, on his deathbed, makes a fool of his credulous confessor. The second story is of a Jew who, before converting to Christianity, wished to gain a picture of the customs prevailing at the papal court in Rome, but discovered there only "lust, gluttony, greed, deceit, envy and pride" – lacking just wrath to complete a sevenfold of vices, but indicating that whoever seeks faith would be well advised to look elsewhere than in Rome. The third novella offers the original version of the story of the three rings, which Gotthold Ephraim Lessing later reformulated as the "Ring Parable" in his play *Nathan the Wise* (1779); in the *Decameron*'s third tale, the role of the dissembler falls to Saladin, the sultan of Egypt, who needs a loan of money from the rich and wise Jew Melchizedek, calculates against making a forthright confession of his need, and seeks to compel the loan by ensnaring Melchizedek with a loaded religious question. The fourth novella tells of a monk who, when chance favors the opportunity, disports himself with a young woman in his cell; the abbot who should discipline him, however, is aroused in turn to the same sense of opportunity and succumbs in like fashion to the call of sin – and thus is forced to concede that he has no right to reprimand the monk under his charge. Boccaccio anticipates Marshall McLuhan's consideration of the mediatory vehicle: the sequence of the stories is the message. To count to four with the novelist and, with the key of the opening quartet in hand, to proceed along to ten times ten – so that the number of secular novellas in the *Decameron* is equal to the number of cantos in the *Divine Comedy* – is to come to know what the Enlightenment is all about. The book of novellas is intended to be read as a second-order exercise in observation: a thesis resonating to the effect that "religion" is a thing that can only be understood in a language other than that in which it explains itself.

A good part of what will be called "culture" in post-Reformation Europe might be understood as hypocrisy developing into a system. It forms a space of simulation in its own right, the finest flower of which is courtesy, in which "critique" awakens – sometimes in the form of a second hypocrisy – and grows into a constant of modern conditions. "Culture" and "critique" then form a "reservoir of themes," to echo Niklas Luhmann, for semi-serious differences that, one agrees, one does not have to come to an agreement about. Karl Marx may have struck upon the right idea with his claim that all critique must begin with a critique of religion; without the critique of hypocrisy, there can be no critique of religion. The critique of hypocrisy supplies an attestation that cynicism goes further than any ideology.

When Friedrich Schleiermacher's epoch-making speeches *On Religion* appeared in 1799, at first anonymously, it had become evident that what was said could be dissociated from what was done to the point of total incoherence. "To have religion means to intuit the universe."[9] There is no liturgical gesture that could ever correspond to a statement of this sort: the inner act through which an individual becomes aware of his being-in-the-universe is indefinite. It remains undecidable whether exposing oneself to the all-encompassing is like an inner upsurge, like giving oneself up for lost, or like a drift into indifference. In any case, the gesture through which the intuition of the universe is accomplished is akin to an inner pantomime of dying. Martin Heidegger schematized it in *Being and Time* (1927) as a figure of the "anticipation of one's own death." The "feeling of utter dependence" invoked by Schleiermacher denotes a waking immersion into the comprehensive. This imaginary euthanasia of the ego does not, as Hegel mischievously insinuated, amount to an emotional enslavement according to which dogs would be the best Christians.

Religions, it would seem, can be engendered by way of kits of different kinds. Schleiermacher argues that because "the idea of God adapts itself to each intuition of the universe, you must also admit that one religion without God can be better than another with God."[10] Hegel will later distinguish – in contrast to the "natural religions" – three great religions of "spiritual individuality": the "religion of sublimity" in ancient Israel; the "religion of necessity or of beauty" among the Greeks; the "religion of expediency" among the Romans. According to Schleiermacher, however, what authentic religion requires, first and foremost, is a "sensibility and taste for the infinite."[11] Its vagueness notwithstanding, this thesis indicates that, although the Augustinian construct of the *vera religio* had faded over the course of the Enlightenment, its power to haunt persisted up to 1800. A religious attitude is now considered true insofar as it is affected by the infinite. Any concept of God in which this taste is not expressed cannot form the crowning glory among the cults.[12] As it turns out, there are blinkered gods, just as there are dull and unworthy visions of the hereafter.

By distinguishing religiosity from religion, by detaching it from historical forms of scripture and cultic practice, by interpreting it as an illumination of the universe in a congenially receptive subject, Schleiermacher makes a breakthrough to a first, as yet romantic-ironic, explication of the principle of theopoetics: "It is not the person who believes in a holy writing who has religion, but only the one who needs none and probably could make one for himself."[13] The only thing missing here is the insight that to "make one for oneself" has been an operating principle at least since the "folk spirits" highlighted by Herder made their contributions to the great chorus of peoples, whether these spirits were expressed collectively, or else were championed by particular authors.

The other side of the theopoetical difference assumes its contours as soon as one envisions a state of affairs that, over the past 2,000 years, has been determinative for the historical realities of ideas and ways of thinking: there are religious constructs which, despite their plainly evident poetic formation, fundamentally deny that they are poems, fictions, myths, projections, or any other work of the imagination. They form the hard core of the "recognized" (mostly monotheistically coded) "religions."

One must state it as frankly as the situation demands: the prevailing "religions" in the narrower sense of the word – what are often referred to as the "great religions," or even "world religions"

– are de facto theopoetic entities strongly characterized by doing
everything in their power to avoid comparison with the myths,
cults, and fictions of other cultures. This they do, on the one hand,
by preserving the bonds between their dogma and their rite in
a strictly orthopractical way (Jan Assmann occasionally calls it
"empractical"), and, on the other hand, by curbing, with the help
of orthodox and absolute norms, all impulse toward any heretical
(i.e., selective and schismatic) rewriting of their scriptures. They
say No to mere religious-sounding notions. Formulated in terms
of systems theory: "It must not come to the point that everyone
asserts something."[14] From this perspective, the religious remains
a question of observance.[15] It was not entirely wrong to claim that
only those who practice a religion "understand" it; for practitioners,
what matters is the correctness of word and action and the close
correspondence of the two.[16]

With regard to the philosophical theology that issued from the
teachings of the Akademia outside of Athens, a formal cultic elaboration of its doctrines was not to be expected – although there are
indications suggesting that post-Socratic teaching was accompanied
by conventional sacrifices – a hypocritical pretense, one might
suppose, aiming to mitigate the risk of renewed accusations of
impiety (*asebeia*) from the suspicious city. Certainly, the late Plato
no longer wanted to hear of gods who could be swayed through
supplication and sacrifice.

When Plato had Socrates speak about the *therapeia theon* before
his trial, Plato had in mind an intellectualization, perhaps even
already a kind of mystical spiritualization, of eusebeian conduct
(Latin: *pietas*; German: *Frömmigkeit*; English: *piety*). Socrates
could proceed, *pro domo*, as if, among prudent believers, popular
rites of blood sacrifice would be replaced by internal acts – and,
in particular, by meditations on the just and the good. The
outcome of his trial suggests that he did not succeed in making
the turn to prudence plausible for a majority of the five hundred
citizen-jurors. Little is to be found here of Karl Jaspers's figure of
a "breakthrough" to a humanly relevant, reflexively heightened
state of consciousness; in truth, the very figure of the breakthrough itself belongs to theopoetries of a second order as an
attempt at their interpretation. The really striking processes in
the history of ideas and ways of thinking take place either in the
mode of a religious-political decree, or in the mode of the ongoing
percolation of sophisticated doctrines, over the course of generations, through to a "public" that could only anachronistically be
described as such.

Where in life, if not in the routine cultivation of conscious existence, should a place be found for exercises promoting the remembrance of the good as such? This is the point of the proposition that wakeful watchfulness is the natural prayer of the soul. Those devoting themselves to its practice could persuade themselves that they were subscribing to religiosity of a post-conventional level. Having been won over to such a stance, Socrates drank his fatal cup.[17] For him, the opposition between faith and knowledge would have been the sort of thing that the jargon of the twentieth century would call a "pseudo problem."

The "religions," in the sense made explicit here of being second-construction poetries that categorically deny being poetry, display in their professional adherents characteristics that make their weaknesses inseparable from their strengths. Often their experts can be wondrously clear-sighted with regard to rival systems. They see through the fictional and functional elements of these systems with a practiced professional eye.[18] The thought that the priests of other cults are, as a rule, no more than well-trained impostors comes so easily to them, one might almost suspect that a lack of spiritual generosity was part of their basic nature. Be that as it may, however, they also tend to be wildly sensitive to the judgment of outsiders with regard to their own doctrinal commitments. It is not uncommon for clergy and theologians to practice identitarian fortress-building in the exercise of self-defense – apologetically, plaintively, lamenting the ungodly spirit of the age and, as occasion permits, appealing to secular powers to impose the *auto-da-fé*, the "act of faith," upon schismatics and heretics.

Since the end of the nineteenth century, advocates of the major religions have sought their advantage in ecumenical dialogue. In that time, they have come to understand that the visibility of their own brand in a pluralistic marketplace contributes to identifications that strengthen client loyalty and mobilize donations. In September 1893, the first Parliament of the World's Religions was held in conjunction with the World's Columbian Exposition in Chicago; since that time, engaging in dialogue as such has come to be elevated to the level of a minimal dogma among clergy and theologians – the Roman Catholics played coy for a spell but, in the end, they too agreed, albeit after voicing due reservations. For most of them, it involves renouncing missionary activity on the territory of the others. This new modesty corresponds with the counsel that, for the time being, each party should minister to the lost sheep of its own flock.

The irony of positive religion shows its administrators constrained to choose between sclerosis and heresy. The long-lived monotheisms have existed for 20 or 14 centuries – to say nothing of Judaism, which has survived 25 centuries in its post-Babylonian forms (though its rabbinic form is younger than Christianity)[19] – but they also owe their resilience to rituals of stigmatization and to castigation procedures that effectively imprint their engrams upon the younger generation and thereby bolster the fitness of the group's memo activity.[20] If they urge their younger generation to relive the symbolic content of tradition, they rejuvenate themselves by virtue of being forced to work through the inevitable eruptions of fermenting symbolic and presymbolic matter – and to do so in a way that is at once conservative and innovative.

9

REVELATION WHENCE?

A cult might indeed reject and deny, with perfect rigor, the charge of being "mere" poetry, including in its doctrine and its theological superstructure – but this option is only available under two conditions: for one, on the condition that "divine things" can be opened up in a way other than that of conventional human assumptions about spirits and of afterlife fantasies born of fear and wish and derived from human, all-too-human sources; for another, on the condition that, in more complex cultures (especially literate cultures), there is a sorting of extraordinary mediumistic talents – in particular, differentiating healing competence from the "prophetic" ability (as construed by the Greeks) to predict what is to come, as well as separating poetic inspiration from erotic enthusiasm.[1]

Traditionally, the other way is called revelation. It enters human consciousness through one of the four doors Socrates describes in his second speech of Plato's *Phaedrus*: erotic rapture, prophecy, healing arts, and poetry. For what follows, the second and fourth are important: the door of prophetic proclamation and the door of poetry, which say more elevated, more exalted things and know better than the popular talk of the day. In the event of revelation (a benevolent mania, in the Platonic view), things are generally arranged in such a way that what is found strictly precedes whatever is invented, what is received strictly precedes the self-thought and the self-made. When Moses received the tablets on Mount Sinai, they had already been inscribed by the "finger of God" – Moses himself was said not to have been the writer. The fact that there were commandments on them – one in the I-am form, some effectively in the thou-shalt form, the rest in thou-shalt-not form – was only set down through the work of redactors at a later date.

Compilers likely took some direction from the ideal of the number ten and from state treaties of the ancient Near East, which are said to have contained similar lists and to have matched the wording of the Decalogue.

Wherever revelation is accepted, one is reliant upon the purity of its reception. Moses may have been regarded as an obstinate individual and his deficiency in rhetorical talent was an established public fact, but in his day no one saw him as an impostor or a charlatan.[2] The ability to write was ascribed to him in later times, when the Torah came to be handed down as the "Five Books of Moses." The light of historical criticism makes it clear, however, that not a single line there can be attributed to an author of this name; this fact, of course, changes nothing with regard to the finding that the (fictive) attribution of those books to the legendary author has established itself as a force in the history of memory. In any case, the logic of the situation requires that Moses would have been able to read because handing written tablets over to him would not otherwise have represented a meaningful gesture; this course of events also falls consistently into the sphere of legend. In the context as given, only one conclusion is admissible: since Moses was not himself an inspired poet, he must have passed through the second door, that of prophetic reception.

The account gives no suggestion that Moses himself set fire to the burning bush whence spoke the voice: "I am who I am."[3] And it would be too much to imply that it was merely in the crackling of the flames that he heard the utterance spoken by the Elohim or YHWH. It burns, it speaks. The fire and the words were there before Moses, even if not independently of him: it burned before his eyes, it spoke to his hearing – both processes can be dated to an age in which the eye and ear could be mystified without a second thought, as passive organs of reception, far from any imputation of independent hallucinatory activity. If Moses remains of great importance in the history of religion, it is because he was one of those who are supposed to have met God, the absolute sender, in the position (or non-position, one might say) of pure receptivity, and because of Moses' devoted acceptance of a meaningful gift from the unconditional elsewhere. The thesis of pure acceptance or the unconditional acceptance of gifts sounds impressive indeed, but it has not been demonstrated that the "whence" of this gift is anything different than the source from which poetry comes. The difference between laws and poems is of a theoretical, not an ontological, nature. That they do not come from separate stars is manifest in the fact that both of them thrive in consistently quoting, reciting, interpreting, and relaying.

Acceptance necessarily transpires on the recipient's terms, which the giver cannot fully determine, even in the case that intermediaries have primed the recipient for the taking. Moreover, it is generally overlooked that the willfulness of the receiving party also includes a longing for absurdity, through which recipients place themselves at the disposal of the wondrous. Faith – in the sophisticated sense that denotes the historically most successful religions of revelation – is articulated precisely at the juncture of functioning plausibility and functioning absurdity. The attempts undertaken since ancient times to prove the reasonableness of belief effectively render the absurd inoperable – wherever, that is, such attempts threaten to succeed. Absurdity disarms; when listeners are dislodged from their anchorage in normal ontology, they are prepared for suasion from above and beyond. Successful rationales roll back the disarmament until there is no more left of the believer than is granted with Sunday indulgence.

The pure welcoming of a gift from an absolute elsewhere is a motif cultically cherished in Islam in particular. The tradition of the revelation of the Quran holds that, through the archangel Gabriel, the Prophet received in his inner ear, albeit auditorily, the recitation and the flow of words, and then and there memorized the words he'd heard. At the same time, the notion takes shape that the angel had brought before his eyes inscribed verses – excerpts, as it were, from a pre-existing book. Muhammad's auditions begin suddenly with the miraculous: what is revealed to him at the beginning are the very un-Arabic teachings of resurrection, judgment, and eternal life. Here there ensues an elaboration of figures established among Christians for half a millennium, and among Egyptians and Iranians for far longer; they are articulated in the mode of a newly granted epiphany drawing upon earlier ones. The fact that Muslims initially prayed in the direction of Jerusalem, before they switched over to Mecca, shows the extent to which the later revelation was shaped by acts of redaction and editing.

Unusual memory skills must nonetheless have formed the basis of Muhammad's proclamations. The heroic feats of the Prophet's memory can be admired in the earlier surahs, notably in the over-long Surah 2, "The Cow," which unfolds without a clear structure and without a recognizable sense of sequence. If this extravagant surah had been compiled by editors long after Muhammad's death – no message from heaven can be delivered in such a fragmented state without being returned to the sender – then the bond between receiving and reproduction would be fissured, to say the least. Of the numerous postscripts to the oral impartations by listeners from the very beginning, the one that was finally canonized – under political orders and with the intention of legitimizing power – was that which most accurately corresponded to the voice resounding in Muhammad's ear and recited aloud by him. How this selection was possible is not to be explained without recourse to higher causality.

If Muhammad is said to have three times protested "I cannot read," before the revelation came down to him, this supported the premise shared by the narrators of the Quranic tradition. This premise was that the Prophet was the missing link between God and the earthly book – or, better, between Gabriel, the intermediating angel who speaks what will later be written, and the many (perhaps more than 20) scribes of the surahs who, at the sound of the Prophetic dictation, materialized it in flows of ink upon papyri, until a single version of it could be circulated as the legitimate one. The Quran as a written event presents itself as transcendently motivated, on the grounds that the unlettered Muhammad could not have been its author. It could not be his work – in the mechanical sense – because he was acquitted of all suspicion of being able to read and write. As with Mary, his ear had remained virginal. Indeed, this was so in an even more exalted sense for the eyes of the Prophet – they had not been deflowered by reading. That is why the Quran could almost be described as the "Book of Allah." One can invoke such a statement in a neutral stance, without entering into the labyrinthine debates of later Islamic scholars regarding the createdness or uncreatedness of the book. The idea of the pre-existence or the uncreatedness of a thing implies the infiltration of the Platonic distinction between archetype and copy, of which one may impartially say that it was located outside the vocabulary and syntax of the Prophet.

The angel who spoke into Muhammad's ear displayed a certain erudition. He quoted uninhibitedly (also without quotation marks) from the holy writings of the Jews, not least the Psalms. The art of paraphrase and allusion to major and minor historical incidents was also at his command. He was likewise familiar with Jesus' speeches from the Gospels concerning the impending apocalypse, and he seems to like to draw upon them. To one speaking in the name of Allah, there seemed to be no appreciable difference between inspiration and compilation. Although the angel declared: "We have not taught him [Muhammad] poetry" (Surah 36:69), the writers and redactors must have counted free composition, compilation, and rhyming among their proper tasks. *Sub specie aeternitatis*, from the perspective of the eternal, one might regard the Quran as a single sentence existing apart from time and space, which, due to the constraints of earthly syntax, frustrates expectations of a logically ordered sequence. Even if the sequential order in it is the message, it operates in a strictly esoteric manner.

The concept of "revelation" is based on the idea that the god or gods who disclose themselves to people are not altogether dependent upon accommodating themselves to human fabulations, even if, more often than not, they content themselves with such an expedience – much as they must also make do with the local languages, at least to begin with. This became apparent after seafarers, traders, priests, and ethnologists fanned out from European ports to all points of the globe and began to inventory thousands of peoples with regard to their ideas about the hereafter. The finding was everywhere confirmed that gods and cult communities, regardless of the form of the latter, whether as tribes, nations, or confederations, lived in economies of give and take – and had been connected thus with one another from time immemorial. What the hereafter announced under these conditions was not only based on vague reciprocity – it was also for the most part concretely transactional in expressions of gift and counter-gift.[4]

And yet, in rare moments and in due time – especially according to his proclaimers in the Middle East – the most high and almighty Lord made use of his sovereign freedom to revolutionarily pre-empt symmetrical, humanly conditioned transactions and to communicate things so superior, so evidently holy, and so mind-harrowing that no poets like Hesiod, no singers from the throng of Homeridae, no philosophers of the Platonic or Vedantic school could have come up with them on their own initiative.

For a god of revelation with claims to truth, exclusivity, and supremacy, the point of departure is always the same: the need to reckon with the fact that people have always been spirit- and god-poeticizing beings. Any goddess who would wish to disclose herself to people, any god who would wish to reveal how he is in accord with his being-in-himself-and-for-himself, will find how very much mortal consciousness is already overflowing with traditional tales of deities, spirits, and heroes. For a connoisseur of humanity experienced in observing from above, such a state of affairs should be found both untroubling and unavoidable. Wherever they might be on the planet, peoples who are furnished with myths and rituals from their own cultural sources – from their local demonic farmers' market, so to speak – move within ingrained "plausibility structures" with regard to their *therapeia theon*. Their life there in established provinces of meaning is to be admitted as a *factum brutum*; since they still exist, it is fair to assume that, as yet, a "good enough god" must have held a protecting hand over them. By contrast, a god with heightened ambitions with regard to loyalty and exclusivity would have to break down existing plausibility structures, or else transform them subversively.

The question "What is to be done?" can only germinate in a god who has revolution in mind. This kind of enterprise presupposes a condition of weakness in the then-existing cults – in sociopolitical contexts, one would speak of a "pre-revolutionary situation." A religiously well-served group – if one might deploy a market-economy expression in this context – could hardly be drawn over to a newly advertised god by mere sermons. To begin with, only individual problematic natures among the peoples and collectives are susceptible to becoming animated with the spirit – broadly speaking, these are the natures who feel the waning, crumbling, and increasing nuisance of their existing system of inspiration. The breakout of a new and unique God, one who admits no others, necessarily follows a putschist-enthusiast tendency, putting into play a God who forces an immediate decision – for or against him.

When this God appears on the scene, a crucial time comes to pass, tending toward the approaching End and the revelation of all things; the certainty takes hold that things cannot possibly go on as before – and, from then on, everything essential is understood to happen between Now and Soon. When sermons of this tenor catch on, the phobocratic shadows deepen immediately. The same God who holds out the prospect of paradise also providently lays down wide avenues to the eternal fires.

The unmanageably complex field of "religions," the revelations implied in the broader sense of the word, can be entered into here only by way of a narrow point of access. The first approach touches only upon the exterior surface of the subject matter: it proceeds from the historical observation that most cults, together with their locally issued revelations, have now vanished, notwithstanding the fact that each had an implicit concept that posed itself as valid irrespective of time. How should one understand the fact that revealed truths, with their ritual realizations and their adherents, emerged, flourished, and then disappeared? In which crypts, which memorial halls, are the extinct words of God deposited? How might one conceive of the archiving (or, to boldly state the cruel truth: the final repository) of the innumerable theopoetics that have been suspended?

Inquiries of this kind hint at a waste disposal problem of dimensions that are difficult to fathom. Just as gigantic eddies of plastic waste have recently formed on the oceans, whose biological degradation will take centuries, if not millennia, so we might imagine mighty eddies of god-residue having formed (albeit less obtrusively) on the oceans of the soul. Their detoxification and recycling is theologically, ethnologically, psychologically, culturally, historically, and aesthetically unfinished. Since many members of present-day humanity carry within themselves, consciously or unconsciously, particles of decomposed cult memories, innumerable individuals are effectively crypts – more or less troubled – for ostensibly forgotten and unmourned relics of a transcendence fallen into disuse. It would be naive to think that the emeritus gods, often having been dishonorably dismissed, could all be permanently sidelined in secular cemeteries, or neutralized within the accounts of religious history. If modern mass culture began with the gothic novel of the eighteenth century and opened up an alternative afterlife with the spiritism of the nineteenth, then might one legitimately speculate that much of it is a semi-serious dalliance with the shades of superseded otherworlds? And how can one avoid the impression that bad spirits are by far superior to the good ones, so far as the power to haunt is concerned?

A second entrance to the field of religion follows dramaturgical considerations. It proceeds from the question of how gods would act in the event of an actual manifestation, entering onto the stage on their own behalf, renouncing traditional mediators such as augurs under narcotic influence and prophets with overactive temporal lobes. If a god were actually ready and willing to step forth with a kind of new directness, a certain pressure would presumably have been felt to motivate the appearance, some inadequacy with respect to the previous medium. Once the Most High could no longer appear behind theatrical masks – something that would be incompatible with the concept of epiphany or *revelatio* – then representations by actors, rhapsodes, and *theologoi* (in the Aristotelian sense of fabulators of the gods) also likewise lost their currency. A *theologeion*, as visitors to Hellenic theatres once knew it, was no longer available to introduce such an event – as noted above, the sermon pulpit did not take architectural shape until the High Middle Ages. Viewed as a whole, the principle of revelation conflicted with the use of special "effects" – excepting signs and wonders,[5] which throughout ancient times were regarded as evidence of supernatural spirit and power, and which have only since the late eighteenth century been ridiculed as the fairy tale's revenge upon factual truths.

Any god who resorts to miracles engages in the conduct of a de facto populist persuader. If the aim is to expand the number of adherents, the god works to convince people more adversely situated. Every belief in signs and wonders relies on the hypothesis that the god does not act periodically through secondary causes and natural regularities, as usually happens, but instead deploys special effects in wholly unanticipated ways. The invisible agent is thereby constituted as a fellow inhabitant in the fairy-tale world. Likewise, the god's occasional appearances before mortal eyes, of which myths of the Near and Middle East like to tell, remain woven into the web of eastern folk surrealism. Even when manifest singularly in the mode of incarnation, God evinced orientalizing propensities: glimpsed from the perspective of the geography of religion, for example, Bethlehem and its comet are quintessentially of the Orient. Quite apart from chronological considerations, God simply could not have become man in Husum (North Frisia) or in Reykjavik.

Without the Greek vector that induced a movement to the westward, Christianity would have remained, like Islam, an eastern affair. The incarnation of God would have been viewed as altogether a matter of the fairy-tale East and it would have been abandoned to the campfires of the caravanserais. "One doesn't cut the blossoms of oriental storytelling."[6] In fact, Christianity also spread along the old Silk Road, eastward to the borders of China. Through the Grecophone world of the New Testament, beginning with the Pauline epistles, the fabulatory fertility of oriental salvation fantasies was coupled with the ontological and truth-theoretical seriousness of Hellenistic-Occidental thought.

While the emergence of Islam in the early seventh century CE marked the provisional end of the road to the de-Hellenization of monotheism,[7] the early Christian church, insofar as it did not become a desert church, consistently relied on Hellenization and the cultural infrastructures of the city. Wherever the Christian God was talked about in the old Occident, he was proclaimed from *theologeion*-like podiums – from ambos, pulpits, and professorial chairs that sought to establish that, following the Greek *logos*, the Gospel had also taken possession of the Roman *ratio*. It was not until the sixteenth and seventeenth centuries, after some late medieval preludes, that the emancipation of Hellenic heritage from Christian paternalism began in Europe – a development called the Enlightenment.

10

THE DEATH OF THE GODS

The question implied in the first approach to the revelation thesis can only be answered in a roundabout way. Future visitors from distant stars might conclude that Earth is a planet for decommissioned gods. Anthropologists estimate that worldwide, since the beginning of hominization, there have been about a million clans, tribes, and ethnic groups in which theogenic impulses will occasionally manifest themselves, in however rudimentary a fashion, so it is not altogether fanciful to imagine the earth as overspread with the relics of millions, even billions, of extinct spirits and deities – even when one excludes from the estimates the baroque Indian inventories for otherworldly agencies.

Linguists predict that, of the 6,000 living languages on earth today (a number to be further multiplied by the myriad dialects), more than half will become extinct by the year 2100 for lack of new speakers.[1] Even if one were to assume that each of the disappearing languages had only one name for otherworldliness, one would be forced to admit that we now (as ever) live in an era of the unnoticed mass extinction of spirits and gods: in less than a century, thousands of addresses for invocations and cult-based conceptions of the beyond will be obliterated – most of them undocumented, unnoticed, and unmourned.

The softer forms – call it a theo-hiatus, in which gods are put to rest through exhaustion – have been noted in the recent past as in the present. These differ radically from the theocidal effacements that were characteristic of Christian evangelizations by the sword (*Schwertmissionen*), and no less of early Islamic expansions. The enthronement of the sole God *in excelsis* was often accompanied by the diabolization of the hitherto existing notions of the gods, and occasionally also by the reclassification of the dethroned powers as servants under the monarchy of the One. In the French Middle Ages, the belief flourished that there was no more honorable recruitment for a decommissioned demon than to serve in the form of a cathedral gargoyle at Notre-Dame de Paris. For elves, nymphs, and intermediate beings of all kinds, the expanded hell offered new job profiles in the field of seduction work.

Processes forcing a coerced theo-hiatus also have little in common with the trivial atheism of the post-Enlightenment, which attended the entry of part of humanity, especially in Europe, into the enclosure of semi-successful provisions for existence. Extinction due to a dearth of offspring, dying off due to dwindling interest, and atrophy in the wake of oppression – these share with one another only the fatally dissolving effects of entropy.

The intellectual history of the nineteenth and twentieth centuries has illustrated how reckless it would be to underestimate the haunting power of the emeritus gods. Hugo Ball, who in 1916 would be one of the founders of Zürich Dadaism, wrote in his diary entry for November 25, 1914, that "all the world has become demonic."[2] Two and a half years later, in April 1917, he articulated his notion more precisely: "Everyone has become mediumistic."[3] Any randomly selected ego of our day could thus be converted overnight into a conduit exposed to the hauntings of a revived power. In modernity, the "metamorphosis of the gods" oversteps the religious field. What has become extinct as a religion can return as ideologized politics, as stage magic, as a technological marvel, and as an informational pandemic.[4]

11

"RELIGION IS UNBELIEF": KARL BARTH'S INTERVENTION

The most profound break with the theopoetic origins of religious tradition occurred in the twentieth century, with the doctrine of the Swiss Reformed theologian Karl Barth (1886–1968). Barth's rustic ingenuity pushed its way to the fore when he sought to remove Christianity – as historically the strongest success story of revealed truth – from the ambit of "religion." In his view, religions are machinations of people in the interest of their self-assurance and hubris – or, worse, in the interest of their self-deification. As a rule, they turn out to be fabrications in support of political violence and organized crime. Hadn't Augustine of Hippo already asked whether kingdoms were anything other than great robber bands – if a shade better than criminal organizations, then only to the extent that they tend to the administration of justice?[1] Even the doctrines of East Asia, whether of Indian or Chinese inspiration, form mere fictions in Karl Barth's eyes – in his words: "religions of lies," "idolatries" – light years away from the sphere of valid revelation. Martin Luther is likewise charged: through his errors concerning the relationship between law and Gospel, he helped the natural paganism of the Germans to gain ideological strength.[2] Karl Barth might indeed be accused of a few things, but lack of combative clarity is not one of them.

Karl Marx would have wondered what consequences would follow from his early thesis that all critique should begin with the critique of religion. In Barth's conception, revealed religion is focused critically against actually existing religion – indeed, more critically than any materialist critique could ever achieve. Barth declared in 1937 that "Religion is *unbelief*: religion is a concern – indeed, we must say that it is the one great concern, of *godless* man."[3] The author does not have to be asked twice to explain how he knows this: "We cannot, as it were, translate the divine judgment that *religion is unbelief* into human terms, ... But we must still accept it as God's judgment upon all that is human." Nor is he embarrassed by the question of how he got his knowledge of "divine judgment." He knows that what he says is true because he was "addressed by God." The subject of the revelatory address is "the word of God and therefore God himself." The revelation of God implies "the abolition [*Aufhebung*] of religion" – a rejection of "religionism." In order to become a receptive vessel for revelation, one must also be its subject – or, better: one must integrate oneself into its true subject, God, or, better still, concede that one has always already been integrated with him.

This operation is called "dialectical," because it is at once impossible and necessary – impossible in substance, and necessary because "we" are already included in the revelation issued to us. "The Truth itself has proclaimed to us that Truth is Truth and that we originally participate in it."[4] Anyone who likes to run in such circles can become a theologian. Shortly before his death, Barth defined the theme of his theology in a more childlike way: what speaks to us is "heaven for earth."[5]

Karl Barth lays bare the trade secret of the putatively non-theopoetic speeches of God by confessing to the fiction of the non-fictionality of such speeches. With energetic naivety, he insists that he speaks as one who has been addressed, in the execution of an absolutely obligatory Relay charge issued from on high. *Deus dixit*: *God has spoken*; there can be no going back to the time before God spoke. Theologism is a kind of non-theopoetic speech that only wants to know, transmit, refresh, and venture the "Word of God"; the procedure of theologism is based on a change of subject in which the ego, possessed by socialization, together with its deep-rooted illusions and its irreparable lapse into the world and death, is exchanged for the ego of faith.

The "change of subject" operation is considerably older than Christianity, but wherever it appears on Christian soil, it is Pauline in character. The most illuminating formula is to be found in Paul's own Epistle to the Galatians (according to the majority opinion, written around 55 CE; according to a dissident view, falsified in the second century CE): "and it is no longer I who live, but it is Christ who lives in me [*en emoi*]." Analogously, the Gospel of John (possibly around the year 100 CE) lets Jesus say: "Abide in me as I abide in you [*meinate en emoi, kago en humin*]."[6] The change of subject – which the Greek Christians called *pistis*, the Romans *fides*, and which formally happens through baptism, a ritual repetition of the scene at the River Jordan– aims to effect an interchange or trans-position, right up to the entanglement of spiritual spaces: God/I, I/God, each in the other. From this entanglement, Paul draws the most extreme consequence when he writes in the Epistle to the Galatians that he has been crucified with Christ (*synestauromai, confixus cruci*).[7] Anything less than the total eversion of one's funda-mental attitude will not suffice to shatter one's ownness through the otherness of God; it requires something comparable to a spiritual heart transplant. Naturally, one cannot operate on one's own heart. Karl Barth: "If man tries to grasp at the truth of himself, he tries to grasp it *a priori*."[8] "But our freedom in God is also our bondage in him."

One might be advised to modulate the tone on such pronounce-ments by joining them together with cooler complementary reflections. A reminder of Johann Gottlieb Fichte's (1762–1814) early *Attempt at a Critique of All Revelation* (1792) could prove useful here, as might a reference to Nietzsche's aphorism from 1888: "I am afraid we are not rid of God because we still have faith in grammar."[9]

For Fichte, it was compellingly clear that religion, understood as life's institution for moral guidance, should not contain anything other than what the rational moral law requires, regardless of whether religion were taught as natural or as revealed; this should shape our "appetitive faculty" and "determine" our will to the good. Belief that a "revelation" has taken place could usefully support weaker minds as an auxiliary idea that might rally the will in the service of the good – but, otherwise, the concept remains cogni-tively empty. Indeed, one recognizes "with complete certainty ... that absolutely no proof concerning the actuality of a revelation, either for it or against it, takes place, or will ever take place; and that no being will ever know how the fact of the matter stands in itself, except God alone."[10] Irony gets the last word here. It leaves it to God's discretion whether or not he wants to start something with revelation as a concept and an event. In the view of the young Fichte, as already for Spinoza, the historical religions are systems of persuasion and schools of obedience, which give the child's mind preliminary indications of what is right, but they cease to be worthy of mature, independent minds.

The problem of a possible self-revelation of God is something Nietzsche approaches even more sharply. He is hardly interested in how people came up with the idea of the existence of other-worldly beings. It is simply to be accepted as a fact of historical culture and ethnology that the thought came to people in varying degrees of rawness or refinement. The presumption of powerful entities that are invisible, transcendent, and open to intercourse with mortals forms a potent layer in human imaginative life and has an elementary, thought-like quality to it. Whether it concerns the near-beyond of ancestors and other spirits who live alongside people in a common locality, or else a regional high-beyond of the Olympus type, or else a radicalized beyond of the *totaliter aliter*, the absolutely otherwise, as one already finds in the emphatic articulations of Philo of Alexandria – experience everywhere imposes upon us the inescapable fact that hiddenness is not synonymous with nullity.

The ethnologist Adolf Bastian (1826–1905) argued that elementary thoughts denote ideas that are spontaneously articulated in various cultures, independently of one another, but based on logically, cosmologically, and socially analogous experiences.[11] Existence without them would be an impossibility – something at best conceivable as a product of a morbid impoverishment of the psyche, as occurred in ancient times with slaves and in modern times with immiserated parts of the proletariat, with cowboys on the prairies, with housewives in the Midwest, or with competitors on German casting shows. Elementary thoughts, like "ideas" from below, interleave pictorial patterns into the "flow" of perceptions. Anyone who can conceive of persons taking action is, *eo ipso*, able to carry the scheme of *agency* (sustained by purpose and the ability to take action) over to spirits, gods, and natural phenomena in the surrounding world. Personification thus forms the basic figure of demono- and theopoetics; it models forces into which an intention is implanted. The more personal the god, the more poetic the depiction. Within the vocabulary relating to these energy-filled "inspirations," one finds stars, deserts, forests; trees, grasses, flowers, insects, reptiles, birds, mammals; rivers, wells, seas; flames, clouds, and lightning – all of them waiting to begin a second life in poetic phrases. Pre-Socratic agencies, like the cold, the dark, the blue, report for the morning roll call of being.

Much as he does with the platitudes of middlebrow popular psychology, Nietzsche brushes aside the conventional early Enlightenment inferences concerning the gods as products of ignorance, fear, and superstition. He is particularly interested in the question of how people at the peak of their vitality could have understood the god hypothesis. Whatever the sound of the poetry that first spoke of the gods, it cannot, in Nietzsche's conception, have been a lament of self-pity and vengeful begging. As soon as enunciations were generated through the unabated impetus of illusion, and the powers opened up avenues for offensive portends, it was clear what religion is made of: "Being thankful for himself, man needs a god."[12]

Construing primary symbol formation in the direction of a god who encompasses an invigorating "we" remains plausible so long as, preceding all complaints, requests, and appeals to the impossible, one finds the impulse of gratitude – or, more precisely: the ingenious association of a collective celebration of victory together with humility in the face of the unknown. Archaic collective gratitude – and, at first, Nietzsche wants to speak only of this – is an impulse or emotion delimited by something internal and moral; where it appears, one finds victors, and their gods among them. The gratitude that a god demands for the gift of being-as-one-is subsists on the experience of victory, wealth, and authority awarded to the people with whom one belongs. Belonging to the god is thus an asset per se. In cultic language, successes are called "blessings" (*eulogia*). They follow from speech acts or the "good speech" of heaven: Greek *eulogein*; Latin *benedicere*; Arabic *barak*. One may of course receive gifts from exchange partners of equivalent status, but some gifts issue from higher sources or date back to the "ground of things" that precedes all chance. When powers are experienced as granted, beneficiaries become sensible of the connection between power, means, and their own apparent chosenness. Hence the primary complement to "We are" can only read "the favored" – and the one who favors us is the Lord of Heaven. God is the address at which successful collectives reckon they can reach themselves. The fact that God – whoever or whatever God may be – always bears an intrinsic address problem is a worry for later, most notably when victories begin to dwindle or come to nothing. Under the aegis of the god, the battles won and the stories about them become figures that constitute collective identity. For this, too, Nietzsche found the formula: "No victor believes in chance."[13]

Nietzsche's arguments show the contours of a bipolar anthropology sketched with the left hand. It aims to explain what victories and defeats make of a people in the long run, considered from a moral point of view. His suspicion is that slave morality – as the modus vivendi of those fixated in defeat – has started a campaign, in the form of the "world religions," against the remnants of free, sovereign humanity; this campaign has already found world-historical success and is on the verge of final victory.

Beyond historical anthropology, the author of *Twilight of the Idols* is engaged with the question of why it is almost impossible, even after the Enlightenment, for people to become wholly unbelieving. Nietzsche discerns the silhouette of God in the syntax of European languages. As a rule, they join a predicate with – and this is not accidental – so-called "noun substantives," or else a grammatical "subject." In the Indo-European sentence, the sun shines from Elea – in every assignment of a verbal statement to a noun, there shines a Parmenidean light. First there is a substance, a permanent something, which philosophically is called a being; attributes are joined to substance; in its attributes, the substance becomes mobile, colored, potent, and active.

What remains becomes actualized as a unity of potency and meaning. The philosophical program of Idealism, which seeks to establish this unity, entails the necessity of developing substance as a subject. To "still" believe in grammar means to still believe in the ubiquity of action and, together with action, in quasi-personal entities as that which everywhere initiate action. It is this belief that forces us to add a doer to an event, a sender to a sign, an author to a work, and a creator to a universe. Hegel called the substantially active subject *Geist*, translated into English as *mind* or *spirit*. Having become self-assured, so to speak, *Geist* can be seen in its "work" – its struggle with itself, its movement within history, and its sedimentation in the outcomes it has effected – as well as in its continuation on the basis of what it has already achieved. When it is more subjective, *Geist* is lively, current, open, and undisciplined; in order to rise to the level of art, it must undertake the labor of discipline and do violence to its unbridled vitality. When *Geist* is more objective, it embodies what has been achieved in science, art, religion, law, and the state. In order to become absolute spirit, *Geist* would have to develop the ability to join – within sovereign syntheses, and at any point in time – its being-active which has become objective and its current reflecting-and-acting. If such a thing were to be accomplished, Hegelians would have shown a capacity for being right such as has not been seen in human beings since their expulsion from paradise.

Karl Barth carried the belief in grammar to extremes by interpreting protestant Christianity as an act of the revelation of the divine subject beyond all human, theopoetic, and cultural components. If Christianity were the absolutely decisive event of truth, it could not have anything in common with "religion" in the general sense – neither as self-praise by winners, nor as a cult of lamentation by losers, nor as an expenditure of collectives' vital surplus, nor as individuals' uplifting experience of God – and certainly not of the kind that some Christians wanted to experience in August 1914 when the war broke out, much to Barth's displeasure. Christianity would have to be like the impact of a meteorite, not like the unwinding of a tightly coiled cult. It should have nothing to do with the casually attended "divine service" of the bourgeois commune, and above all no relation with the cult of an aesthetic church that would transform itself into a concert hall for religiously musical minds.

It was as timely as it was consequential when the young Karl Barth turned vehemently, resolutely, away from Friedrich Schleiermacher and his epigones in the culture-blessed Protestantism of the nineteenth century. He directed his "neo-orthodox" fire against ecclesial sclerosis and its employees, who had made themselves comfortable in a world that had become untenable. It was no longer possible for the church to remain a conservatory in which the well-disposed enjoyed the ease and steadiness of their God-friendly impulses; being addressed by the Good News would no longer be misunderstood as the result of gifts and moods. The time of mere aptitude was over. The beautiful, all too beautiful souls were too much like the corrupt world from which they thought they had turned away. The young Karl Barth stood on the edge of the impact crater of meteoritic revelation and waved the crowd on as they ran past – as if to say: Move along … "There is nothing here for romantics to experience, nothing for rhapsodes to enthuse about, nothing for psychologists to analyze, nothing for the storyteller to tell."[14]

The empirical reality of Europe and the Old World's loss of moral bearings had been catastrophically exposed during the First World War. Henceforth, the crucial task would be to experience the Word of God as an even greater catastrophe. In view of what the agents of the world and its nationalized religions had wrought, Karl Barth, like a church father fallen out of time, brought heaven's last chance to the concept that human participation in the truth goes further, in spite of everything, than the harm humanity has itself caused.

Whether Karl Barth made the right choice with respect to theopoetics remains an unanswered question. A man who spent a good part of his life in church pulpits and university chairs of theology could not have believed that he was himself the word of God speaking in a Swiss accent. Luther's reproach against Huldrych Zwingli, following the failed Marburg Colloquy of 1529 – "You Swiss have a different spirit" – would have been bestowed upon Barthes. Then again, Barth could never have taken himself for an actor gliding in on an updated *theologeion* into the midst of a listening congregation. One cannot avoid the suspicion that he fundamentally misjudged the question of the theopoetic consti-tution of "religions." He even composed a work of religion – albeit a religious work despite his will. His magnum opus, *Church Dogmatics*, published between 1932 and 1967, can only be understood as a lifelong rearguard battle, in which he tried to compensate for the neo-prophetic surge in his early writings, *The Epistle to the Romans* (1919) and its heavily reworked second version from 1922. The monumental *Church Dogmatics* implies, as it were, the reversion into "ordinary" theology of the Holy Spirit, which had been present in the moment; but even in the prefaces of subsequent reprints of the brilliant *Epistle to the Romans*, the author denied that he was, in the Gnostic sense, a "pneumatic" who overflowed the boundaries of his discipline – he only ever spoke as a theologian. The later Karl Barth felt an embarrassment with respect to his early prophetic phase (his spiritually overweening phase, as his opponents would have it): in it, under the impact of the disaster of war, Barth had elevated his tone in imitation of Paul,[15] who himself wrote under the impact of a Judaism trapped in a depressive cycle of law and guilt, and who evoked Christianity as a cult of relief from this wreckage – with the result being an expansion of the zone of guilt.[16] Barth's strikingly forward dismissal of "religion," from the start of the 1930s on, as a machination of the unbeliever, is an indirect self-criticism:[17] he, too, had once been a theopoet in action, concertizing in two-part harmony with Paul, borne by a time-bound impetus to proclaim, excited by dithyrambic passions, and propelled by the fury of under-standing and the zeal of the deputized, 6,000 feet beyond war and time.[18]

The new situation – in retrospect, one airily calls it the "interwar period" – made it necessary to counter the resounding declamations of countless crisis speakers with stricter forms of *therapeia theon*. Barth in the 1920s was repeating a late antique drama. By the end of the first two centuries of its history, the early church synods and councils had already noted that, in order to silence discussion of Egyptian and old Iranian influences, it was necessary to crop the rank growth that had emerged in the interplay of Jesuism and Jewish motifs with various Hellenistic and Middle Eastern sources. Around 1914, an era of rank para-religious growth had dawned in Europe (and far beyond the Old World) – as if a thousand voices strove at once to refute Nietzsche's ill-tempered remark from 1888: "Almost two thousand years – and not a single new god!"[19] In later genera-tions, historians of ideas and religions are likely to conclude that, from the early twentieth century onward, more religioid movements were launched in the West (as in the rest of the world) than at any other point in human history since the pharaonic cults – as if to contest the dominant narrative of secularization. Readers wishing to become better versed in these things will find a vast panorama of neo-mythological discourses since European Romanticism compiled by the theologian and historian of new religions Linus Hauser[20] – especially in the second volume of his *Kritik der neomythischen*

Vernunft [*Critique of Neomythical Reason*], which covers the broad spectrum of "new myths of becalmed finitude" in the post-1945 era. Even before that, Bazon Brock referred to this set of issues in his polemical treatise on the "God-seeking groups" of the twentieth century.[21]

In his search for something lasting beyond the crisis, Karl Barth's presence of mind involved him in an epoch-spanning war of minds and media. Even after nearly 2,000 years, we are now farther than ever from any kind of peace accord in the war between the designers of religions, full of ideas, and the disenchantment therapists, heresiologists, and inquisitors opposing them. From time immemorial, the guardians of "orthodox" tradition – on Christian soil, their patriarch is Irenaeus of Lyon (*c.* 130–*c.* 202 CE), who came from Asia Minor and whose book *Against Heresies* had been in circulation since around 180 CE – were concerned with the proliferation of narcotic, fabulatory, and schismatically-tending factors, and wanted to put a stop to them by establishing essential beliefs, called "dogmas," which precede any discussion. In dogmas, factual truths and moral directives are laid down as such and drawn together. Their announcement presupposes that those who issue them are strong, or at least powerfully determined, in daring to submit their addressees to such statutes for their own good. They count on the existence of persons inclined to believe who are also receptive to clarifications in the form of binary decisions. In the sphere of western Europe, the main sources of authority capable of transmitting dogma are called Catholic, Lutheran, or Protestant; in the sphere of eastern Europe, Orthodox; in the Islamic sphere, rightly guided. If the pathos of dogmatic integrity had to stir for systemically understandable reasons, it was because those early theologians who were gifted with strategic foresight had to fear the disintegration of their "movement" – unstable and difficult to organize as it was – so long as special doctrines (such as those of the so-called Gnostics or the Marcionites) could spread without being opposed. Even Irenaeus polemicized against Marcion of Sinope, like Marx against Bakunin – and like Stalin's creatures against Trotsky and the "revisionists." In such disputes, tolerance plays no part in the rules. In its struggle to establish proper discrimination, the Catholic Magisterium availed itself early on of the weapon of *anathema*, the curse of expulsion; what this meant in practice was revealed by the young Marx when, for his part, he laid it down that the criticism being realized does not aim to refute its opponent, but to annihilate it.[22] This suggests that the will to form a church was not alien to the critical school either.[23]

12

IN THE GARDEN OF INFALLIBILITY: DENZINGER'S WORLD

Leaving aside here its legal aspect, one can define dogmatics as a special ecclesial form of magisterial speech, arising from the will to reduce what is to be said to the indispensable, the clearly distinct, the carved-in-stone, with the delimiting of counter-theses as errors or false doctrines and the sanctioning of their representatives through an exclusion understood as a curse (*anathema*).[1] This restraint engenders a stylistic genre of its own that is marked by sovereign barrenness. Connoisseurs of medieval aesthetics would assign it to the plain, unadorned, *dépourvu* style.[2] Among diplomats from early European countries, it would have earned respect as the officialese of an empire that impressed with its unflappability.

To get an idea of the tone, scope, and shape of the production of Catholic dogma over the span of almost 2,000 years, it suffices to consult the magnum opus of the magisterial pronouncements of councils and popes: the *Enchiridion symbolorum: definitionum et declarationum de rebus fidei et morum* – in English, the *Compendium of Creeds, Definitions, and Declarations on Matters of Faith and Morals* – first published by Heinrich Denzinger in 1854, updated for its 37th edition in 1991 by Peter Hünermann, and provided with parallel vernacular translations. The 45th edition was released in 2017 with numerous additions, having grown to include over 5,000 documents. It begins with findings of the earliest Coptic professions with regard to baptism, and it closes with a selection from an apostolic exhortation published by Pope Francis on November 24, 2013.

Those who immerse themselves in this work will lose themselves in it, as in a Celtic magic garden on whose bushes there blossom bizarre distinctions. Some of them are still familiar to us from a distance, but most have long since appeared impenetrable, like bulletins received from a remote star. The contemporary reader cannot easily escape the impression that many of these doctrines have assimilated the most colorful fictions of the ancient *theologoi* from Hellas, India, and Persia, no less than the mythopoetry of Africa, the Americas, Asia, and Oceania – although they are generally not present at the level of even second-rate poetic articulation. In Denzinger's world, the pronouncements that pass themselves off as the spirit and letter of orthodoxy – what are they but blossoms on the old, often cropped-back bush of orthopoetry?

The bishops of North Africa who met in Carthage at the Council of 418 issued the following doctrinal canon concerning original and hereditary sin: "Whoever says that Adam, the first man, was created subject to death in such a way that, whether he sinned or whether he did not sin, he would die in body, that is, would go forth from the body, not as a penalty for sin, but due to the necessity of nature, let him be anathema."[3] This canon was formulated at the urging of the bishop of Hippo Regius, Aurelius Augustinus – by now known for his intransigence – to abjure the teachings of Pelagius (*c.* 354–418 CE), his rival from Britannia who had taught an anthropology of freedom not completely corrupted by sin. What mattered to Augustine was the strict adoption of his grimly conceived doctrine that not only must death be understood as a consequence of sin (without burdening himself with the question of why animals incapable of sin also die), but, more than this, that sin also already darkens the existence of human children from the moment of their birth – hence the insistence on infant baptism, through which the newborn is to be wrested from the dominion of evil.[4]

Pope Leo I, bishop of Rome from 440 to 461 CE, attested in a didactic letter to Bishop Turribius of Astorga on July 21, 447 that it was a fallacy to believe that the devil:

was never good and that his nature was not the handiwork of God, but that he emerged from chaos and darkness; because, of course, he had no one who made him but is himself the beginning and substance of all evil: although the true faith … professes that the substance of all natures, whether spiritual or bodily, is good and that there is no nature of evil, because God, who is the establisher of the universe [*universitatis conditor*], made nothing that was not good. Whence even the devil would be good if he had remained in that state in which he was made. But because he made bad use of his natural excellence [*excellentia*], … he was not transformed into an opposite substance, but he fell away from the supreme Good, to which he was obligated to cling, just as those very persons who make such claims rush away from the truth into falsehoods and blame their nature for their having gone astray intentionally and are damned for their own voluntary perversity [*voluntaria perversitate*]. And evil will certainly be upon them, and the evil itself will not be a substance, but the punishment applied to a substance.[5]

For the Second Council of Orange in July 529, Pope Felix IV, bishop of Rome from 526 to 530, submitted a number of doctrinal statements (canons), of which the synod approved 25, including this one:

> Can. 7. If anyone asserts that to be able by one's natural strength to think as is required or choose anything good ... without the illumination and inspiration of the Holy Spirit ..., one is deceived by the heretical spirit and does not understand the word said by God in the Gospel, *Sine me nihil potestis facere*: "apart from me you can do nothing" (John 15:5).[6]

In 1169, Pope Alexander III wrote a didactic letter to the sultan of the Seljuk Empire, who lived in Iconium (present-day Konya, Turkey) and who was interested in the Christian faith; in it, he reported the following about the mystery of the body of Mary: "[Mary] indeed conceived without shame, gave birth without pain, and went hence without corruption, according to the word of the angel, or rather [the word] of God through the angel, so that she should be proved to be full, not merely half filled [*non semiplena*] with grace."[7] In a letter to Bishop Simon of Meaux, Pope Lucius III, bishop of Rome from 1181 to 1185, answered the question of a prioress as to whether a young lay brother who had been deprived of his sexual organs could be ordained to the priesthood with the approval of the canon law:

> We, therefore, wishing to observe the canonical distinction on this point, mandate Your Fraternity by apostolic writing to inquire diligently after the truth so as to know whether he was cut by enemies or by doctors or, not knowing how to struggle against the vice of the flesh, he laid hands upon himself. The canons admit the former cases, if they are otherwise suitable, but they provide that the third is to be punished as a homicide against himself.[8]

At the Council of Florence (1439–44), the most holy Roman Catholic Church anathemized and cursed once again the early

Christian Gnostic theologian and heretic Valentinus, whose effect had been palpable in the Middle East since the middle of the second century CE, and "who declared that the Son of God took nothing from his Virgin Mother but that he assumed a heavenly body and passed through the virgin's womb like water flowing down an aqueduct [*sicut per aquaeductum defluens aqua*]."[9] A few lines later, the most holy Roman Catholic Church anathemized all those who do not accept "that in Christ there are two wills and two principles of action. / She [the holy Roman Church] firmly believes, professes, and teaches that never was anyone conceived by a man and a woman liberated from the devil's dominion [*diaboli dominatu*] except by faith in our Lord Jesus Christ, the Mediator between God and man."[10] In August 1896, the Holy Office affirmed, at the request of the archbishop of Tarragona, that "spirits of wine" (*spiritus*) may be added to sacramental wine to raise its natural alcohol content, so long as the resulting alcohol content does not exceed 18 percent of the whole.

On May 29, 1907, the Pontifical Biblical Commission published a brusque No to a sensitive question posed to it by advances in historical and philological learning:

> Question 3: Can it be said, notwithstanding the practice that flourished constantly in the whole Church from the earliest times of arguing from the fourth Gospel as from a truly historical document, ... that the deeds related in the fourth Gospel are totally or partially so invented [*ficta ad hoc*] that they are allegories or doctrinal symbols; but that the words of the Lord are not properly and truly the words of the Lord himself, but theological compositions of the writer [*compositiones theologicas scriptoris*] although placed in the mouth of the Lord?
> Response: No.[11]

The 1907 Commission's answer in the negative cannot conceal its increase in embarrassment. The reach of the theopoetry-conjecture has extended sufficiently far as to affect a Gospel whose affiliation with the core revelation had seemed untouchable from time immemorial. Even among theologians (and it is needless to call them Catholic), it has long been known that religions are invented – and for what purpose they are invented. Augustine, for example, tore through Roman notions of the gods[12] – not least to counter the reproach that Rome's military debacles in the Gothic Wars were signs that the old gods, having been displaced by the Christians, no longer extended their protective hands over the empire.

The prophet Isaiah preceded Augustine when he established the prototype of critical debunkery in his denunciation of Mesopotamian idols. In his eyes, they were nothing more than carved wood and he insinuated that the Babylonians, like other peoples devoted to images before them, especially the panentheistically disposed Egyptians, worshipped the statues as such – "Shall I fall down before a block of wood?"[13] – whereas, like most later zealots militating against images, he could have been expected to understand that divine images, statues, icons, and scenic representations were here, as elsewhere, cult aids for uplift to higher attainments. Iconoclastic episodes in the later history of art and religion show how mobs, inflamed by disdain, operationalized their hatred of the imposition of accepting the sacred objects of others.

Protestant Reformers of the sixteenth century similarly adopted the unsparing language of critical debunkery deployed earlier by Isaiah and Augustine. Martin Luther in Wittenberg, Huldrych Zwingli in Zürich, William Farel and John Calvin in Geneva – they felt they had to convince themselves that the Roman Catholic Church had created a mess of insidious distortions; indeed, that the precept of fasting, celibacy, the clergy as a whole and in its hierarchy up to the papacy, and even the Holy Mass with its ceremonial contrivances and its Latin hermeticism – all were biblically unfounded fabrications, no different from the veneration of saints and the cult of Mary – to say nothing of the fictions of purgatory and the fraudulent letters of indulgence. It was plain from all of this that, in order to reform faith and restore it to its true form, these things needed to be cleared away as additive corruptions of human devising. But how can one distinguish between poetic fictions and truth if the newly instructed faithful are to discard as fiction and additive a large part of what has hitherto been considered the right *religio*, while only a remnant, delimited by the principle of "by scripture alone," is to be exempted from the suspicion of fiction? And who protected scripture from historical decipherment, from wild reading, or even from demythologization?

Fictions are always other people's fictions. One's own faith plays on a field boundlessly different, insofar as *it* is founded in holy scriptures and carried by the tradition of the evangelists (presuming one does not completely reject the Catholic as a now-superseded convention). This conviction remains held in common by the most baroque Catholic and the most austere Protestant. In the antimodernist oath that Pope Pius X made his clergy swear in 1910, priests and theologians loyal to Rome had to vow to keep away from "the inventions [fictions!] of the rationalists" and to credit the audacious methods of modern textual criticism only with the most restrictive of clauses;[14] it was not until 1967 that this oath requirement was suspended.

One cannot possibly do better than to study Denzinger–Hünermann if one wishes to find out what theopoetics sounds like when it strives to suppress the sense that it is composed of inspired poems or strategic fabrications. It is unrivaled as the strangest book in the history of old and new European ideas, pervaded by hypnotic monotonies and clever oddities. In its pages glisten the scintillation of a synod-devised gynecology, which grants the one woman beyond women the good fortune to receive in her uterus the angelic word whispered into her ear.

The columns of the monumental work, in impeccably justified typesetting, drafted largely in elaborate committee-Latin, reverberate with condemnations and words of demarcation. Unseen prefects, as if concealed behind the veil of non-ignorance, indulge in hypnotic litanies, incanting their refusals of a large part of what has made its mark on the intellectual life of the past 1,000 years – and, in particular, inveighing against the tendencies of the eighteenth and nineteenth centuries: neo-Aristotelianism, Protestantism, rationalism, pantheism, fideism, Quietism, Indifferentism, agnosticism, mesmerism, naturalism, socialism, modernism. In frequent succession, thunderbolts ring out against the onanistic use of marriage. In addition to the abiding care for the purity of church teaching, one feels the efforts – as enduring as they were futile – made by the guardians of faith to encircle the primally rebellious genitals of the faithful within a ring of admonitions.

Denzinger takes his bewildered readers by the hand and leads them through a city of errors, scarcely much different from Virgil accompanying Dante through the Inferno. One learns of false paths more numerous than one would be able to tread in a tripled lifetime of wayward wandering. Anyone who wishes to experience Catholic surrealism at its peak point of development – thus, the sum of poetic fictions that will not, for anything in this world, admit to being what they are, according to their deep structure as well as their first impression – cannot avoid delving into this book of unbelievable things. In it there unspools the endless melody of sacred self-quotation. Where else would later additions be so tightly bolted to what was said earlier? The curial syntax is relaxed mediocrity, as it corresponds to an oration of majestic speech: it would be incongruous to sparkle with punchlines in the manner of younger authors. What God himself uttered long ago through cooperative earthly organs with regard to himself and humanity returns in the *theologeion* of the admirably even-tempered recitations of the Holy See and its quite infallible commissions. Whoever speaks for God has no ideas. Only in the Quran – and in no other construct – is the art of presenting oneself as completely right developed at the same high level as in Denzinger, and one can see there the labor involved in entrancing and capturing addressees in the loops of its self-reference.

To return here to Karl Barth's "neo-orthodox"[15] maneuver, the one which led him to the broad field of the interpretation of dogma: one cannot avoid the impression that Barth wanted to check the proclamatory expressionism of his early years so as not to validate the suspicion that, after the Great War, there was once again a "prophet in the German crisis"[16] who had arisen from among a throng of so many others. Wasn't there, in the commentary to *The Epistle to the Romans*, another ingenious *Homo religiosus* clamoring on the restless Swiss periphery to create a mood for irruptions of the *totaliter aliter*, the totally other, into the this-worldly, the all too this-worldly?

Barth's anti-theopoetic and anti-religioid turn led to the conviction that everything in matters of religion must be started anew from the ground up. From 1927 onward, the undeveloped parts of *Church Dogmatics* took shape; the first volume came out in 1932, and by 1967 there were 13 weighty volumes piled high. Those who peruse its pages will know soon and with certainty: the spirit that still wafts where it will cannot settle its affair with gravity in this way – especially not with the uncomprehended multiplicity of religioid structures all over the world, to say nothing of Barth's remoteness from everything that older and contemporary arts have to show. In its ungainly monumentality, in the specific detachment and the awe that one feels before its monological excesses, Barth's dogmatics can be compared more readily with Richard Wagner's *Ring des Nibelungen* or Thomas Mann's tetralogy *Joseph and his Brothers* than with a catechism that projects God's word onto the widescreen.[17] If Barth miscarries at great heights – or, more precisely, if he lapses into theological idleness, generating misplaced verbosity without advancing insight – it is because he does not sufficiently appreciate the provenance of poetic creation and the world-forming accomplishments made by restless hearts beyond number.

II

UNDER THE HIGH HEAVENS

13

FICTIVE BELONGING TOGETHER

One might be tempted to infer from the foregoing deliberations that the realm of religion should be incorporated into belles-lettres; this, however, would be a misunderstanding – and also a superfluous worry. One may indeed find Dante's *Divine Comedy* in the "Fantasy-Fiction" section of the Stanford Bookstore, but no bookstore would readily shelve Denzinger or Karl Barth's *Church Dogma* together with fine literature. The present proposal for a redescription of "religious facts" in theopoetological (or daimonopoetological) terms seeks to advance a goal which leaves the booksellers' classifications in peace. The redescription proposed here rather concerns itself with the ill-considered boundaries between theology and theories of poetry, as these have been marked by historical incidents and accidents and stabilized by factors that now appear largely anachronistic. Because it finds theology in the defining elements of these anachronistic formations, some remarks concerning the field may be found to carry ironic strains (Greek – *eironeia*: understatement). This, one hopes, represents the lesser evil as compared to what usually prevails in theology: saying-too-much (*alazoneia*: boastfulness, empty presumption) and ultimately-knowing-everything-better.

The undertaking of "theopoetics" should not be reproached with making its task easy for itself when it sees at work in all known versions of *religio*, without exception, a poetry-like (and originally directly poetic) operation of the powers of vision, imagination, and formulation. Nor can there be any question of a hostile takeover of the sacred by the profane – it is, rather, a question of a friendly acceptance of the all too serious. The sphere of activity for poetizing, dreaming, and hallucinating, like that for reciting, impersonating, rephrasing, and restaging, is herewith taken more seriously than is usually the case with conventional distinctions between truth and poetic fiction. As we have already observed, Herodotus did not shy away from saying that Homer and Hesiod had given the Greeks their gods; Johann Gottfried Herder's ideas about the proximity of world poetry to the religious beginnings of cultures, like Goethe's and Friedrich Rückert's, translated the Herodotean thesis into a program that lives on in fruitful forms of contemporary cultural studies. Against such a backdrop, the present deliberations claim an almost classic unoriginality.

A far greater misunderstanding would ensue if one were to conclude, from the dense contraction here of poetry in the broader sense and religion in the stricter sense, that "religious things" should be construed as decorative artifacts or ornamental idealizations of a prosaic life that could manage without them. In fact, it is not a matter of attaching poetry as a superstructural phenomenon to some social basis, however one might wish to define it – whether the emphasis is placed on kinship systems, procreation, care for the dead, the division of labor, the exercise of physical and symbolic power, or anything else.

Those who take into account how, from the origin of languages onward, poetic activity is bound together with worldmaking, do greater justice to the scope of primary poetry's impact. With each new entry into its vocabulary, poetry has a new reality-shaping effect; with the formulation of every phrase that it allows, it contributes to a constitution of "realities." It forms the first architecture of collective existence long before it becomes a decoration and an accessory – much as "culture" is a total competence before it narrows into a field for higher education in differentiated civilizations.[1] It represents the characteristic ability of *Homo poeta*[2] to establish "regimes of meaning" and to inhabit them. Active poetic thinking, from its beginnings in gesticulation and word-formation, establishes habitable worlds for speaking collectives by distributing names and articulating rhythms, rhymes, and relations. Martin Heidegger's dictum borrowed from Nietzsche, about language as the "house of being," is thus more than a metaphor for domestication.[3] The self-enclosure for the tamed night is complemented by exits from the cave and the house: it is on this account that language can be called the abode or the house of being – and yet it might be even more aptly figured as the window of being. Speaking poetizes from the outset and, in speaking, an activity appears that segues from the sounds and gestures of primary naturalness into culture as a process of articulation. It is also physiologically effective in an autoplastic way, since the human larynx could not have developed without speaking and recitative song.

Grammar is a sociology before Sociology; it deals with actors, actions, and consequences, with attributes and similarities, with compatibility and incompatibility. It allocates individuals to positions within structures (genealogical, division of labor, etc.), like syllables in words or like clauses in units of meaning. As in parts of a sentence, individuals are actors within the human structures we now call "societies," where, until about 200 years ago, one spoke instead of *ethnoi, tribus, gentes*: ethnic groups, tribes, families, or clans.

Since the late eighteenth century, once expressions like the *populus, peuple,* and *people* came to denote the population of emerging nation-states, what is typically meant is a body of people, relatively lax in structure and no longer able to assign distinct positions and tasks to the individual – except to acclaim leaders, to send delegates to representative assemblies, and to bring an ordinary or skilled workforce to the market. Populism implies an attempt to impute a character (a We) to a character-weak aggregate (a non-We).

What procedures of We-formation meant for a group of people living together in ancient cities and lands can be helpfully elucidated by recollecting a few pronouncements by the Greek philosopher Protagoras of Abdera (*c.* 490–420 BCE), who is conventionally counted among the early "sophists." Since his writings were destroyed, one can no longer properly conceive his thoughts in their internal cohesion.[4] The general tendency of his thought, however, shines through in two isolated quotations that survive as cited by other writers. The first contains the well-known and difficult to interpret principle of *Homo mensura*: *Anthropos metron apanton*, "Man is the measure of all things." Humanistically minded readers in more recent times have sought the source of western individualism in the dictum, which they take to mean that the individual measures the surrounding world against the standard of personal preference.

That such an interpretation misses the point of the thesis is suggested by a second quote-worthy passage: "if anyone is incapable of acquiring his share of these two virtues – the sense of justice and fear of the gods – he shall be put to death as a plague to the city."[5] If the first passage could be interpreted with a little good will as an axiom of the pragmatic attitude that would later typify Atlantic rationality, the second indicates a coercive collectivizing *polis*-attitude, about which modern admirers of classical Greece would prefer not to know.

And yet the two propositions do not contradict each other. Together, they show why Protagoras should be appreciated as the father of *polis*-functionalism. His *anthropos* embodies the city dweller whose "own city" imparts the standards for what is important (that which exists) and what is not important (that which does not exist). Whether these are true or false standards – regardless of the criteria used – does not matter for present purposes. To be or not to be is simply not the question here. The only thing that matters is that the *polis* is always right. From a functional point of view, political collectives have the form of self-reproducing know-it-all communities. In order to assert themselves as such, they take upon themselves the necessity of stifling dissent that crosses over into the impermissible – and, as in later centuries, atheism was the refusal of consensus that was seen almost everywhere as beyond the pale.

For all its coarseness, the second proposition of Protagoras illustrates this state of affairs by evoking a first functional theory of religion. What Protagoras calls "fear of the gods" forms the psychopolitically relevant affect in the service of "social synthesis." It has nothing to do with what would later be called "faith" or "conscience." The ordinary Greek *eusebeia* is a habitual value that exists independently of personal conviction. One can recognize in it – as in the Roman *religio* – the unremarkable adaptation to a people's strictly inculcated collective patterns of perception and protocols for behavior. Whereas the Romans were aligned predominantly with the examples laid down by their ancestors, the Greeks can be forgiven for orienting themselves by way of timeless myths. The common feature of Greek and Roman cults (leaving aside a few more serious secret rites) consisted in there being nothing "deep" about them except their having been ingrained from the earliest days. Initially, the sacrifice of animals on altars had a harrowing effect on those involved, especially in the case of the hecatombs, in the course of which a great number of large, first-rate cattle were slaughtered in solemn carnage. The We-forming impact of witnessing sacrificial killings was bound to fade over time, however, and over the course of the centuries, altars became mystified butcher blocks.

The personal piety of individuals would only have become conspicuous in this context if they comported themselves "more religiously" or "more irreligiously" than typical members of the collective, of whom no one asked how serious they were. Serious or unserious made no difference, so long as fundamentally dissonant doctrines did not emerge. As is well known, religious dissonance first led to intractable conflict in the Roman Empire with the entrance of Jews and Christians upon the scene. Since a multiplicity of gods existed in relaxed coexistence, all concern about a possible weakness in the faith of others was initially pointless. Those who particularly venerated Athena probably neglected Poseidon, lord of the wine-dark sea – but this fact did not trouble cult companions on either side. Every piety addressed was invested with some kind of unilluminated aspect, but one could live without worrying overmuch about such areas of latency. In the numerous cults devoted to individual gods, all the rest were included too in vague nuances. The phenomenon of partial atheism simply did not appear in the field of vision for ancient and classical practical and popular "religion."

"Religious" individuals emerged as specialists with respect to the fear of the gods in the more intense sense of the phrase; the phenomenon of an organized clergy was unknown in western antiquity. The emphatically pious of that time were those who were the first to worry when fundamental alternatives to the beliefs of the country became apparent. They issued indictments of "godlessness" (*asebeia*), and made accusations against those who deviated from the common cult through their unwelcome innovations (their suspicious private altars, new and foreign gods, or secret cults) or through their strained disregard (their derision, skepticism, or denial of the otherworldly). Since, in older times, Athens had no public prosecutor's office, indictments were initiated by private individuals who felt or simulated a personal stake in the collective interest in enforcing cultic conformity. Plato's *Apology* recorded the names of Socrates' accusers – Anytus, Meletus, and Lycon. They are stored in the archive of the humanities like blank index cards that contain no more than an indication of the poisonous mediocrity of the citizens of a defeated city.

Protagoras proves to be a pragmatist on the *asebeia* question – supposing the second fragment expresses his actual opinion – and, one might almost say, a precursor to "political theology"; thus, as hinted, he stands at the beginning of functional conceptions of "religion." To begin with, *eusebeia* and *religio* mean nothing more than performatively embedded programs of consensus that ensure that "peoples" endure both synchronously and diachronically. Hence the "truth" of a cult was manifest in the survival success of the cult and its core group of supporters, whether an ethnic group or an urban commune. What the individual believes *in detail* is of no consequence to the philosopher-sophist. The decisive thing is that the "citizen" takes part conventionally in justice and the fear of the gods, together with their rituals. Those who comport themselves like the others, as participants in the language games of the community, don't infringe upon the "social synthesis," the medium of the local community spirit, regardless of whether one understands that as "kinship" or as a "religious commune" – or, in a more modern spirit, as a "community of values." By contrast, those who deviate from the consensus further than the customary bounds of tolerance will be conspicuous as "a plague upon the city." In cult conformity – as in public speeches – the problem of hypocrisy passes beneath the threshold of public notice. The everyday hypocrite is indistinguishable from the true believer. More precisely: a generalized hypocrisy, based on the habitus of participating in the participatory game of others, is the soul of "political" or "cultural" "unity." Before the invention of the "individual," existing in the mode of taking part [*Dabeisein*] is everything. For members of cult-bound communities, one sees the pertinence of Martin Heidegger's observation in his analysis of the They in *Being and Time*: "Everyone is the other, and no one is himself."[6]

To put the matter rather pointedly, in warlike cultures (and not only in antiquity), there prevailed a hypocrisy toward death, which older and more recent Europe stylized as heroism on the Greek model. As a rule, heroism by the book produces not heroes, but nameless fallen; it leads to conditions in which one takes action with an average degree of heroism – whereupon one invokes the gods of war such as Týr, Indra, Ares, Mars, etc. In trading cities, heroes and their followers are not in demand; there, what is needed are people who can calculate, organize, and debate – and such talents seek connections with cognitively robust denizens of the world above, such as Thoth, Hermes, Apollo, Athena, or Minerva. In his late dialogue *Statesman* (from around 360 BCE), it was Plato's merit to have intertwined the two competencies (formerly: virtues) that are most important for successful political life – namely: martial valor (*andreia*) and civil prudence (*sophrosyne*) – and he intertwined them in a visionary educational–psychopolitical project that is particularly useful for modern democracies *cum grano salis*, with *andreia* referring primarily to the courage of conviction.

Where "religion" is retrospectively presumed to have been present, one is dealing in most cases with semireligious forms. Even in ancient times, one had to take people as one found them, in all their diversity. A religious arbiter might have said of them: forbear with mortals, for they know not what they believe. The cities of middle and late antiquity lived thanks to a synergy of zeal, suspicion, and folklore. Hypocrisy, syncretism, conformism, fanaticism, esotericism, curiosity about the afterlife, irony, and a vague sense of the exalted – all this formed a mixture in which none of the participants was fully versed. Jörg Rüpke, reflecting on this juxtaposition and intertwining of religions, semireligious forms, and non-religions in the late Roman–Hellenistic era, called them "opaque gray zones."[7]

Claude Lévi-Strauss seems to have been right when he insisted that only "from the outside" can one understand a given culture in its functioning: one understands it only to the extent that one does not oneself share in that culture's stabilizing self-mystifications. In relation to individual ethnic groups, only observers whose non-native background fortifies them against the temptation to join in with the group's well-rehearsed self-delusions can grasp the difference between the group's myths and their real structures. Admittedly, "objective" ethnography is impossible, since the relationships between peoples and their observers from elsewhere inevitably retain an element of inter-hypocritical tension. As a general rule, ethnologists at the research site are the more acutely hypocritical because they can never explain to the people – whether "primitive" or not, whether honored or aggrieved by the attention – why, exactly, the ethnologists visit, describe, inventory, and translate these people.[8] The appearance of the ethnologist always marks a moment in which the ethnic groups visited must come to grips with the imminent appearance of rather less reserved visitors who may threaten their existence. Lévi-Strauss's most characteristic declaration consists in his confession that he detests traveling and explorers. The implication is that one may deal with strange cultures from a suitable distance as intensively as one thinks is desirable and possible, as if little were to be gained from physical proximity except to make it clear to oneself that, for all their otherness, these people are ultimately quite like the ethnologists themselves. In Lévi-Strauss's eyes, all conceits of superiority through higher development remained self-satisfied delusions.

On the other hand, the cultural anthropologist overlooks a fundamental fact – one wants to suppose this is due to some strategy of self-reserve, as among followers of Rousseau – a basic circumstance in the western history of ideas and western social history: that, for two and a half thousand years, "our culture" has been waging a titanic battle against its own inheritance of Paleolithic, Neolithic, and Bronze-Age mystifications – occasionally even in the name of philosophy. This continuing and as yet undecided battle has been fought under the banners of empirical science, critical history, the realistic novel, and, not least, general cultural theory – and it is with the philosophical auxiliaries of this latter camp that the present endeavor has enlisted itself. In this "gigantomachy," neutrality is neither attainable nor desirable. Here, as in most things that concern the drama of knowledge and life, it is again Nietzsche who expressed the essentials: "Alas, it is the magic of these struggles that those who behold them must also take part and fight."[9]

It is seldom remarked that the social-functionalist approach of Protagoras' thesis continued to produce effects even in the older

Plato. When he set down his late, pragmatically more subdued version of the doctrine of state and law in the *Laws* (*Nomoi*, c. 355 BCE), more than half a century had passed since the death of Protagoras. Protagoras' concern for social cohesion through "fear of the gods" (*eusebeia*) and the waning invocation of the gods in civil cults was more topical than ever. His maxim, according to which man is the measure of all things, is opposed to Plato's guiding principle, according to which the measure of all things lies with the divine. The contrary propositions coincided insofar as they claim, each in its own way, to name the grounds for the possibility of life in the *polis*. His older colleague's relative lack of concern with respect to the "truth" of the cult was a stance Plato had been unable to support. He saw the need to replace conventional city piety and its hypocritical double with convictions grounded in truth. The reformed *polis* could exist only on the strength of post-conventional insight – that is, thanks to philosophically guided prudence at the apex of the commonwealth. If the orientation toward truth, justifiability, and objectivity were just one nebulous, semireligious consensus among others, the projects of "philosophy" and "science" would lose all meaning. Truth and society would be forever parted.

The new, post-conventional, truth-saturated, *polis*-forming convictions that are at stake for Plato could most readily be made feasible by conceiving the commonwealth as a work of art or as the academy expanded into a state – or even as a higher organism with a soul, as a collective *res cogitans* (much as, centuries later, the church wanted to be substantialized as *res orans*, the praying thing). In Plato's view, the philosophically guided commonwealth formed a whole that should withhold autonomy from its parts – or cede them only as much as necessary for all constituents to voluntarily agree to the overall plan. Plato has nothing better to offer here than faint suggestions in favor of totalism as the casting mold for truth. His era's real rule by advocates in the court was something he countered with an unreal epistemocracy, a dream of the dispute-free rule of the knowledgeable. The experience that has emerged incisively since the Middle Ages – that even knowledge shaped by science remains contentious[10] – passes over into the hard-fought Basic Law of cognitive democracy.

Plato, however, knows what he is talking about when he writes distrustfully of the hollowness of "democracy," or (in more modern terms) an "open society." This kind of hollowing out starts with giving false designations for the true state of affairs. In Plato's *Laws*, for example, it is an "open society" that gives the name of "peace" to perpetual war.[11] This is the Cretan's argument, with which the Spartan[12] tacitly agrees. The Athenian, introduced in the text as a foreigner (*xenos*), counterposes to this only a utopian vision of the durable victory of a minority of the good over a majority of the bad. The objections are clear: was it not a "democratic society" that charged the most prudent citizen of Athens with godlessness, put him on trial, and, with latent panic conformism, voted for his execution? Socrates probably maintained more serious intercourse with his inwardly perceived, indefinable divinity (*daimonion*) than ordinary Athenians had with their standard gods. For them, their "religious" content was hardly more demanding than that of the cultural sites then yellowing in decay. Wasn't it also true that, for at least a generation, Athenian satire had been hollowing out Olympus? What dominated the tribunal was a sham piety. At the end of its democratic era, Athens had transformed itself into a complex of furious litigation, lay justice, and mood-politics, guided by experts in parajuristic rhetoric and a more or less venal pedagogy. The latter was supposed to ensure that the sons of the wealthy learned what was required to stay on top.

More than 40 years after the death of Socrates, Plato composed the *Laws* and set down the detailed sum of his reflections on the capacity of the many for being together in a *polis*-type community; it seems the judicial catastrophe of 399 BCE had taught him the distance necessary for stating in tranquil reflection, like a retired constitutional judge, what was at stake when the question of Socratic *asebeia* was being debated.

In the regard of his pupil Plato, it is beyond all question that the verdict against Socrates would not have been possible without the deluded indolence of the 500-strong judges. By now, however, he knows that the convention-driven conduct of the many goes back to a comprehensible reason deriving from the *polis*'s pursuit of self-preservation. Self-delusions with majority appeal are arrangements among opinion- and habitus-parties – and, without them, more complex commonwealths are hardly able to exist at all.

Socrates' tragedy followed from the fact that he dared to consider a higher form of conceiving or hearing the divine precisely at a moment when the older figure was faced with the danger of perishing in an ironic twilight. It bears remembering: a good 20 years before the trial of Socrates, in Aristophanes' comedy *The Clouds* (423 BCE), the poet had amused himself roughly at the expense of the erratic thinker. And yet the poet's more intense derision was directed at Zeus, first among the gods, whose privilege of bearing thunder and lightning was reassigned to the chorus of clouds. Was it likewise comedy that there was already meteorological atheism in the air? Moreover, it seems significant that the comic poet stages the sophist Socrates' first appearance on the scene by floating him over in the hanging basket of the *theologeion* – without, very plainly, being a god himself. Shortly thereafter, Socrates lectures that it was the clouds who were the new Olympians: they were the ones who sent down ideas, empty flashes of thought, and the blue haze.

One may presume that many of those who came out against Socrates in 399 BCE had hardly a closer relationship with figures such as Zeus, Ares, Artemis, or Poseidon than today's Germans have with the federal eagle. In its mental constitution, the classical *politeia* around 400 BCE was much like the modern one: a community of hypocrites and a convention of the clueless. The tacit law of feigning equality and performing piety in the service of the whole applied even to them; this does not preclude the existence of a minority who were serious about the gods and the laws of civic being-together. Already at that time, it was the vaguely committed participants who granted, to a handful of the more resolved, the leeway for great gestures of faith. With their new temple buildings erected on the Acropolis, and swollen with a sense of their own power, the Athenian elites since 450 BCE had achieved a religious-imperialist luxury that was expected to impress the ordinary locals as well as amazed and awed visitors from all over Greece. The buildings of the "Acropolis" were supposed to suggest to anyone looking up at the "high city" that this *polis* must be favored by the gods. It is hardly out of the question to wonder whether, even back then, temples were built partly with an eye toward visitors, as is common enough today, when museums are built in the anticipation of tourists seeking to let art work its magic on them. The Athenian illusion was crushed in the Peloponnesian War (431–404 BCE). If the residents of the *polis* were seldom afflicted by scruples with regard to their overstretched indoor/outdoor civic games, it was because they rightly feared that anything other than the current regime would turn out even more contentious and would inevitably involve them in the greatest evil – civil war. Only this would have been worse than the deplorable state of affairs which up to that time had produced the endless conflict with the Peloponnesian League dominated by Sparta. A hollow vacuity capable of attracting majority support had become the spirit of the times for the inhabitants of the democratic city.

Plato in his older years achieved a degree of clarity in the *Laws* that borders on the unfathomable. How should one – in a pragmatic commonwealth – proceed with those who insist that the stars are not gods visible from afar, but rather large fiery stones? What could one say to contest the smiling sophists, who deny the existence of gods as a whole and declared humans to be the orphans of heaven? How to deal with the bold who, by openly denying the existence of immortals, threaten to degrade the capacity of mortals for being-together? Plato's wisdom in old age approached tragic consciousness, in a non-theatrical sense, by teaching that one had to reason with unbelievers repeatedly, as if they were deeply ignorant, in order to win them over with the thought of all-connectedness. If obstinate persons refused to the bitter end to join the *eusebeian* consensus, they would have to be eradicated – although to render such severe sentencing would not be easy for the wise men in power, pledged to benevolence as they were. The graves of the *atheoi* or *asebeians* should be relegated to the middle of nowhere, outside the territory of the state, unvisitable, unlocatable; their thoughts to be held as worthless, empty, and unquotable.

The unseen scandal becomes the more visible when one regards how, in his late years, Plato extended a hand to his erstwhile antagonist Protagoras. They met on the grounds of a highly problematic insight: at the level of more complex communities, social cohesion arises through the shared beliefs in gods – even if gods, conventions, fictions, and strategic lies can no longer be effectively distinguished. Both thinkers welcomed the productive imprecision of the *therapeia theon* for its socio-functional value. For them, God is the "generalized other" – the Lord of opaque gray zones and vague affinities; as a generalized other, God is also the generalized self – only as its Olympian or Uranian counterpart, so to speak. Those who relate to divinity through cult participation are fellow citizens who affirm their We-being in the name of Athena, Apollo, Zeus, and other noble improbabilities; as it turns out, they are the ones ready and able to pledge themselves to being together with other people beyond family and clan. With whom exactly? Most narrowly, with fellow citizens of Athens, with whom the kinship fiction had to be accepted, for better or for worse – citizen standing was generally not granted to newcomers, called *metoikoi*, and, in any case, it could not be granted to slaves who had been bought and brought in as living tools. But also, more remotely afield, they might consider themselves akin with the linguistically related Hellenes from the mainland and from the islands and their local gods, who had no fewer than 700 *poleis* to inspire – and in the end perhaps even with humanity as a whole, to the extent that its outer reaches were not considered barbaric and dismissed as a hodgepodge of hordes of grunting subhuman creatures.

The reproach to be leveled against atheists can now be more precisely articulated: those who resolutely refuse to affiliate are on strike against the *koinon*: the common, the unifying spirit. If, to the bitter end, they refuse to make concessions, then, according to Plato, they deserve death as saboteurs of the fragile We.[13]

The unnoticed scandal of Plato's return to Protagoras – in substance, we might call it the resignation of philosophy in the face of sophistry – was preceded by a scandal that was both visible and long and keenly remarked: even at the peak of his intellectual and literary energy – as in his earlier dialogue, *Republic* – Plato had given unabashed priority of care to political and social cohesion over "truth." The notorious theory of the "Noble Lie" (*gennaion pseudos*) is reminiscent of the historical compromise of philosophy with calculated illusion.

To find how expressions such as "truth," "religion," and "justice" (among others) acquit themselves in the political stress test, one would be well advised to return to the passages of the *Republic* in which Socrates elucidated the salutary political impact of fairy tales for adults. Like every subsequent observer of social matters of fact within complex "societies," Plato's Socrates knows that inequality is the prime characteristic of hierarchically stratified and functionally differentiated social groups. In such groups, the "law" of inequality is stamped on every scale of reality, beginning with differences between the sexes and between age cohorts, through access to political participation (which, even in the golden age of Athenian democracy, excluded immigrants, women, and slaves), up to the training of the next generation. Here, the gulf between the classes reveals itself most nakedly. While the children of the wealthy were objects of costly care, the offspring of the poor were mostly cast upon the meager resources of their basic cultural helplessness. To insist on designating such groups as "nations" or "peoples" suggests that kinship orders or kinship fantasies play the decisive role in the cohesion of the "social" whole. In this way, inequalities in the allocation of positions within the commonwealth are given a sense that people are willing to tolerate. Where kinship – whether concrete or imaginary – constitutes a primary cohesion machine that one experiences as still producing reasonably substantive effects, belonging generally carries more importance in the social fabric than the particular status of the individual.

In the fairy tale of the *polis* from the third book of the *Republic*, Plato, through his mouthpiece Socrates, attempted to make a plausible case for the priority of kinship over the idea of equality (*isonomia*). This he did through a kind of geosophical fraud of sympathy. Mother Earth, on whose soil Athenian citizens live together, had long ago furnished specimens of her childbearing strength when she brought forth into the world children of gold, children of silver, and children of iron. From these metal offspring, there issued forth the three officially designated classes of the ideal state – the rulers, the sentinels standing watch, and the craftsmen or the farmers. If they were able to live in harmony with one another, it was because the binding energy of their fiction of origin was able to predominate over the inequality of their functions and positions. Children of the same mother must be conciliated with one another pre-politically, if not perfectly reconciled – by virtue of blood ties, if that's what it takes.[14]

Socrates admits that, to begin with, such a story cannot be seriously believed by any adult. In later generations, however, the fairy tale will also be acceptable for non-children, for better or for worse, since better explanations for the inequality of citizens are no longer admissible. With the help of censorship, an artificial *therapeia theon* was to arise – the oldest prototype of the "civil religion" called for by Rousseau. From a sophistical-philosophical point of view, it would prove what had to be proven: in stratified commonwealths or "class societies" of the *polis*-type (later *res publica* or *state*), there can be no sense spontaneously common to all unless it draws on the basis of contrived illusions. The only alternative to the idealistic–illusory animation of the new city would follow from the real stress of war, which would clarify for citizens at all levels of social standing which side they belong on.

When Plato composed the *Republic* (sometime after 390 BCE), the latter supposition very nearly corresponded to the status quo. At the cost of enormous sacrifice, a war of nearly 30 years' duration had been brought to a grievous end. Any Athenian in those days was forced to identify with the city, like it or not, if only out of hope that it would emerge victorious from the ongoing battle with Sparta. In his program for the ideal republic, Plato tried to think beyond external war as the binding force of a stress-community, by exploring whether and how an inescapably stratified *polis* could cultivate a viable public spirit. If he had Socrates inquire about the nature of justice, it was also because the real *polis* had long since turned into a theatre of agitation for lawyers, in which the speakers taking the floor relentlessly perverted democratic procedures for judicial findings and political decision-making – with the result that external war and internal litigiousness had become constant companions of the democratic modus vivendi.

It is not without some embarrassment that Socrates offers his fairy tale of classes of different metals being "related" to one another on the maternal line. An unhappy awareness reveals itself in his argument, if one may refer like this to a thinking existence caught between the times: if there were once conditions which saw the spontaneous blossoming of the gods who endow both the community and society (the Lares in families, the state gods in the *poleis*), such conditions are obviously by now as long gone as

the Golden Age. The New Republic, for its part, which is supposed
to be based on philosophically grounded insight into the divine and
the just, can only be posited through ineffectual and unpopular
anticipations – it will take 700 years before the heirs of Constantine
the Great will put some of the Platonic postulates into practice with
their Christian religious policy.

The embarrassment of this position between the times can be
explained in terms of the history of consciousness: with all due
respect, so long as the adults themselves were in mental terms
like big children, they could, without much bother, give credence
to their myths and their narrators; to the extent that they came
of age as thinking beings, they outgrew the sphere of myth. The
divine, however, did not develop synchronously – it presented itself
predominantly in the mode of auto-suggestive, half-rational, half-
fairy-tale mystifications. Their breeding grounds, in the ancient and
classical western world, were the metropolises, which were teeming
with cult benefactors, expositors of scripture, and importers of
myths – all of them vying for influence over a small class of educated
people, for whom established religious conventions had to give way
to an interest in the new syncretisms then in fashion. Symbolic
amalgamation supported a post-conventional adaptation for the
new religioid formations. There was, moreover, a free-floating will
to believe that accommodated the combinatorial fictions promoted
by the city's religious traffickers in their ceaseless struggle for
differentiation.

Socrates' embarrassment with reciting the fairy tale of the metals
testifies to a burgeoning discontent with "good faith" – as the
expression *eusebeia* was best translated: so long as members of the
people enjoyed bona fide belief in what their ancestors had told
them, they were in a happy state of being misled; they were doomed
to believe, in any case, because there were no better explanations
available for the constitution of the world and its evils. Faith, as
such, became awkward thanks to era-specific increases in reflection
and praxis, and became distressing to the extent that the faculty
of understanding distanced itself from the sphere of myth and
fairy tale, especially in the metropolitan cities, where comparisons
offered themselves to reflection and the free word circulated: in
post-mythical (or "alternately mythical") times, believers are put
in the position of believing, with knowledge and will below their
potential. This is the main motif of the much-discussed "individu-
alization" of religiosity in later antiquity. "Individuals" are people
who "need" private metaphysical illusions and who, in order to
satisfy their "religious need," resort to the offerings of local mysta-
gogical or philosophical circles. The "metaphysical need" falsely

generalized by Arthur Schopenhauer is in truth produced by a decay – it compensates for a void left after the evaporation of belief in myths. What Schopenhauer calls "need" appears at the same time as a kind of human right, grounded in the postulate that individuals left deprived of a former belief are allowed the liberty to rest in the arms of their preferred illusion.

"Unhappy consciousness" does not come into being, as Hegel lectured, from the inadequacy attending both late antique stoicism and skepticism – both understood as philosophies of a subjectivity that go no further than an ideal of self-mastery in the face of insuperable fate. In fact, it ensued much more directly from the intelligentsia, who were now detached from myth, yet tasked with imposing participation in its socially requisite self-deception. Unhappy is the consciousness faced with the choice of shrinking itself for the sake of belonging to a community of the ignorant, or of emigrating into the solitude of an unpopular knowledge.

In no individual in the world of late antiquity can the effects of the devout semi-faith typical of the era be read more clearly than in Constantine the Great (c. 272–337). His interest in Christianity – regardless of whether it expressed personal conviction, or was motivated principally by strategic considerations – can only be grasped from his search for a *religio*-framework that would be suitable for the imperium. After the elimination of his rivals in his struggle for the title of Augustus, it was the analogy between monocracy and monotheism that bound the success-obsessed field commander to Christian doctrine.[15] Even if one knows next to nothing concrete about Constantine's inner life, notwithstanding the eulogistic fictions of his biographer Eusebius of Caesarea (in whom Jacob Burckhardt thought he recognized "the first thoroughly dishonest historian of antiquity"[16]), it is plain to see that he was "a man under influence" – a little too devoted to his postmenopausally pious mother, Helena. Pious legend provides only vague information about her career, from a stable maid and officer's concubine in Byzantium, to the saint who discovered the True Cross in her advanced years (and thereby launched a trade in relics that flourished for more than 1,000 years), and finally to her appearance unduly transformed in a magnificent statue in one of the niches of St. Peter's Basilica in Rome. It is also evident that, in accordance with his position at the apex of the empire, Constantine sought contact with Christian *eusebeia* or *religio* because the Christian God evinced the potential to be launched as the god of success in the imperial world.

To the older eastern titles of Christ, notably that of the Savior (*soter*), Constantinian propaganda added the Roman predicate *victor*, which resonates with the word *invictus*; this originated with the cult of the Undefeated Sun, which had been thriving since the middle of the imperial period. *Sol Invictus* had been a favorite of Constantine's from the bazaar of late antique gods; a coin with his portrait, minted around 309 CE, shows on its reverse the emperor with the radiate crown on his head and the *sphaira* of the cosmos in his left hand. If Christ came out ahead with Constantine on the score of invincibility, it was because Constantine demanded a higher consecration for his performance as a soldier. He had eliminated his rivals on the battlefield, but the religious text for this was still lacking – Constantine did not believe in chance either.

The Roman state in the imperial era has rightly been called a military empire; since the days of Augustus, its permanence had also been secured by religious-political measures – foremost among them, the cult of Caesar; one would describe this today as a soft-power strategy. Religious integration offered a clear cost advantage over robust military-administrative dominance. Constantine's religious policy moved along the line of this insight of power-economy. His most consequential decision was not the "shift" named after him – denoting the Edict of Milan in 313 CE – or the gesture of being baptized on his death bed (337 CE) by a bishop of Arian tendencies; it was the declaration in 321 CE elevating "Sundays" (*hemera heliou*) as a public holiday across the empire. Two generations later, in the territory of the imperial religion (instated as Christian after 380 CE), and presumably because it still sounded too pagan, Sunday was rebranded as the "Lord's Day" (*kyriake hemera, dies dominica, dimanche, domingo*). In this political calendar-decree, one encounters the ambivalence of the Constantinian phenomenon: from the center of power, it gave Christian parties the satisfaction they sought. The sun could be related to Christ without much difficulty, if one so desired, yet it still left devotees of older cults (the *peoples*, the *pagans*) with the illusion that the cult title "Sun" might refer to Apollo, Zeus, or an array of other addressees of worship and sacrifice of Iranian, Egyptian, and Hellenic origin. The double address was maintained with an explicit choice of symbols: when Constantine inaugurated his new capital in the Greek city of Byzantium on May 11, 330 CE, there was raised in the center of the new forum a column bearing his statue with a seven-pointed radiate crown, corresponding to the iconography of Apollo – but, according to legend, craftsmen had worked into its rays nails preserved from the Cross of Christ.[17] It was not until 60 years later, after Sun-day had been rechristened as the "Lord's Day," that the ambivalence seemed to resolve in favor of the Christian reading.

Constantinian equivocation survived the era of Christianity as an imperial and state religion. On Sundays of the modern age, Christians and non-Christians enjoy the right to do as they wish – without too much troubling themselves as to whether Sunday marks the seventh day of the week on which the Creator rests for a well-deserved sabbath, or else the first day of the week dedicated to the Lord's resurrection. For all of them, this is the day when they want to be left in peace by gentlemen of all ranks, and going to church is becoming an option ever less frequently chosen. Hegel fancied that attending his lectures on the "Sunday of Life" was the most sensible thing to do – and Sunday was always when Hegel lectured. For that matter, in the harmless impropriety of Dutch peasant weddings – as rendered in Dutch paintings of the seventeenth century – there prevailed, according to Hegel, an air of the Sunday-of-Life mood: if the one urinates under the table during a boisterous meal and the other snatches at a maid's skirt, nonetheless, a spirit of forgiveness radiates over the scene, for people so whole-heartedly cheerful cannot be altogether evil and base.[18]

At the time of Constantine the Great, Christians in the empire probably constituted little more than a "5 percent party,"[19] so to speak; Christianity was, however, already more strongly represented in the army, and in the larger cities parishes were established that could support transmission. In the East, processes of Christianization had advanced rather further and might have accounted for a third of the population. When a co-religionist could succeed in rising to the rank of court theologian – whether this was Eusebius of Caesarea or Eusebius of Nicomedia – there was the potential that, within a generation or two, quasi-totalitarian majorities could emerge from the relatively few. The apodictic demeanor of Ambrose, bishop of Milan, toward Theodosius I, emperor of the East, following the Massacre of Thessalonica (390 CE), soon gave evidence that the highest moral authority could be claimed by a high official in the church.[20] Constantine, for his part, entrusted the education of his children to clerics, probably underestimating the consequences. The rest came to pass in accordance with psychological likelihood: from the first third of the fourth century, many who had been previously persecuted were recruited into highly motivated cohorts of persecutors in the reverse direction. Under the successors of the Christian-educated *Augusti* of Constantinople, the threat of punishment hung over even the mere viewing of pre-Christian statues and temples (insofar as these had not been destroyed). But Eusebius already commended Constantine himself for his efforts to purge the world of "enmity against God."

The demise of the pre-Christian regime of gods was signaled by the decades-long dispute over the removal of the Altar of Victory from the vestibule of the Senate House in Rome. This had been provisionally ordered by Emperor Constantius II in 357, counter-manded by Julian the Apostate in 361, contested at a higher level between the urban prefect Quintus Aurelius Symmachus and Bishop Ambrose in 384, reinstated again by Emperor Gratian in 393, and later decisively imposed by Valentinian II. Those who know *Christus-Victor* to be on their side have no need for a separate goddess of victory.

Monarchs of later formations of the empire had no need for anyone to explain to them the synonymy of faith and victory. Wherever one finds an empire, a *Victoria* is likewise there to be found. At the beginning of the fifth century, after the debacle visited upon Rome by the Visigoths in 410 CE, Augustine of Hippo was there to supply a nuancing of the imperial idea of success with his major work *The City of God*: even if the Earthly City cannot be secured against defeat, there are no setbacks that can impede the City of God on its way through time. The existence of the City of God is exemplified by the earthly church, whether as embattled, as struggling, or as triumphant. It generates the scene for the "community of saints" in which the still living non-saints profess to believe. In the gallery of places proximate to God, those arrayed closest belong – according to promise – to the martyrs and apostles who have passed away.

Among those who most nearly approached God, Augustine is assigned a distinguished place, even though he never won a martyr's crown. Augustine excelled only partly as a consequence of the fact that – with the assistance of his wayward students Martin Luther and John Calvin, more than 1,000 years later – his *City of God* provided cues to roil the sphere of the Earthly City. His supreme triumph is manifested in Dante's *Paradiso*, where Augustine enjoys a privilege that can only be granted by the illuminated poet: to abide in the company of John the Baptist, Benedict of Nursia, and Francis of Assisi in the nearest vicinity to the Most High.[21]

14

TWILIGHT OF THE GODS
AND SOCIOPHANY

Whoever seeks enlightenment regarding the state of religious affairs at the present time – supposing for the moment that a general state of affairs can be captured from a single point of view – cannot avoid dealing with the general spiritual climate that has spread across Europe since the late eighteenth century – namely that, in the wake of Columbus's voyage, one could no longer so blithely refer to Europe as the "West" knowing that the setting sun continued on its wanderings across the Atlantic.

To remember the closing years of the eighteenth century implies the task of viewing the American secession, the French Revolution, and early German Romanticism not just as phenomena close together in time, but also as votes cast in the never-ending struggle concerning the future political and cultural forms of human coexistence. What were, in effect, the greatest tendencies of the age – one could call them, along with industry and science, the futurisms that continue to shape the face of the world – form a synergy of imperatives which point to the modern age as the epoch of unbounded self-activity in all areas: Learn to establish states and political systems without kings! Let us crush the coercive institutions of ecclesiastical infamy![1] Write your holy books anew using your own ink!

If Claude Lévi-Strauss long ago unsettled the human sciences with his declaration that one could discern and understand the functioning of a "culture" only from an external vantage point, his thesis has lost most of its controversial force in the years since. Over the course of the twentieth century, to stand as if at a remove and see oneself as if from the outside has become the basic characteristic of our own positionality – especially in relation to the legacy of Christianity with its classical and European influence. The position

of standing at a remove also falls to us in relation to "humanism,"
which from the fifteenth century to the Prussian reforms of the
early nineteenth century developed an educationally successful
recasting of Greco-Roman motifs. So it has been quite some time
since humanism and the humanities could credibly claim the spirit
of the times as their own. After 1914, it became manifestly clear how
very much classical education in the national empires of Europe
had alienated itself from the technical, political, and mass-media
conditions of modernity. Homer's *Iliad* was still being assigned in
academic high schools, but Karl Marx was not the only one who,
in the middle of the nineteenth century, saw the impossibility of
an Achilles or a Hector in the age of artillery and the advent of
unheroic death brought by ballistics fired over great distance: "Is
Achilles possible with powder and lead?"[2]

This "culture of ours," *nous autres européens*, has spoken bluntly
– and forcibly shown us out the door. The unbounded wars on
European soil imposed lessons that dispelled our humanistic illusions
and the sense of superiority associated with them. Whoever wants
to find out who we are need no longer play the cultured traveler
from the Orient who visits us and finds us to be living curiosities,
as Montesquieu affected to do in his *Persian Letters* of 1721. Since
the 1920s, the surrealists have shown their contemporaries how,
even while remaining in place, they might become self-strange to
the point of incomprehensibility. Dadaists and surrealists have
been followed, blow upon blow, by generations of self-subversives,
endo-ethnologists, and artists of disconcertment. In the name of the
transgressive arts, a critique of the system, the unconscious fissuring
of the subject, sexual variability, and the postcolonial condition,
they perpetually supply new evidence of the impossibility of being
identical with ourselves without contradiction.

It should come as no surprise that the current confusion derives from
a long prehistory, but the door to understanding the present had
already opened a crack around the middle of the nineteenth century,
when two motifs developed whose connection is still obscure. Let us
call them the twilight of religion and the post-revolutionary twilight
of social coherence; the latter shall be referred to here as sociophany.

Since the French Revolution, it has become evident that, after
a millennium and a half of political, moral, and educational
dominance on the European continent, Christianity is on its way to
becoming a minority *religio* once again, as it was in its beginnings
in middle and late antiquity. The discrepancy in the count between
Christians in the registry offices and statistics and those in practical
life opened up continuously over the course of the nineteenth

century, only to gape open spectacularly by the end of the twentieth. France, once proud to be "the eldest daughter of the Church," had seen Sunday Catholic Mass attendance fall to less than 5 percent of the general population by 2010. Meanwhile, the (Orthodox) national Church of Greece is still producing (statistical) Christians en masse by summarily stamping the state population as members of the church. The national churches of Lutheran northern Europe, on the other hand, have learned to survive discreetly and conservatively amid long winters and well-padded social welfare systems.

Public measures to offset growing secularization first took shape quite tentatively. The "Cult of the Supreme Being," which Robespierre "inaugurated" on the Champ de Mars on June 8, 1794 as a deistic alternative to the Christian folk religion, could of course result in nothing more than a fleeting improvisation. A nationally respected "civil religion" cannot be installed like a Parisian opera in a matinee. In terms of its ideological content, the cult contrived by Robespierre offered a silhouette-like restaging of "philosophical theology" – the modern revivals of which ranged from Spinozism to Freemasonry to German Idealism and early socialist rational "religion" – with a brief epilogue on the Jewish wing of neo-Kantianism.[3] The derivation of the Cult of the Supreme Being from the political idealism of western antiquity was disclosed in the ceremonious burning of a monumental doll representing atheism: Robespierre was ready to allow individual religious freedom, but not public irreligiosity. As with the compulsory unanimity of classical antiquity, the unbelieving non-We was to be consigned to the flames. It was kitsch that came off the field as the winner that day: when the paper husk of atheism had been burnt up, there was revealed a larger-than-life statue of Wisdom, robed in red, seated, but with its right arm raised in instruction.

A few years later, intuitive insight into the weakness of philosophically devised cult-fictions formed the basis of Napoleon's decision – not without cynicism – to come to a new accommodation with the Vatican in the Concordat of 1801: Catholicism was to be validated as the traditional cult of "the great majority of the French," even if the expression "state religion" was avoided in the document. This Concordat (and being crowned Empereur des Français in December 1804 in the presence of Pius VII) did not inhibit Napoleon from capturing the Pope and confining him for five years – from June 1809 in the Ligurian city of Savona, then from 1812 to 1814 at the Château de Fontainebleau, southeast of Paris. Napoleon's unrestrained demeanor with respect to the Holy See fit in with the tendency of the age to recast Christianity as a kind of ersatz religion to be formed around himself, since he was convinced that even a modern "society" could not do without a transcendental support for collective morality – a view not alien to conservative sociologists of the twentieth century such as Talcott Parsons and his school. Under the impact of the Revolution's dechristianization policies and its depredation against the churches, François-René de Chateaubriand produced his *Genius of Christianity, or The Spirit and Beauty of the Christian Religion* (1802). When, in that book, Chateaubriand celebrated the Christian cult as the matrix of the European arts of antiquity, he had already been captured by the contemporary movement toward aestheticizing apologetics. The beautiful had to serve apologetics as a second-tier ground for truth. Its office was to demonstrate that Christianity "is capable of enchanting the imagination as divinely as the deities of Homer and Virgil."[4] Since that time, beautiful religion has come to belong to the sphere of the arts.[5] It is supposed to veil the ugly truth. Again, it is Nietzsche who provides the formula: "We possess *art* lest we *perish of the truth*."[6]

For those casting about for a way to conceptualize the effects of these developments, the title of the fourth part of Richard Wagner's magnum opus, *Der Ring des Nibelungen* (1848–76), will soon suggest itself – *Götterdämmerung: Twilight of the Gods*. The dramatic conception of this monstrous work, which unfolded its self-will beyond composition and decomposition, beyond edification and dissolution, fell in the middle of the century, while the score was composed only later, between 1869 and 1874; the opera made its premiere in 1876 at the Bayreuth Festspielhaus. It was the key event in the course of the festivalization of modern art; it brought along with it the enthronement of synthetic integrity, which was to replace the waning Christian cult context.

At that time, the author of the *Ring* could look back on a good part of the epoch in which, as a cult and as a modus vivendi, the modern religion of art had alienated itself from Christian tradition. It would have been no secret to Wagner himself that his own work was both a symptom and a driver of this tendency. According to its manifest meaning, the expression "Götterdämmerung" refers to Nordic mythology: it spins out the idea of a cosmic conflagration in which the exhausted world together with its corrupt gods must perish in order to make room for a new cycle of growth and decline.

At the same time, the talk of "Götterdämmerung" forms a figure of thought for interpreting the progress and decay of plausibility structures in "hot societies."[7] It evokes the incineration of the fictions that helped historical peoples (or endogenously stabilized cultures) to fabricate their housing in the world context. The *Dämmerung* – the twilight – denotes the end game of cultural collectives that have exhausted their stock of unifying naivety (or their sociogenic capacity for simulation) – until they approach the zero point in their common willingness to stir and be uplifted. "Every world of gods is followed by a twilight of the gods."[8] Where such twilight falls, it becomes noticeable that the sphere of symbolic orders and ethnogenic structural poetries can also be grasped through their entropic effects. It is not only organisms that carry the potential for decomposition – organizations and "social systems" likewise cannot be conceived of without regard for their tendency to decay.

To call such processes "secularizations" would mean to succumb to a simplification reflex; it imitates the legal figure of the transfer of church property into the hands of bourgeois owners or state organs. So long as one speaks only of "secularization," it remains completely unintelligible which "object" (evidently also some of a non-spiritual nature) is demised to other holders in the "giving over" (Greek: *paradosis*), or (better yet) the "transmission."[9] Modernization in the more complete sense of the word denotes an epoch-spanning process in which generational changes are superimposed upon more or less abrupt changeovers in work processes, life forms, semiospheric effects, and ways of thinking. In some parts of the world, the changeover happens in such leaps and bounds that they expect people to jump from a kind of late Middle Ages to postmodernism within a single generation.

One point calls for further clarification: through which procedures and by way of which concepts are former cult communities and religiously animated (or religiously accoutred) cohorts, of the type found in monarchical states, to be converted into resilient, cross-generational political-economic success teams under constitutional government? It would be nice to deploy the term "democratization" for this alchemy, but it is empirically observable that, before large collectives manage to make the transition to existence under a pluralistic-democratic constitution, they are inclined to resort to nationalistically draped We-fictions. Until something substantial changes, the "concept" of "nation" can be understood as a labile, semi-genealogical metaphor for the misunderstood capacity to belong together and to mutually privilege one another in varying degrees: among non-relatives, as first-degree strangers; in an environment of integrated "foreigners," as second-degree strangers; and with new migrants, as third-degree strangers.[10]

It was not by chance that the nineteenth century turned out to be a golden age in thinking about language – initially under the presidium of philology.[11] If "language" rose to become a metatheme on the religious, social, and cultural philosophical horizon, this was because language was the most concrete way to grasp the something-shared-in-common with unknown members of the same political and cultural We-fiction. Philology came into the world as the older sister of sociology: it is the speakers of a language who first manifest what it means to abide by common rules. In fact, the written grammars of national languages were older than their explicit political constitutions. Antonio de Nebrija, author of the first grammar of the Castilian language, which appeared in 1492, the year of Columbus's voyage, presciently remarked that language was "the companion of the empire."

The philological age, with the help of historical criticism and source studies, hatched something that emerged in the first third of the twentieth century in an intensified form as *Sprachkritik*, or language criticism, pioneered by Ferdinand de Saussure, Fritz Mauthner, Ludwig Wittgenstein, and Ernst Cassirer, to name just the most prominent thinkers. Almost two generations later, and from across the Atlantic, it was Richard Rorty who, with the label *linguistic turn*, summed up the effects of the twilight of gods, signs, and regulatory regimes. From a European perspective, one could say that Wagner's intuitions reached their pragmatic phase on American soil.[12] It appears that the gods do not perish in a conflagration of the world; instead, they are stored in lexical containers, archived in cool temperatures and low lighting, and available to be reactivated on the occasion of presidential inaugurations and oaths of office sworn and solemnized with hand on Bible. Cultural entropy will flow into ecumenical negotiations where there prevails only weak differentiation. Negentropic tendencies in the human sciences thrive on the islands of experts, far removed from anything that could become popular – there is no need to speak of an identitarian racket of neo-nationalist separatist groups in the filigreed context of language criticism and comparative cultural studies.

One would do an injustice to the polyvocal nineteenth century if, from the point of view of the early twenty-first century, one were to emphasize only its aspect of "Götterdämmerung" – regardless of whether one proclaims it, with Ludwig Feuerbach, by means of robust back translations from the divine into the human; or whether, as on the Bayreuth stage, it is placed before viewing audiences as a vast conflagration and the extinction event of the Nordic House of the Gods. It was not just the twilight of decomposition manifesting itself in the progressive unchurching and the countless new tumors of religion that gave shape to the nineteenth and early twentieth centuries; at the same time, what historians of the French Revolution called the *ancien régime* began to perish. In a narrower sense, this meant the epoch that stretched from Henry IV of France to Louis

XVI, the time in which the lawyer Jean Bodin and the executive cardinals Richelieu and Mazarin suggested to their royal charges blueprints for the so-called absolute state – so-called because the power of the royal state in the seventeenth and eighteenth centuries comprised only a fractional part of the authority of later republican and democratic states, to say nothing of the plenitude of power enjoyed by dictatorships in the twentieth century and the present. In a broader sense, it referred to the monarchical age of the West, which – after the prelude of Alexander III of Macedon – began with Julius Caesar and Caesar Augustus and came to an end with the fall of the Tsar in 1917, and the abdications in 1918 of the German emperor and the emperor of Austria.

The evening twilight of the Old Order was overlaid by an initial twilight in which the emergent meta-object "society" began to outshine all other institutions and associations. The upheavals of 1789 and 1793, followed by the era of the Napoleonic Wars with their mass armies and mass graves, offered striking evidence that the principle – not to say the secret – of being able to be together had never really been properly grasped by the very many who had lived in "commonwealths" from the beginning of recorded "history"; one mostly contented oneself with family, fealty, and community metaphors in order to outline the *synousia* of the countless millions in state-like associations; the motifs of the guild association, the workshop commune, and the fighting community (the "nation in arms") were added from the distillation of everyday experience. That none of them adequately explains the hyper-complex phenomenon of "society" at the level of the more advanced nineteenth century should be perfectly apparent. Such failure of understanding in relation to the now so-called "social bond" (*lien social*) and its hidden threads, knots, and patterns – none of this should be assessed as evidence of an intellectual weakness among our cultural forebears. It was, as one began to understand, "social conditions" as such which had not yet sufficiently "developed" in a way that would provoke an investigation of adequate depth into the grounds of their own possibility.

One cannot inquire into the principle and the "ground" of "society" before it really exists. "Societies" in the modern sense of the word only emerge when the mass of participants in the commons have sloughed off the old tissue of genetic, genea-logical, group-cultic, and state-religious commonalities, in order to constitute themselves as systemic ensembles formed politically, economically, and by the media – beyond community, reciprocity, and proximity to one's community of compatriots. For such large bodies, national literatures, currencies, market relations, and media in the local vernacular come to the fore of their experience of "self." How these are coordinated from subsystems to "systems" (perhaps even to meta-improvisations) is, notwithstanding the efforts of Niklas Luhmann, a problem not yet fully plumbed.

After the beheadings of Charles I of England (1649) and Louis XVI (1793), contemporaries no longer had at their disposal suffi- ciently suggestive explanations from above, even if writers from the reactionary wing tried to reanimate the social synthesis from the top down by promoting family-romance motifs and offering dynastic suggestions. Explanations were pushed from below, from outside, and from the side, revolving around immanent motifs, even if it was the "invisible hand" introduced by Adam Smith that first captured the cybernetic motif of "self-regulation." Where should one localize the working principle of being together on common soil, once it had become implausible to locate this in the suggestive synthesis of a monarch who ruled by the grace of God? If "society" is an entity which must appear before itself in order to also be there "for itself," then in what way could the appearance of the social take place in the organs of its self-observation? How should one think what Georg Simmel called "the possibility of society" and what Niklas Luhmann discussed in impressive detail in his book *Theory of Society*?[13]

In the twilight of society in the late eighteenth and early nineteenth centuries, new gods dawn and radiate verbal halos: the people, nation, trade, industry, press, literature, art, freedom, boldness, radicalism. Was Nietzsche thinking of such eminences when, with a prophetic sigh, he noted in 1888: "And how many new gods are still possible!"?[14] One thing was certain: the new gods would be un-Olympian. To be effective as gods, they had to remain incognito. Like the powers personified and transfigured into stars through apotheosis, they appeared on the stage but as partial drives of one incredibly complex and overwhelmingly complicated "social reality."

Even before July 14, 1789, the new situation had manifested itself in the pre-political straining of a collective tension. It discharged itself in a cascade of violent events, which were consistently embedded in the stressed atmosphere generated by national media. All of a sudden, the primary "social fact" turned out to be the almost violent dissatisfaction of the restless masses who, for want of a better term, called themselves "the people." This, in turn, provided the nutrient solution in which political symbols, careers, slogans, parties, and programs could crystallize. Because "the people" is a diffuse, never self-identical parasubject, the publication, stimu- lation, collection, and organization of its tendencies to defiance, its hatreds, and its hopes in leagues, clubs, camps, and parties reveals itself to be an ambivalent and interminable undertaking. When the small activated portion of the people who call themselves "the people" threatens other parts of the population with revolutionary acts, or sweeps them along, the "people" are always confusedly threatening the people – threatening themselves, as it would seem. Before the play begins, how can the actors know who will assume the role of the hangman and who the hanged man? Since the beginning, modern "society" has the psychopolitical structure of a self-tormentor, *heautontimoroumenos*: it cannot appear before itself without instilling anxiety into itself; its members suspect that calm surfaces conceal frozen violence, to be loosed at the first thaw; where violence is openly exposed on the extremist fringes, appointed and self-appointed augurs pontificate that it cannot come from anywhere else than from the "mainstream of society." Violence is both the ghost and the haunted building at the same time. Moreover, the "whole" that wants to represent itself in the mirror of its delegates must accept the risk that its "representatives" have only their clients, and ultimately themselves, in mind.[15] One way or another, "society" – like God – is always to blame for itself.

The "twilight of society" means that the revelation of what is true and essential no longer comes from above – no longer from priestly custodians of the authoritative word, from official eulogists of the status quo, from princes and clerical proxies of God. The new spokespersons are children of the world who speak to the world around them. An age of self-appointments begins, of spontaneously claiming the floor to speak, of testimonials, of projections and agitations from below, from inside, and from without. Empirical description of conditions and secular sermon converge on each other to the point of confusion. Those who think they know something, expounding in cold print about what it looks like "in society," how this something is bubbling up in society, and what is waiting to erupt at its epicenter – such persons speak from the lectern of "reality" per se. Reality, now as the ultimate point of dispatch, sends along its witnesses in advance, so that they can acquaint the world with reality and its tendencies. A new *theologeion* hovers over the politicized scene: the press. The heavens made to speak had arrived at the kiosks.

From a mediological point of view, late antiquity (as the real "Axial Age"[16]) ended only in the nineteenth century, even if one continues to see its traces through the twentieth – in White Houses, Imperial Chancelleries, and houses of government. If late antiquity was determined by the force and authority of the discourse of its theophanies – that is to say, determined by the supplementary force afforded by the appearance of the divine on cult stages, in cathedrals, in palaces, and in sacred writings, as late antiquity ended – from the late eighteenth and early nineteenth centuries, the power – indeed, the authority – to tell the real truth devolved upon sociophany. To this day, it can be referred to as "literature" – including scholarly journals in science, research, and political theory. The new *alethes logos*[17] has no higher aim than to make "society" appear before "society" – not infrequently under the tendentious pseudonym "humanity," later also often under the code name "system." From Johann Gottlieb Fichte's *Characteristics of the Present Age* (1806) and Friedrich Engels's studies on *The Condition of the Working Class in England* (1845), to Alexis de Tocqueville's *The Old Regime and the Revolution* (1856), to Marcel Mauss's *The Gift* (1925), Walter Lippmann's *The Phantom Public* (1925), Walter Benjamin's *Arcades Project* (1928–40[18]), Simone de Beauvoir's *The Second Sex* (1949), David Riesman et al.'s *The Lonely Crowd* (1950), Frantz Fanon's *The Wretched of the Earth* (1961), Marshall McLuhan's *Understanding Media* (1964), Ulrich Beck's *Risk Society* (1986), Francis Fukuyama's *The End of History and the Last Man* (1992), Amartya Sen's *Development as Freedom* (1999), Yuval Noah Harari's *Homo Deus: A Brief History of Tomorrow* (2016), etc. – a good part of the "essential texts" of the past two centuries belong to the sociophanic type. Such scholarly journalism inevitably takes the form of briefings and crisis counselling. Self-alarm is the first duty of the sociologist. There's no need to stress that an important branch of the genre of messages that "society" sends to "society" has shifted to realistic film and engaged visual arts.

True, nothing guarantees that "society" will recognize itself in the descriptions sent to it. It is so deeply fissured by differences in lifestyles, attitudes, property relations, and educational standards that no message "to everyone" can ever reach its addressee. Given such a situation, it seems perhaps more plausible to forsake vivid pictures and instead to reveal social structures by way of numbers, slopes, and statistics. Aided by the language of numbers and graphs, quantitative social research dispenses with everyday knowledge, intuition, tacit knowledge, and likeness to life, in order to demonstrate regularities, constellations, and flow directions in its hybrid and elusive object that might otherwise escape perceptive and sympathetic observation.[19]

Publications of the sociophanic type modulated the elementary notion of the modern age, such that the present came to be assigned the status of a transitional period. As soon as "society" came to understand itself as a "society," it could only see itself as a society in transition to its next state. In being what it believes itself to be, it also opens the door to the "society of the future." From the eighteenth century onward, intellectuals who gave definition to culture interpreted their time as a time of gestation and, *eo ipso*, as an era in transition to new, more favorable, more advanced forms. In 1920, the Lutheran theologian Friedrich Gogarten, then 33 years old and soon thereafter a colleague of Karl Barth's, deemed himself to be expressing the most significant things when he proclaimed a triviality that had been trotted out for centuries: "This is the fate of our generation: that we stand between the times."[20] By this he meant – undeterred by its theological implications – the sense of existence within a breach, littered with ruins, between a revelation depleted and a new revelation upon which his own generation had yet to enter.

Against this backdrop, a second event of the nineteenth century becomes comprehensible for the way it shaped the history of ideas: the birth of social science out of the spirit of sociophany. The model here is the Christian proclamation which, together with its theology, rested upon the highly improbable hypothesis that one could explain to people *in statu corruptionis* their scarcely very promising position before God – a position to be relieved only on condition that they convert to faith in the risen Christ and thus be incorporated into eternity. In similar fashion, the early sociophanics, especially those in the socialist current, proceeded from the postulate that one could clarify for members of bourgeois society their "true position" in the "relations of production" (today: in climatic conditions, ecological conditions, microbial conditions, mediological conditions) – but at the risk of provoking a split in consciousness in the beneficiary of this social enlightenment. The individuals thus addressed would have to consciously assume or take on their alienation: either by trying to migrate to an alternative world, a counter world, a desert, an underground, a heterotopic zone, a new territory – like the ascetics, hermits, monks, and pilgrim fathers once did – or by persevering in their places in the social machinery and cultivating the melancholy they'd learned from systems theory.

Protosociologists of the first generation after the Great Days displayed little embarrassment. Among their spokesmen – Henri de Saint-Simon, Félicité de La Mennais, Étienne Cabet, Charles Fourier, Robert Owen, Wilhelm Weitling, Bruno Bauer, Moses Hess, Friedrich Engels, etc. – there was hardly anyone who would have made a secret of his para-Christian inspirations. The real *père fondateur* of sociology as the science of the commonwealth for the commonwealth, Auguste Comte (1798–1857), author of the *Course in Positive Philosophy* (1830–42), seemed to feel the trespass of sociology concerning its real subject matter more acutely than did the other sociophanists of the age. To the groundwork of his science of the social, he added the foundation of a religious movement: that atheistic *religion de l'humanité*, which – under the slogans "order and progress" and "living for others" (*vivre pour autrui*) – sought to make amends for what the *esprit positif* had done with the disenchantment of mythical-theological and metaphysical worldviews. No one would reproach the author with having forgotten the social question when he founded sociology. In his *Catechism of Positive Religion* (1851), he set retirement age at 63 as one of nine sacraments that would be obligatory for rational religion. For this arrangement, no council of sociologists proved necessary – profane trade unions would achieve in later decades what the *grand prêtre* of the self-founded church had demanded with impotent verbosity; in daring to make himself ridiculous, he cleared every hurdle; his belief in victory through defeat reached early Christian heights. From Comte's fabulations, it can be deduced how it sounds when progressive philistinism advances into the comprehensive. They indicate the tendency of the epoch in the European sphere then still dominating the world: the transition of "religion" to the phase of parody.

15

GLORY: POEMS OF PRAISE

In 1803, Friedrich Hölderlin wrote one of his greatest poems, the hymn "Remembrance" (first published in 1808); there, the suggestive and ambiguous final line – "But what is lasting the poets provide"[1] – imposed the suspicion that the line he had formulated could be symptomatic of a culture living through a devastating crisis of the enduring. How unstable must a form of life have become if what endures is no longer derived from the matrix of the old, no longer descending from times immemorial, which had once seemed to be endowed with all the vigor necessary for a welcome return? And if it is no longer nature that prescribes what is durable, shouldn't it be the ancestors, gods, or heroes who establish what is worthy and enduring in the forms of clanic, tribal, or ethnic ways of life? Where does this scarcely plausible recourse to the poets come from? Why should the durable order of the world be entrusted to members of a will-o'-the-wisp group – and, in particular, a group that Plato's "republic" had excluded on account of its notorious unreliability? Not so long before Plato founded the academy, Solon, the lawgiver of Athens (c. 630–560 BCE), had issued the caution: *Polla pseudontai aoidoi*, "Poets are much deluded!" – or, as one often finds it (taking *pseudontai* as "lies"), "Poets tell many a lie." The Quranic ayah sounds like a distant echo of that old declaration of distrust: "As for the poets, they are followed merely by deviants."[2]

In the era of the Napoleonic Wars, the erosion of that which endures had clearly crossed over a critical threshold, as slipping and falling came to assume priority of position over abiding and enduring. The "Holy Alliance" – the stability pact signed by the European thrones in 1815 – postponed the growing unrest by a few decades. In the spring of 1848, Marx and Engels stated in the

Communist Manifesto: "Everything that would exist in stasis and everything of the order of social standing evaporates."[3] Almost 40 years later, Nietzsche had the madman ask: "Are we not plunging continually? Backward, sideward, forward, in all directions? Is there still any up or down?"[4] The canonical metaphors of movement in the nineteenth century – evolution, revolution, progress – were heightened into the uncanny by corrosive verbs like "evaporate" and "plunge."

The hallmark figures of "Götterdämmerung" (the fading away of the world above) and "Gesellschaftsdämmerung" (sociophany as the rise of universal immanence) are not the only possible figures to characterize the nineteenth century, but the overarching philosophical signature of the epoch is revealed in the twilight of stabilities. If one were to address in philosophical terms the question of what constitutes modernity, one possible answer might be this: modernity executes the program of thinking and acting in functional terms. In place of fixed substances, modernity calculates with variables in diverse and adaptable fields of practice. From an epistemological perspective, it wants to move from essential things to functional determinations. From an ethical point of view, it relies on innovation, differentiation, mobilization; and in technical terms, on optimizing efficiency, standardization, and economies of scale. Modernity invites one to do as one likes with things, and not just to leave them as they were found – unless they are understood to have been set aside in reserve, as belonging to the category of antiques.

In order to appreciate the typically modern pre-eminence of the project, of the critical overachievement, and of the *plus ultra* in its historical and psychological unusualness, it is useful to recall two classic monuments of western and Near Eastern antiquity which invoked the goodness of beings writ large: the biblical Genesis (composed as the "Priestly source" probably during the sixth century BCE in Babylonian captivity or shortly after the return to Yehud), and the philosophical cosmology of the Platonic dialogue *Timaeus* (written *c.* 360 BCE). Both texts suggest that the progressive–critical, activist, anti-ontological negativism (or futurism) of the modern must have arisen from a relatively recent revaluation of older values – although there were already approaches to this in late antiquity, particularly in the gloaming of Gnostic and hermetic speculation.[5] Of these, the most impressive was the Valentinian gnosis, according to which the afflictions of this world are the consequence of a miscarriage suffered by the lower Aeon Sophia (wisdom). Five centuries earlier, Cynic street philosophers in Athens had created a furor by adopting as their slogan "deface the currency" – a trope calling for a change of current customs and morals in the direction of natural [*physei*] simplicity.[6]

The biblical narrative of creation is condensed into an absolute act of affirmation. It has been recited innumerable times without arousing the least suspicion that creation was clinging to any shadow of a need for repair, to say nothing of improvability. At the end of the sixth day of creation, when God saw everything that he had made and saw that "it was very good" [*valde bonum*] (Genesis 1:31), he bestowed upon his work the applause it deserved. It was not the self-applause of a virtuoso who retires to his dressing room after the exultation of the audience to reconcile his superhuman performance with his grounded personality. The Elohistic *valde bonum* after the work accomplished is more nearly akin to the client's speech of thanks at a building's topping-out ceremony.

The creation, in the Israelite redaction, did not have the quality of a performance or a dramatic spectacle – or, insofar as it did, it was at most simply to highlight the superior cosmic competencies of the Jewish god by surpassing the Babylonian myth of the creation of the world from out of Marduk's battle with the primordial dragoness Tiamat. The *valde bonum* on the evening of the sixth day is assigned the value of an absolute predicate. It is not said of the work in external reflection, it is materially inherent within it. When heaven and earth were separated from the formless void and distinguished one from the other in beautiful dissonance, and when the waters brought forth swarms of living creatures and the earth brought forth living creatures of every kind, cattle and creeping things and wild animals, and birds flew above the earth, and trees of every kind bore fruit, then the summary view on the evening of the fifth day speaks to the sense of a felicitous whole. Once the silhouette of the first couple has been added to the tableau toward the end of the next day, the work may be considered to have been accomplished, not only in the sense of having been completed, but also in the sense of having been consummately successful.

The *valde bonum*, with which the active part of Genesis closes, invites those creatures gifted with mind or spirit to approve the judgment about that which exists. While the being of the creation that has been brought to light as "very good" implies a mild tautology for its author (albeit one that was indeed worth articulating), the creature made of clay and breath can only react with bewilderment and discomposure with respect to its position in the middle of this *Gesamtkunstwerk*, this total work of art. At first the creature is unable to perceive itself as part of the tableau, still inhabiting it in paradisiacal immersion. The creature's survey of the field is palpably felt as the Open, and it awakens the premonition that there are great and unspeakable things to be said. What is shown announces abundance, superabundance, superiority. That Adam is allowed to give names to the things that lay before him is a privilege that derives from his resemblance to the Creator. His vocabulary would have been meager at first – it just sufficed for the trees, grasses, and animals in the near vicinity; there is no record of what expressions he used to address Eve. What was decisive, however, was that what was disclosed on all sides stretched beyond the horizon. If it were enclosed by a wall, it would be called a garden. Without a wall, it is the world as Openness in general. Surrounded by a panorama suffused with evidence of majesty, there emerges in the creature the outline of a power, greater than any power of poetry to express. In speaking of it, the matrix of glorifications is formed. From there proceed the hymns, the songs of triumph, the apotheoses, the adorations, which in civilizations given to exaltation are inscribed in the registers of laudatory speech.[7]

The biblical Genesis showcases a creation that was a consistent consequence of monotonously parallel words of power – archetypally: "'Let there be light'; and there was light"; "Let the earth bring forth creatures of every kind"; etc. – and thus of an expeditive logocracy, in which conditions are produced promptly by fiat, excepting the creation of man, which necessitated a switch to handicrafts and a kind of higher ceramics, analogous to the production of vases and statues. By contrast, the Platonic myth leads from the creation of the *kosmos* (Greek: splendor, honor, ornament, order) to formal, mathematical, constructivist terrain. It is open to question just how seriously Plato the physicist-philosopher meant his story of the *demiurgos*, the world builder and his methods. Indeed, there is plenty that speaks against taking it in earnest – among other things, the fact that the Greek logic of questions has always been far removed from inquiring about a first author; one searched with passion for the basic materials, the "elements," the indivisible smallest particles, and for the forms of their composition – but not for a primary maker or builder. The tendency of Hellenic beliefs about the origin of the world inclined toward the presumption of eternity; Aristotle – *nonostante Platone* – also came in on this side.

An eternally existing world in all its constituent parts implies a structure that is venerable in the highest degree: in it, all beings can imagine themselves under the title of nobility: "von Time-Immemorial." This idea of deriving nobility from the eternal is rivaled by Nietzsche's suggestion in *Thus Spoke Zarathustra*, according to which it could only be the old Persian founder of dualism who returns and restores to things the true *titre de noblesse* to which they have been entitled since Fortune's roll of the dice: "'By Chance' – that is the most ancient nobility of the world, and this I restored to all things: I delivered them from their bondage under Purpose."[8]

Plato's decision to discard the traditional and comfortable thesis of the eternity of the cosmos and to introduce a hitherto unknown world architect long seemed rather random. The philosopher wanted to interpret creation as an act of divine intelligence in order to sustain the thesis that the congenial proportions of the cosmos could neither have existed from time immemorial nor have arisen by accident; rather, in this argument, they presuppose the deliberate decisions of a mathematically competent and ontologically empowered master craftsman. With Plato's *Timaeus*, there begins the explicit infiltration of technical feats into being.

The speculations of Plato were to evince their momentous importance only after the eastward expansion of the Hellenized Roman Empire: the demiurge myth of *Timaeus* turned out to be compatible with Jewish and Christian assertions about the world as a creation – under the banner of having been made, the order of the biblical genesis and the conceptual cosmos of Athenian natural philosophy could merge. Certainly, discourse about the demiurge could be easily repurposed into the cosmo-critical fictions of the Valentinian and Ophitic gnosis of the second and third centuries: in them, it was considered to have been proven that the Creator God must have been an inferior spirit who had abandoned humanity to the darkness of his miscarried creation; the Redeemer God, meanwhile, had sent his messenger to show those wandering below the way back home into the light.[9]

So far as the cosmogonic deliberations of *Timaeus* are concerned, their execution has little in common with the biblical Genesis. Their point of confluence lies in the fact that the two writings award the predicate "perfect completeness" not through an external attribution, but rather as a quality to be discerned in the very making of the product. Neither one nor the other could exist if it were not, in each case, the best possible. While the Genesis god declares his *valde bonum* at the end of the procedure, the *Timaeus* world builder would not proceed to business without first clarifying the suprematist premises. It is better to create no cosmos at all than to create one that fails to be the most excellent. The final assessment is known and firmly fixed from the outset. Admittedly, the demiurge (Greek: literally, one who works for the people) is not identical with the unconditional *agathon*, but rather constitutes its executive, as it were, and in this function must transfer the qualities of "the best" to the work itself, to the extent that it succeeds in making the transition into the material. Hence the cosmos per se comports with a self-praising form of appearance: because God is good, the cosmos must enjoy a flawless round perfection – this applies to the world body as well as to the world soul, which pervades the world body and envelops it like an atmosphere. The double roundness: the world body within the world soul provides the place where intelligent beings can establish themselves at home – hence the analogy of *oikos* and *kosmos*. The morphological suprematism is binding in every detail. All other classifications are oriented by firm a priori theogeometric principles. In this way, it is guaranteed that everything that exists is good – and, indeed, not just in the sense of being well made, but as in principle participating in the best possible soundness, from which only further soundness can ever follow.

The two stories of creation, the first of ancient Near Eastern inspiration, the second of western imprint, exhibit one feature in common: they put the praise of what has been created in the ontological mode of a corollary – the world has been accomplished perfectly by the evening of the sixth day of creation – or else in the principles of its construction, which were consummately unsurpassable already before their execution. Nothing better could have been formed. In both cases, a factual description corresponds to the highest praise. In Genesis, one hears the dynamic jubilation in plain statements: that there is a power that could do such deeds. In the *Timaeus*, one feels a mathematical exhilaration: that an intelligence exists that is capable of making sovereign dispositions that can be read from the meridians of that which exists. The two lines of jubilation later intersect only once: in the oeuvre of a thinker situated at the end of the seventeenth and the start of the eighteenth century – Gottfried Wilhelm Leibniz.

In the millennia that followed, there unfolded a parallelism of the jubilations – along one line for God and the gods, along the other line for kings and charismatic leaders. Mirror effects appeared due to the quality of the things. In the *Hymn to Zeus* by the Stoic Cleanthes (*c.* 330–230 BCE), the father of the gods is eulogized as the ruler who sovereignly pervades whatever is in any way capable of obedience – first and foremost, those endowed with reason. In the opposite direction, Alexander III of Macedonia was already in his lifetime surrounded by the nimbus of a god and son of god: the priests at the Egyptian oracle of Amun, in the western oasis of Siwa, had guessed his inclinations when they greeted him, upon his visit in 331 BCE, with the address "Son of Zeus-Amun." Visual artists, storytellers, and eulogists transferred attributes of Zeus to the conqueror. Alexander had at his command the same privilege as his "father," the hurler of lightning – holding in his fist the concentrated force of nature like a directed-energy weapon. The old authors tended to brush aside all thought that a Son of God will naturally also have a mother, as if this were an almost negligible consideration. But the fact that she too had her big moment could not be entirely concealed. Olympias, the Molossian princess, one of the wives of Philip II of Macedon, is said to have given herself to God – as the Greek versions of the *Alexander Romance* aver – in the course of which God intimated that she would give birth to a divine child.[10] Thereafter, nothing more is heard concerning the mother's contribution. One had to wait until Mary, mother of Jesus, to learn in more detail about a mother of God.

The history of exalting speech can be told as the history of the two-way transposition of praise of king and praise of God. It was first and foremost the great kings, the Caesars, the rulers who, with the help of their appointed panegyrists, kept in motion the flywheel of extolling discourse. The concurrency of monotheism and monarchy can be figured as a historical "constellation" – like a binary star system in which speeches about God and speeches about the king each shared their warmth and light with the other. The men at the top of the "social" pyramid – and the few women who made it there – responded to the constraints of their position by referring to a higher order of sovereignty from which they themselves acquired their legitimacy. That there is divinity could be taken as the premise of the being-together of many in associations of "political," non-familial coexistence. That there are kings became plausible when these specific persons (and not others) were brought into their position by divine providence. Postulating a God serves to minimize any sense of contingency with regard to the head of the state.

The royal and the divine function as co-variables. Here the divine plays the role of a shell that envelops the royal.[11] Technically interpreted, then, monarchies are built like vacuum flasks: rays are deflected by the outer shell, which inhibits cooling for a long time. In this way, well-established monarchies can be understood as systems of entropy delay. So long as the monarchies remained active in their theologically reinforced self-praise continuum, their radiant splendor rebounded to the cause of their continued survival. In order to create grounds for self-praise, they had to be militarily, economically, and aesthetically–theatrically successful – or, at least, not obviously unsuccessful. Even Louis XVI's wars of conquest were emanations of the theo-royalist system of grandiosity typical of a European state on the threshold of modernity.

Into these contexts, one places the rhetorical performance of orators, who, because of their profession, draped the mantle of extolment and doxology upon the mighty. It is one of the peculiarities of the civilization of Western Christianity that in it, unlike in the Byzantine Empire (to say nothing of the boot kissing in the aristocratic houses of the East), those who offered the mantle and those who accepted it as their due – the legitimizers and the legitimized – seldom stood on the same side, notwithstanding attempts at co-optation made by those who received the mantle.

The European development of the "critical spirit" follows from this inevitable split between self-praise and praise from others. What is today called "critique" arises not only from the structural detachment of the *clercs* from the monarchs, and of the monks from the "world," but also from the shift in praise to non-monarchical individuals and groups. The old division of labor between praise of God and praise of the king relaxed as the experts in the praise of God discovered new objects of exaltation: the divine was henceforth to be found not only in the branches of church institutions with their foundations in the holy scriptures, nor only in the kings as the political Vicars of Heaven; the divine could henceforth be encountered also in the arts, in learning in general, and in a philosophy that more and more lost its willingness to serve as the maidservant of theology.[12]

Because of these developments, there ensued from the fourteenth century onward a fragmentation in the praising of the king. Experts began to wonder whether there weren't heads more worthy of coronation than those sitting on the official thrones. As this line of speculation gained ground, interest came to be aroused in the cause of non-political coronations. In April 1341, after complicated preliminary negotiations with Robert, king of Naples (who in the end was not in attendance), and the Roman nobility (notably the Colonna family), Francesco Petrarca was crowned poet laureate at the Palazzo Senatorio on the Capitoline Hill in Rome. With this coronation, the pursuit of paramonarchical eminence had become a public fait accompli for a man of the pen: with the *éclat* of a grand debut, a Delphic laurel wreath was placed on his head and he was draped in a royal mantle. In his first enthusiasm, Petrarch fancied that even the old stones of the Capitol would happily take part in the ceremonial rite – even more recent poetry cannot entirely dispense with animism. The pageantry and the paeans in his honor made him blush, though he admits he wasn't altogether averse to hearing them. He later noted that his existence thereafter had been envenomed by the mob of jealous persons.

Petrarch has been rightly portrayed as the first intellectual in Europe.[13] The title of intellectual, however, does not adequately describe his presence on the stage of public life: he was also one of the first to manifest a shift in the idea of royalty from the political to the poetic-artistic realm; here, the revival of the Roman concept of genius played a mediating role.[14] From the advent of modern times, the figure of genius had some attraction for the great lords: "How does one spirit speak to another?" was a question that the gifted readily asked of the world above, suffering a confusion of the Holy Spirit with genius. For 400 years, emperors of the Holy Roman Empire – as well as rectors of universities – would exercise their privilege to place laurel wreaths upon the heads of their versifying contemporaries, based on that scene in Rome in 1341.

The ritual coronation of poets by monarchs and universities died out in the seventeenth century. By the age of Goethe, one already finds it ridiculous. The fading of the laurel cult follows from a change in the conditions of praise. Praise came to be understood as valid only when bestowed by audiences and their critically educated elite. No genius after Goethe and Beethoven would feel elevated by the compliment of a monarch – unless his name was Napoleon; in any case, its conferment, as with Napoleon's tribute to Goethe at the Congress of Erfurt in 1808, remained episodic.

What was later called democracy began with an expansion of the zone of veneration. Thomas Mann called the enlarged area – for once, without irony – the "nobility of the mind or spirit." At the onset of this development, it was not easy to foresee that "democracy," sufficiently well established to appear as a triviality, would one day bring forth the popularization of contempt for higher things and for the elite themselves. The twentieth century gave some semblance of wanting to end the secondary monarchies of geniuses, bosses, directors, and leaders that had outlived the first ones; as events transpired, however, it offered them more comprehensive spheres of activity than ever before.

In his textbook on rhetoric, the Roman master orator Marcus Fabius Quintilian (*c.* 35–*c.* 100 CE) defined *laudatio* as a form of artistic speech. Its *proprium* consists in exalting and heightening the beauty of the object of the speech: it is part of civilized competence to be able to meet an object with the verbal arts of enhancement. Anyone who has learned to speak should also have learned to sugarcoat: *amplificare et ornare* – this is what the profession demands.[15] The business of rhetorical pragmatism was so advanced in Quintilian's time that to make things, cities, and people greater and more beautiful could be viewed as an artisanal task; to a large extent, this could be mastered independently of the qualities of the object. With the early imperial era, following on from republican traditions,[16] a market for laudation had developed, in which – at a proper distance from Caesar Augustus – high officials, senators, officers, wealthy benefactors, and men of letters asserted their claims upon praise. The less such people could stand out in the political arena – where the imperial monopoly was inviolable – the more they wanted to benefit from rhetorically available aggrandizements in the free spaces of "culture." Whereupon "culture" emerges as a sphere of secondary and tertiary glorification. Its wellspring is the *analogia augusti*: as there above with the emperor, so here below in the city. In a further extension of the analogy, the scattered Christian subcultures came to develop new genres in their hagiographies of saints and martyrs. They praised a God who assured his witnesses of ascending to the hereafter, certain of their salvation; at the same time, the legends exalted these witnesses to such great heights that the danger of approaching them was fairly remote for "ordinary mortals."

Up to the fifth century CE, Rome remained the Silicon Valley of orators; aided by combinations of Ciceronian, Quintilian, Platonic, and Stoic programs, they experimented with a plethora of verbose simulations in existential sovereignty – drawing on the sophists' motto from the fifth century BCE, that man is a being who must never sink into wordless helplessness (Greek: *amechania*, the absence of tricks or resources to help oneself).[17]

It was in this climate of a categorical never-at-a-loss-for-an-answer that the most gifted individual of his century, the North African Aurelius Augustinus, received his training as a speaker. He used it to praise the lucidity of the Most High and the obscurity of his election of grace – and to such an extent that he lost the certainty for himself with regard to his own admission into the ranks of the saved. Augustine cannot be denied intellectual integrity. When he died at the age of 75, his city under siege by the Vandals, he is said to have passed away in racking uncertainty of his own salvation. With him, the "will to believe" had already rushed on ahead of the sheer ability to believe. Nor could the trace of unhappy consciousness be erased from the doctor of the church – unhappy is the consciousness in which naive faith, unfamiliar with deeper doubts, can no longer overtake the reflection that blossoms in doubt and its dangerous excess.

Dissolving subjectivity can now and then be bolstered by plain and public formulas:

Holy God, we praise Thy Name;
Lord of all, we bow before Thee!
All on the earth Thy scepter claim,
All in Heaven above adore Thee.

The Catholic hymn, composed by Ignaz Franz in 1771, adopted into Protestant hymnals and sung worldwide thanks to German emigration (as "Holy God, We Praise Thy Name"), dissolves doubts and fluctuations into a powerful melodic affirmation for the duration of the common singing.

Franz's song of praise sounds like an echo of the lines at the start of the most enchanting book in world literature, an almost authorless work from Indian, Persian, Greek, Egyptian, and Arabic sources, the stories of the *Arabian Nights*, which opens with an invocation addressed to Allah:

> Praise be to God, the Beneficent King, the Creator of the world and man, who raised the heavens without pillars and spread out the earth as a place of rest and erected the mountains as props and made the water flow from the hard rock. ... I praise Him the Supreme Lord for His guidance, and I thank Him for His infinite grace.[18]

16

POETRY OF PATIENT ENDURANCE

Two thousand years before Plato issued the dictum translated by his interpreters of the Latin Middle Ages as *omne ens est bonum* – "All that *is* is good" – poets from the ancient cultural land between the Tigris and Euphrates undertook some of the first attempts to illuminate the presence of the Not-Good in the midst of what is given. From the debris of forgotten cities, their poems were brought to light by British, German, French, and other excavators from the nineteenth century onward, and they attest that Mesopotamian thought had discovered nothing less than the problem of "theodicy." In its fully developed form, this is an inquiry into the problem of evil: *unde malum?* Whence evil? In the early period, it arose as the wish to understand how those who are not aware of any sin should comport themselves when misfortune comes along.

By the second half of the second millennium BCE, there had formed in Babylon and other cities of Mesopotamia a milieu of priests, scribes, and scholars who could be defined as professional hymnodists and experts in ritual. In their verses, whether for private or for public cultic use, one of their tasks was to realize or make present the relationship between people and the sphere of the gods. The context in which such poems were recited is unknown. Some chants, however, refer to the main thoroughfare of Babylon, on which, so far as is known, funeral processions were formed; there, a verse like the following may have had its *sedes in vita*: "May everyone who sees him [the dead] in the street praise your divinity, may they say: '(Only) the lord ... (Only) Marduk ... can revive the dead."[1]

One work from the Kassite dynasty (1475–1155 BCE) stands out among Babylonian literary creations in the elevated tone. It is

named after its opening lines – *Ludlul Bēl Nēmeqi*: *I Will Praise
the Lord of Wisdom* – and prevailing opinion among Assyriologists
dates it to around 1300 BCE. The work is thought to have been
commissioned by Šubši-mašrâ-Šakkan, an official close to the court
who wanted to memorialize his piety through a donated poem. The
poem achieved canonical status over the course of the centuries;
duplicate copies made over the span of at least 700 years and its
presence in the clay tablet libraries of multiple Mesopotamian
cities attest to its success. Even in this epoch, "theology" (here:
Mardukology) is a matter of scriptural exercise. Those who passed
through Babylonian writing schools at that time were required in
the course of their training to absorb and assimilate – to the point
of automation – numerous prayers to Marduk, time-honored lists
of gods, and excerpts from the 600-line *Ludlul* and the 1,000-line
creation myth *Enūma Eliš* (*When on high the heaven had not been
named* …).

If Egyptian "paper" endured patiently, the Akkadian and
Babylonian clay tablets endured no less so. The believing self
inevitably internalized the form of the clay tablet. Just as the
scribes made the soft clay speak with their reed pens, so Marduk
inscribed with signs of fate and power, with sorrows and blessings,
human existence as a whole – one might refrain in this context
from speaking of the "soul," as if it had already acquired its later
metaphysical sense. The "Lord" of Israel is said to have given
Moses the revelation on Sinai in the form of two "tablets of stone"
written by the finger of God; this fact indicates, on the one hand,
the imaginative appropriation of Babylonian formats by Jewish
narrators, and, on the other hand, a backdating of the deportation
of the Jewish elite, from Babylon in the sixth century BCE to an
unspecified era in ancient Egypt, which, in the view of historians,
could never have existed in the form depicted. Nor, indeed, is
there any lack of Christian appropriations of the tablet motif. It is
believed, for example, that John Climacus's text on monastic discipline, *The Ladder of Divine Ascent* (*c.* 600 CE), was initially called
plakoi pneumatikoi: spiritual tablets.

That the history of the figure of inscription did not end there is
shown by the dogmatic central passage, "On Old and New Tablets,"
from Book III of Nietzsche's *Thus Spoke Zarathustra*. The author
is aware that Paul of Tarsus, the only rival whom he places on equal
footing with his own claim to epochal impact, has in mind a letter-
and tablet-writing God: every living individual, says Paul, is a letter
from God, "written not with ink but with the Spirit of the living
God, not on tablets of stone [*en plaxin*] but on tablets of human
hearts."[2] From this, it follows that the Christian heart cannot be

thought without Babylonian formatting, even if the writing implements, the inks, and the vowels have changed.[3]

The point of departure for ancient Babylonian exercises in dealing with the Unseen is indicated in the fact that the gods, including Marduk, were addressed initially only as guarantors of success – in modern parlance, as superior "social partners." Max Weber rightly called them "function gods"; their jurisdictions were strictly rooted in region, clan, or ethnos, or concentrated in one city, one temple metropolis, one dynasty. For their worshippers, they served as patrons and protectors of their quality of life:

> My father is the great lord, Marduk,
> The one who watches over me. May he command my favour.
> May the finger of justice stretch out over me.
> May my descendants be enlightened.
> May he make my offspring prosper.
> May goodness, wealth and good health meet me.[4]

Such invocations are not yet bound to any notion of Marduk being the absolute sovereign. He stood before his believers as a deity of choice – eminent, but not singular; in this respect, he resembled Israel's YHWH, who was likewise one god among others. But, where YHWH's singularity came to be enforced through the alliance with "his people," and his incomparable peerlessness through the prohibition of representation, the Babylonians obviously did not succeed in creating a similar relationship with their main god – one that was tightly bound and that could be embodied anew down through so many generations. Initially, the adulation of Marduk was something one decided upon *pro domo*, as if settling upon a heavenly provider of tribal security services. Only in later dynasties does the Marduk cult appear to have been adopted as the official religion of a Babylonian kingdom; previously, for example, the Kassite rulers in the Sumerophone city of Nippur on the Euphrates worshiped Enlil as their main god. Once this change in cult address was instituted, the fate of the empire would be handed down by its transcendent ruler and be received and accepted by the king of Babylon. In the empire's own creation myth, Marduk bears, in addition to 50 other names, epithets related to basic social policy: "avenger"[5] and "provider."

Nebuchadnezzar I (reigning 1125–1104 BCE) appears to have been the first to invoke Marduk as the "King of the Gods."[6] Presumably he was also the one who included Marduk's bipolar power politics in his program of rule over the retinue of the black-headed (i.e., the people). As the *Ludlul Bēl Nēmeqi* makes plain, this includes the power to make any of his subjects suffer inexplicably, and then to deliver them from suffering just as inexplicably. From commentaries on the book of Job made by scholars of the Hebrew Bible, narratives of this sort have come to be described in terms of "suffering a test of virtue." One may think of this expression either as schoolmasterly or as profound; it is distinctive, in any case, that it points to processes of indissoluble irrationality.

The turn to Marduk marks a significant turning point in the history of religion. Under his name, there comes to be a divine addressee who can be expressly asked why, in the domain of his rule, blessings and punishments are found so closely together – and with a sense of the *why* that is moral, not causal. In response to this, the Mesopotamian *Ludlul* poem elaborates an idea familiar to Jews and Christians from the Tanakh poem of Job, which is about 800 years more recent. Job, too, shatters on the questions that fissure his existence: Why must the righteous bear an exorbitance of suffering, while the wicked enjoy their beautiful days unchecked? Why do the ungodly have the advantage over the pious, such that they enjoy the good life, at richly laid tables by day, between the knees of concubines by night, while the faithful are too exhausted to lift their heads? Some Jewish authors, who could not get over the absence of an answer, tended, like some philosophers of Hellenism, to skepticism and indifference: "All is vanity," says the unknown author of the book of Kohelet, which Luther called "Der Prediger Salomo" [The Preacher Solomon] – alias Ecclesiastes. Anyone who still believes in God under such premises sees in him a rigid mask of cosmic incomprehensibility.

Even Šubši-mašrâ-Šakkan, the righteous suffering man of the Babylonian era, was not conscious of any guilt, no matter how earnestly he examined himself. No matter how carefully he scrutinized himself, he could not acquiesce to the insinuations of his friends that he must have transgressed without knowing it. Nor could he credit the rebellious thought that God's work might harbor some element of injustice. Afflicted as he was by the inability to understand, he suffered above all from suffering as such, since, according to his own judgment, it could not have been occasioned by his moral conduct. For him, the only thing that was evident was that in this world there can be no suffering without the implication of a divine agency behind it all. He is in no doubt that what has happened is a punishment sent by Marduk or a penance-like ordeal – the modern god of "Chance" was still unknown in the old realm where purposes had been laid down from above since time out of mind. The reason Marduk turned so violently against him will remain forever a mystery to Šubši-mašrâ-Šakkan.

Conversation with friends about the whys and wherefores of his agonies does not bring him any useful insight. Suffering, questioning, weakened, and unable to understand, he reaches the nadir of his endurance. He plunges into the depths of wretchedness; he has moved about on his knees since walking upright became too difficult for him; he crawls in the straw amid the excrement of sheep; he passes his days on the ash heap, his nights in the stables. He wanders around and everywhere finds only his inability to rebel. Enfeeblement and resignation converge. The powerful kneeling of later heroic tenors of faith – as exhibited by the Iberian conquerors of South America – has no prototype among the suffering righteous of Babylon. He endures what befalls him and, with the remainder of his exhausted existence, he bears what continuous degradation has made of him. Even if he himself knows nothing of sins committed, such things could have slipped in unwittingly and, with head bowed and eyes opened questioningly, he would have to accept the consequences. How can anyone know oneself down to the last detail?

Then the page turns: the god has decided that the trials have reached their conclusion. His servant Šubši-mašrâ-Šakkan has proven himself loyal; the god reinstates him in his previous functions and restores him to a life of abundance. Already with Babylonian thought, there developed a suspicion that faith settles in the space between final resignation and a readiness for the impossible.

The parallels of the *Ludlul*'s Šubši-mašrâ-Šakkan narrative to the book of Job in the Tanakh are too conspicuous for the latter to be taken as simply a chance later consideration of similar subject material. The Job narrative thus testifies to the spiritual receptivity of the Jewish community during its Babylonian exile, with respect to their "host" culture. One may, of course, cast a skeptical eye on the legend maintaining that exiles by the rivers of Babylon were occupied first and foremost with mourning the lost Zion – after the edict of restoration issued by Cyrus II of Persia in 539 BCE, it appears that more than half of the deportees nonetheless remained in Babylon. Hebrew names soon emerged on the lists of the prosperous families there; one knows the names of Israelite banking houses in Babylon that prospered both during and after the exile. Still, it makes sense that a forceful memory of better times was formulated among the more resolute and nostalgic of the Israelites. The book of Psalms illustrates the combined effect of longing for one's homeland, praise of God, and a wish for vengeance. At the time of the post-exilic editing of the Psalms, a version of the book of Job would also have taken its initial shape. In contrast to the verses of vengeance, in which the unrestrained hate speech of the aggrieved is cast outward and the Lord of Israel is implored to visit the worst upon their enemies,[7] Job's grief is directed auto-aggressively against his own fatal having-to-be-in-the-world. The final redaction of the book, to which authors of later generations also contributed, came at the beginning of the Hellenistic era – as allusions to Cynical, skeptical, and early Stoic motifs indicate.

On the first tablet of *Ludlul*, the primacy of Marduk is formulated in terms that resemble a theory of mind in the relations of the gods among themselves: Marduk is able to see down through to the bottom of his inferior colleagues, whereas no ordinary god is capable of comprehending the judgment of the superior Marduk. This goes to show that Babylonian theology, in its own way, has a stake in the movement that raptures God ever upward. The epithet *hypsistos* means "the Most High"; the later Greeks conferred it upon Zeus, but in circulating around the Hellenized Near East, it encountered a thought structure that, from time immemorial, had already been figured in terms of elevation or height; it was particularly well suited to come to an accommodation with the rigid monotheism that, with the doctrines of Zoroaster, had shaped the ancient Iranian cultural space and its surroundings. One and a half millennia later, it was possible to lodge a figure like Allah within this resonant space – he, too, an exalted singleton, and the only one to know what he does and doesn't do.

It is upon Marduk's impenetrable orders that the personal protective gods withdraw from Šubši and abandon him to his fate. The sovereign God retires to a height such that no call can reach him. His disappearance into zones beyond all possibility of address signifies neither a breach of covenant nor a regression into indifference. Marduk avails himself of the privilege of the heavens – gaining an overview by overlooking a lot.

Faced with a heaven that owes no explanation, abandoned by spirits hitherto favorably disposed and helpful, Šubši sinks into wretchedness; his rivals triumph over him and appropriate what is his; his family is ashamed of him; he stumbles out of his house to wander in a wasteland of withered grasses; his "cheeks were burning with the tears" (Tablet I.110). A band of demons weaken his body, they kindle a fire in his belly, his arms are palsied: "In my own dung, I spent nights like an ox; I was mixed up in my own excrement like a sheep" (Tablet II.106–7).

The account of nascent healing begins with the text of the third tablet. The voice returns, breath flows freely once more, the intestines – gummed together through privation and intertwined like a reed basket – come to be open once more for ingestion. The head is uplifted, virility returns. The fifth tablet resembles a psalm of praise: "My Lord absolved me (of my sins). / My Lord revived me" (Tablet V.3–4); "From the hand of my burier, he took away the spade" (Tablet V.18). People from all quarters called out: "Who would have predicted that he would see his sun?" (Tablet V.71).

Among the conclusions of *Ludlul* is the observation that, for their author, patient endurance reaches deeper than comprehension. One could speak of a Mesopotamian ur-Stoicism: what cannot be grasped must be borne. Nevertheless, in this proto-Stoic stance, which appears to be coded throughout in a religioid way, no providence (*pronoia*) and no world soul (*psyche tou pantos*) ensures confidence in the intelligibility of the whole.

As paradoxical as it may sound, the Mesopotamian high gods are indeed assigned to the Eternal, but they cannot get out of improvising; they vary and vacillate from capital to capital, from temple to temple, from dynasty to dynasty. The principal of the *Ludlul* does not take the floor himself, but lets an expert narrate under his name; this first-person narrator intimates that, in the matter at hand, he has not made any headway with his god Marduk. After the happy escape from annihilation, he merely knows more profoundly what ought to have been presupposed in the first place – the Lord is pure ambivalence *in persona*: excessively fury-prone, punitive, and relentless – and "at the same time" gracious, mild, approachable, and tenderly caring like a mother cow to her calf. The nature of the "at the same time" cannot be broken down. Those who want to understand Marduk run into a wall of ambiguity impervious to all analysis. God is from the beginning both one and the other, only in higher potency: more destructive than the ordinary kinds of terribleness – illness, wretchedness, dispossession, war, death; more life-giving than the ordinary power of childbirth and blessings – youth, fertility, prosperity, high status, triumph. His portraitists devised the sophisticated attribute "inscrutability" in trying to describe him.

It is not unreasonable to sum up the theopoetic work of those willing to believe in gods of this type – Marduk, YHWH, and ultimately Allah – as confrontations with the predictable unpredictable ambivalence of a transcendent sovereign. The opening verses of the *Ludlul* emphasize the facts of the matter from the very beginning:

The one whose wrath is like a devastating *gale*,
but his blowing (wind) is gratifying like a morning breeze.

In his anger, he is irresistible, his fury is a deluge,
(but) his mind is *caring*, his *heart* is lenient.
(Tablet I.5–8)[8]

Against the backdrop of such statements, it becomes clear: the early formulators of Mesopotamian para-monotheisms (also called summotheisms or henotheisms) were faced with the task of contending with the ambivalence of God – a god who consists entirely of willfulness, able to do everything, and allowed to do anything; he appears sometimes on the scene like a berserker, playing with a giant toy of catastrophe. He scatters his affections and his aversions like a super-Croesus facilitated by his plenitude.

From the clinical perspective of modern times, it is obvious that the first figures of the imperial gods, not unlike their rivals of equal rank, suffered from what one might call a severe dissociative identity disorder that made it impossible for them to face their devotees with a coherent profile. With just minor cult infractions, they lost their composure, raging and rampaging their grievance in an infantile, destructive manner. Much as one saw the *furor Caesarum* take shape with the Roman successors to Caesar Augustus – Tiberius, Caligula, Claudius, and Nero – so portraits of the gods in the ancient and more recent Near East, from Marduk, Ahura Mazda, and YHWH up to Allah, betrayed a kind of *furor deorum*, raging in a continual state of *lèse-majesté*, that failed to differentiate between petty offenses and crimes: thus, Adam and Eve's bite into the wrong apple is punished with expulsion from paradise – implicitly a death penalty – while Cain, the murderer of his own brother, survives untouched, under God's protection, and active as the founder of cities.

The furor can be interpreted as an effect of forcing together under one cult name a mélange of incompatible qualities, generating a distinctive overload syndrome. Just as the attributes of omnipotence and omniscience mutually repel each other – something which was generally passed over in silence during the 2,000-year empire of theological half-thought – so justice and mercy must sit uneasily together under a shared roof; this is why it was said by later rabbis that God prayed to himself – namely, that his mercy should prevail over his angry justice.[9] What god would not be torn if, at one and the same time, he were to lovingly protect the people of his dominion and yet, in the case of the least misdemeanor, already felt the inclination to subject them to the cruelest torment? Even the God of the Tanakh, whom one has to keep in mind as an idealized father figure for Jesus, behaves so unspeakably in sending the Deluge, in the destruction of Sodom, and during the phase of the Israelite conquest of Canaan, that trust in him can only be preserved through a darkening (or a moral neutralization) of the memory of his dictates and deeds.

One sees the monotheism candidates of the Near East run, one after another, into the omnipotence trap to which they are predisposed by their function and conception. The protomonotheistic gods – Nietzsche described one of them as an "honor-craving Oriental in heaven"[10] – behave like inexperienced parents who themselves have infantile fixations and who traumatize their children early on with overly strict punishments, but telling them all the while that nothing equals their love for them. They suggest that their inability to let their children grow up without being beaten is a sign of their being faithful to the covenant: "Those who spare the rod hate their children, but those who love them are diligent to discipline them."[11] The axiom of pedagogical beating retained its prestige into the twentieth century – for example, among some benighted flocks of Irish Catholicism. Its rationale can be reformulated in terms of memory theory: it is the concern that whatever is not beaten in early on – that is, fixed in place through the association with painful memory – will not have "sunk in" later.

The peoples between Babylon and Jerusalem behaved, in short, like smart young people who, over time, learned to evade paternal incoherence. They managed to show the heavenly ones prone to decompensation that, if children can grow up, then sooner or later the gods should follow suit. It is no coincidence that the theopoetically gifted peoples of antiquity spoke of earlier and later generations of gods, whose succession corresponded to a civilizing of the infantile, jealous power gods who succumbed to piques nearly to the point of obliteration, followed by a maturation in the bearing of their sovereigns. The domestication of God by believers, which is at stake in every *therapeia theon*, is far from complete, even long after the era of Mesopotamian, Persian, Jewish, and Christian dramas. Atheism plays a creative role in this domestication because it emancipates the divine from the constraints associated both with the impositions of reality, appearance, and availability, and (even more) with the imperial mandates of heaven. The poetry of inexistence cannot be adequately discussed here – however much the poetizing-away of God would be instructive with regard to the modes of his calling-into-existence. And even the poetizing-away of complications suffers great difficulty – Nietzsche, for his part, announced his suspicion that the shadow of God may still be shown for thousands of years.[12]

The most important projection between God and his cult group (his "people") unfolds through the elevation of patient endurance to a core virtue of piety. If it is practiced among the pious sufferers as a stance toward the impenetrable, it can be projected onto God: in such a case, one extols God's forbearance and praises the restraint of his righteous wrath; he could have prosecuted much earlier his judgment against the unrighteous and have extended much further the afflictions that test the righteous. Patient endurance is the human counterpart to what is marveled at as God's "inscrutability." In the face of the inscrutable, which is particularly present in disaster, the human intellect learns to suspend its questioning and to resign itself to the answer that God thinks altogether differently than does humanity: "For my thoughts are not your thoughts, nor are your ways my ways, says the Lord" (Isaiah 55:8).

The inference from the unintelligible to the mysterious makes theology possible by sustaining the belief in a God for whom there can be no imputation of deprivation or deficiency. If he remains incomprehensible to his own, it is because his abundance of ulterior motives cannot be exhausted. If we were to understand him rightly, we would see that God is planning a campaign for the benefit of mankind – since the days of Augustine, there has been no lack of attempts to tell it as a comprehensive, future-oriented "salvific history" moving toward the day of judgment. To want to understand the calculations involved would be presumptuous – those who make the attempt inevitably get sucked into a maelstrom of paranoid ideas that everywhere take for granted conspiracy, ciphers, remote control, secret logic, and counterintuitive demonstrability – all of them traits of an irrationalism marinated in a higher, more refined knowledge.

At the base of faith, beneath the desperation that strives toward the end and beyond the further hope against all reason, there is found an unanalyzable layer of resignation – Latin: *resignare* (lower the standard, give up the fight), German: *Ergebung*, English: *surrender*, Spanish: *sumisión*, Arabic: *islam*.

One should see resignation not only as a stepping back from the struggle that follows from one's powerlessness once everything possible has been exhausted, but also as the original synthetic achievement of patient endurance, which bears up under God's unfathomable incoherence. Patient endurance goes beyond the zone in which, between God and humanity, that simple analogy of caregiving could be accepted, as attested by the folk logic of a proverb of the first millennium found in W. G. Lambert's *Assyrian Collection* (ii, 23–6):

When you take good care of (your god),
your god is yours.

> When you do not take good care of (your god),
> your god is not yours.[13]

Transactional mindsets of a similar cast are likewise present in the Psalms of David: "Therefore the Lord has recompensed me according to my righteousness, according to the cleanness of my hands in his sight. / With the loyal you show yourself loyal."[14] The suffering among the righteous people of Mesopotamia played a pioneering role in the simultaneous darkening and exaltation of their deity of choice: they translated him up out of the sphere of simple transactions by making him more asymmetrical, more irrational, more idiosyncratic, and more ironic than usual in the case of gods with whom one could negotiate (Pauline–Lutheran: "dispute") on the basis of continuous reciprocity.

The authors of the book of Job went a dramatic step further by integrating Job's unprecedented lament into the patient submission of the sufferer, and by amplifying his lament by temporarily silencing it into a signless fermenting monstrosity, as known by people who have become uncertain about more than themselves and their internal and external coordinates. During Job's seven-day silence, the asymmetry between what lies above and what lies here below deepens in the most abysmal way. His no-longer-speaking conceals the possibility of questioning creation, challenging its terms. While God permits the test and therewith retires into the heights of complete otherness, the sufferer plunges into a hell-like abandonment of meaning that pushes his burden to infinity. In Job's lament, there rings forth what remained unsaid in the darkness of the week of silence: "Let the day perish in which I was born, and the night that said, 'A man-child is conceived.' ... / Why did I not die at birth, come forth from the womb and expire? ... / Or why was I not buried like a stillborn child, like an infant that never sees the light?"[15] And again: "Why did you bring me forth from the womb? / "Would that I had died before any eye had seen me, and were as though I had not been, carried from the womb to the grave."[16] Job speaks here as someone to whom the burdensome character of existing has been demonstrated to the uttermost limit of endurance. One can read this as a subjective version of the question of being: Why birth? Why the world? Why being in the world? There is no room here for philosophical speculation, any more than for Gnostic support structures.[17] Intelligible answers are not to be expected. Indeed, what is given in response sounds like the opposite of a clarificatory disclosure. Does one not hear the tone of priestly

Cynicism, when the Lord humiliates the plaintiff with counter-questions? Or is God's reply the earliest example of a paradoxical intervention?

> Where were you when I laid the foundation of the earth? Tell me, if you have understanding....
> Or who shut in the sea with doors when it burst out from the womb? –
> when I made the clouds its garments, and thick darkness its swaddling band,
> and prescribed bounds for it, and set bars and doors,
> and said, "Thus far shall you come, and no farther, and here shall your proud waves be stopped"? ...
> Can you lead forth the Mazzaroth in their season, or can you guide the Bear with its children?
> Do you know the ordinances of the heavens? Can you establish their rule on the earth?[18]

Job's questioning lament has made the god more loquacious than in any other part of the Tanakh – indeed, the questions seem to have provoked him like a poet who wants to tame the sea with metaphors. Like a Greek actor, the God of Israel, called the "Lord," arrives on the scene, confronts Job the non-Israelite and his friends, and declaims – as if from a *theologeion* – a monologue full of mockery at the presumptuousness of comprehension; his torrent of words overflows with rhetorical figures that speak of cosmic self-assurance and a self-congratulatory mood. This is no longer the serene *valde bonum* of Genesis; it corresponds more nearly to the summation of a lawyer who holds the very idea of an allegation against his client to be absurd. With arguments from nature as well as morality, the Most High – the all too high – crushes his would-be accuser to the ground. What, after all, would be a meaningful response to ironic questions such as: "Is it by your wisdom that the hawk soars, and spreads its wings toward the south? / Is it at your command that the eagle mounts up and makes its nest on high?"[19] After that, all that remains is for Job to reply: "I lay my hand on my mouth."[20] The one rebuked wants to remain silent, repent, and back down from the presumption of asking questions. Thereafter, there can be no suggestion that asking questions is the piety of thought. One of the curiosities of the Lord's self-presentation in his reply to the man from the unknown land is the detailed way in which God on high presents himself as the creator of animal life; this includes the monsters Behemoth and Leviathan, two erratic monsters that plow through land and sea. Presumably, they represent a remnant of titanoid power that could not be taken into account in the Genesis creation narrative. They are a reminder, however, of how very much the world chaos needed an organizing hand before the mythical six-day labor of creation. The fact that the Lord highlights them at this point, as if they belonged in some unexplained way to the Lord's entourage, fits in with the tendency of persuasive and overpowering rhetoric which lends the book of Job its special profile among the books of the Hebrew Bible. It shows a pleading God – even, one might say, a God who wants to make an impression. The fact that he does not rule over a political empire is a reminder that the ancient Jewish attempts to form an empire had by then definitively failed. The motif of the covenant between God and his chosen people now formed a surplus that tended toward dysfunction, bearing unsuccessful imperial ambitions in constant remembrance – and, what is more, setting up chronic friction with the theologies of other peoples in the world who were more successful at power politics. With an emphasis that he commands over the animal kingdom and its horrific spawn, the politically disempowered Lord reclaims his sovereignty over the kingdom of animals and over two surreal super-animals.

From Behemoth and Leviathan can be read the signs of what had never been expressed before; in these two figures, there becomes visible the really sensational part of the book of Job – namely: in the creation, more had gone wrong than just that which followed from the serpent's conversation with Eve. Evil was, to be sure, present in the well-made world from the beginning through the serpent-mediated infringement of the ban on apples, together with its well-known consequences. The very banality of the ban provided the invitation to transgress, as if it had been Eve who had introduced the first negation into the pure Yes-world of God, while it is evident that the original founding of the negation was accomplished in the ban itself, in which a No to the No was laid out like a trap into which one could not not fall. But now, into the discussion, significantly belated, there entered further evil in the form of two monsters, which can be interpreted without further ado as symbols of the maritime and terrestrial realms.

The book of Job reveals the need to think further about problems of power concealed in the book of Genesis; initially, this could only be done through the symbolic visualization of atrocious beings of monstrous size, who enter the picture as anomalous domestic animals of God, separate from the harmless fauna of paradise. They have to be conceived as the empires that came epigenetically into the world. What is more, they are creatures of the first hour, like the cunning serpent, yet they are serpents on a massive scale, created malignities, which were elevated to their enormity only after paradise. In the book of Job, the God of Israel presents himself as having mastery of them, as if they were walking beside him on a leash, though he had not successfully led his people to dominate them.

Still, the fact that Israel was not completely crushed by its powerful enemies might already be taken as some evidence of providential care. In much the same way, God had pulled strings with the Egyptian pharaoh, hardening his heart; he had played his game with Cyrus II of Persia to bring some of the Jews back from Babylon to Jerusalem. After the sojourn in Babylonian exile and its (partial) discontinuation thanks to the divine surprise of the Edict of Cyrus in 539 BCE, the flame was extinguished for expansive ambition among the post-exilic Jewish elite; during the next half-millennium, there followed periods of Persian, Greek, and Roman domination, and finally diaspora. It was the de-imperialization of the covenant between God and his people that first called for theopoetic coping, then later the (provisionally) final deterritorialization of Judaism.

The fact that the Leviathan, under the pen of Thomas Hobbes, became the emblem of the modern seafaring imperial state in the seventeenth century speaks to the topicality of the monster from the depths. The twentieth century should probably have discussed less about "political theology" and more about monstrosity. The mention of the monsters Behemoth and Leviathan, in a description to which the author of Job gives his poetic utmost, reveals a secret not disclosed anywhere else: the six-day labor, after its completion, and notwithstanding its predicate *valde bonum*, has produced an unresolved excess. It is to this that Philippe Nemo's so-called "excess of evil"[21] can be related, as something inseparable from God's underived decision to create. In order for there to be anything at all, it was inevitable to give what succeeds a surplus element of the amorphous, the misshapen, and the unmasterable; this includes an excess in ambivalent political violence, as was manifested in the empires of the Egyptians, the Babylonians, and others. And yet: if, in the creation, God had already intended the later emergence of empires, why did he let his people get into a situation in which, more than other peoples, they suffered from the existence of these powers? If the behemoths of Egypt and Babylon are really his "creatures" too, then why did he not allow Israel to become a behemoth, or even a superbehemoth? Was it his wish to make Israel a Job among the nations?

The poetry of patient endurance, which is spread across both ancient and more recent narratives of righteous people in their suffering, goes one momentous step beyond the economy of *do-ut-des* thinking – whose importance for the quasi-universal system of gift and counter-gift can hardly be overestimated.[22] Job, a man in the land of Uz, does not belong to him – the covenantal relationship with God pertains to the believers of Israel. Whatever reciprocity this covenant might imply can no longer be understood according to the simple logic of *do ut des*: "I give so that you may give." It is apparent that God stands in no binding obligation, no strictly contractual relationship, with the pious sufferer, not least because the covenant was made with the people, not with its individual members; it is likewise clear that Šubši-mašrâ-Šakkan and Job are not punished for manifest misconduct, nor even for latent or "unconscious" rebellion. The "Lord" takes due advantage of his right to impose a trial, since the frailness of people in (and outside) the covenant can be no secret to him. Since, for his part, he kept his main promise to "give" land to the people by allowing the bloody conquest of Canaan, or by leading them to triumph as their warlord, no further claims can be lodged against him.

The basic material fact about the trial is that it cannot be passed. The subject is not even supposed to know for sure that it *is* a trial. Holding out is not to be ascribed to any merit of one's own. Simply bearing it is everything. For the suffering person, as for the dying, there is no project, other than the hopeless hope that what is to be endured will pass. This supposes that the patient sufferer deals with the imposition of staying alive without the kind of despair implied in resorting, on one's own authority, to the voluntary peace of the grave – the despair that has a sense of time that is inherently angry and attached to the violated ego.

The poetry of patient endurance has qualities, as the conclusions of these stories show, that are not only proto-Stoic but also proto-evangelical, addressing the question: is there life after disaster? An answer in the affirmative will not fail to materialize, so that the stories are more than pieces of "wisdom" literature: they already exhibit a trace of good news. Readers might recognize a trace of the messianic in the book of Job – but, for those who want to do so, can they resist the temptation to overinterpret?[23] Stories like these about the righteous enduring a trial are not about the coming of a redeemer – to say nothing of rising from the dead. It is wonderful enough just to recover from disaster – as might be attested by those among the Israelites who returned to Jerusalem and recovered from the disaster of exile in Babylon, thanks to Cyrus the Great, the messiah who came from Persia.

From the poetry of patient endurance there follows the poetry of restoration, in every possible sense of the word. It heralds the poetry of resilience, which for more than 2,000 years will be concealed under the ciphers of tales of good *fortuna*. They are about the grounds for hope in general, whether attended by a messianic factor or not. How could one live humanly without in any way having (or expecting) good fortune? Hope cannot be a principle, notwithstanding whatever Ernst Bloch has advanced in its favor. As the daughter of patient endurance, hope depends on preconditions that it cannot itself create.

If eking out a miserable existence in calamity already corresponded to social death, then complete recovery from misfortune is tantamount to resurrection. In no way do Marduk and the "Lord" admit, in restoring the *status quo ante*, that the immiseration of Šubši-mašrâ-Šakkan and Job had all been a willful experiment; they indicate that in both splendor and misery it is the same sovereign who exercises his power – or, as it may be, allows it to be exercised – for the gods of both Mesopotamia and Israel act through secondary causes: through enemies, through helpers, through "Satan," through ailments, through the human, all too human. Development does not take place. At long last, Job finds himself twice as rich as before and, after the reintegration of his household, he lived 140 years, and saw his children and his children's children down four generations – but after all that, it still cannot be said that his second fortune was merited. Nor can one even claim that he understands it more deeply than before. This second happenstance of good fortune remains, even more than the first, a sign of plenary power on the part of the superpotent Lord, who now bears a proper name: the "author" of the book of Job sometimes refers to the Lord as "Shaddaï" – "the one from the mountain."

The difference between the first and second fortune lies in the proselytic effect: for the first time, the law overspread the boundary between peoples. In this piece of early ecumenical literature, the God of Israel was experienced and recognized by a non-Israelite. Straitened by the Lord, the man from the land of Uz was compelled to adopt a new conception: this Lord on high is able, as Marduk was before, to take the spade from his burier's hand. He also allowed a near-dead man to see the light again.

17

POETRY OF EXAGGERATION: RELIGIOUS VIRTUOSOS AND THEIR EXCESSES

If patient endurance were the last word on "religions," there would hardly be any grounds for people in the modern world to be more than superficially interested in them. Apart from a few sentimental festivals, they would have dissolved in the shallow Stoicism of finitude becalmed; in terms of their therapeutic effects, they would have been replaced by anxiolytics, analgesics, stimulants, and any number of intoxicants – the discreet benefactors that Aldous Huxley called the chemical "Grace-substitutes." Faust's curse on patient endurance is closer for contemporaries than the Christian exhortation to bear the Cross. Of the millennia spent longing for redemption, what remains in the culture of the welfare state is the striving for alleviation and commercial forms of the principle of relief. What seemed specific about religion, the surplus of revelation granted from above, is lost in the basic empirical mood of recent times. John Locke expressed the Enlightened view when, anticipating Immanuel Kant and Johann Gottlieb Fichte, he asserted that religion reveals no truth that human reason could not have come to by its own means; religion must settle for a lesser degree of certainty than that claimed by the truths of reason or observation. There are no assurances for its statements, other than those it proclaims on its own behalf.[1]

If, in the present day, "religion" is often still honored with the predicate "of interest," it is certainly not because there is any deeply felt popular inclination for being schooled in patient endurance. It is not individuals' willingness to suffer that still draws their attention – indeed, it is precisely their unwillingness to patiently endure. Heavenly patients, like those of medical practice, have become impatients, so to speak: they consider themselves entitled to claim well-being and healing as if these were covered by insurance contributions based on life expectancies.

"Religion" remains noteworthy so long as it tends to its capacity for fascination – in other words: so long as it displays the ability to attract attention to itself through irrational enchantments, bizarre rituals, and a careful measure of absurdity. Besides its normalizing component – to which it owes its reputation for obscuring things in routine or for serving some indefinite need for meaning – it still has, usually discreetly veiled, an extravagant side that tends toward the obscure, the terrifying, the rationally unacceptable. Especially in their founding phases, the state of exception seems to be permanent, so far as particulars have been handed down from those times. In them appear an abundance of personal revelations, psychotic episodes, collective contagion, group hallucinations, and miraculous overpowerings. The ability to fascinate is something that "religion" shares in common with theatre, circus, and sorcery – especially when, as in archaic initiation rites, it presents itself as a sacred and cruel theatre turned against the actors. Where it works most disconcertingly, it allows glimpses through the half-open door to the wondrous.[2]

As a rule, the fascination produced through the crossing-over of boundaries does not come from the "excess of evil"[3] one sees in the wretchedness of the poor and infirm and in the victims of natural and social catastrophes; most witnesses prefer to turn their eyes from it, as if proximity to disaster could expose the observer to a kind of like contagion or malady. Brahmin from ancient times regarded the mere sight of strange suffering as a defilement to be kept at bay. In the magic of avoidance, repulsive force asserted itself along the lines of an escape reflex, upon which would later be imposed neurotic fixations on purity. By contrast, as soon as the *fascinosum* was attached to the sphere of the sacred and deployed its effect, it set in motion a kind of attraction, a bewitchment by way of a disconcertment, from which participants hardly knew how to withdraw themselves. The bundling of religious actors into unusual, non-everyday situations transfixed not only those who were similarly attuned, but also often witnesses from outside that frame.[4] Moreover, those who had been once in the light sought out others who knew of such things, and with whom the otherwise unheard-of and unseen could be shared.

As with most forms of active life, the practical field is divided into the few who come to prominence through the display of their passion, and the many who remain sheltered in the crowd, albeit with elevated pulse. The separation of the actors from the onlookers concerns not only the theatre and its visitors, it is also of anthropo-logical relevance, since the culture-forming work of articulation is initially propelled only from the side of those who step forth from the crowd.[5]

The poetry of excess opens up a decisive chapter in the study of the premises and forms of religious poetry. In so doing, a non-everyday definition of "faith" comes to assume its contours: what is commonly referred to as faith not infrequently arises as a result of the fascinated observation of subjects in a spiritual state of exception by members of an audience that is affectively moved from a distance. Conventional faith believes that what is called "religious experience," in the eminent sense, is something that has befallen others – regardless of whether this experience is construed phenom-enologically, psychologically, or paranormally.

Such experiences extend over a spectrum of states in which the everyday personality loses sovereignty over itself and, in moments of varying duration, becomes permeable on ecstatic frequencies to quasi-self-less experiences. It should go without saying that the distinction between people who have experienced ecstasy and those who are denied or spared it is not the same as that between priests and laity; the latter distinction is, to speak with Luhmann, "internal to the religious system" – it characterizes the incipient differenti-ation of the "religion" system. The ecstatic element goes back much further than any ritualized and constituted *religio* and it manifests itself long before the establishment of sacred professional roles, hierarchies, holy scriptures, and the emergence of rigorous ascetic movements. Where higher cults were established, as in Brahmanism, Zoroastrianism, Buddhism, Christianity, and Islam, ecstatic and ascetic moments merged and begot a pandemonium of sacred extremisms; these, in turn, ushered in a new willingness for extreme exertion. On the left-leaning extremist wing of Shiite Islam, for example, tendencies toward anarchic gnosis appeared on the scene, tendencies which more prudent Muslims referred to as *ghuluw*: to exaggerate, to exceed reasonable bounds. Fakir phenomena from the Islamic and Hindu spheres caused a stir, so long as they were attributed more to the realm of the sacred than to that of physi-ological show business.

In the early Christian world, the paradigmatic case of a "religious experience" is presented in Acts 9:3–9, a few decades *post eventum*; it came to pass when Saul of Tarsus, a persecutor of early Christians, was dazzled and overcome on the road to Damascus:[6] suddenly a light from heaven flashed around him, blinding him, and he fell to the ground and heard a voice saying to him, "Saul, Saul, why do you persecute me?" – while the men who were traveling with him heard the voice but saw no one. By contrast, in Acts 22:9, the other men who were with him saw the light but did not hear the voice. The fall is common to both versions. The narrator himself seems to have been content with the fact that higher agencies played a part in casting the traveler to the ground.

The discrepancy between the versions affects the authenticity of the reports: in the first telling, Saul's traveling companions heard Jesus himself speaking to his persecutor, mentioning his name; in the second version, Saul alone heard the voice. Shortly thereafter, the traveler was led into Damascus and lodged with a disciple of Jesus; after three days' blindness, his sight was restored, he was converted and baptized and, thereafter under the name of Paul, began to proclaim the news of Jesus: his messiahship, his resurrection, and his ministry.

What Saul-Paul experienced on his approach to Damascus – provided that one is not concerned here with the fictions of a miraculous milieu – was an incident that was both relatively uncomplicated and psychologically easy to interpret, measured against the enormous internal states of emergency in elaborate ascetic cultures, especially those of the East[7] and in the narcotic cultures of the global South: his gift for zealotry was something he simply redirected in the reverse direction and little changed in the structure of his personality. What was distinctive about Saul's "experience" was that it seemed to befall him suddenly in the middle of life – which is not to say that it was entirely unprepared; what Paul had learned as a persecutor served him well as a proclaimer. Since he had empathized with his opponents, he knew how to realize the omens. In between, there lies the moment not mentioned by the author of the Acts of the Apostles, when ideas suppressed within Saul began to surface: What if the other side were right? What a beautiful sea of plagues and glorious labors would open up, in the event that one could finally preach old Jewish truths even to non-Jewish souls! Since the Jesus-Christ hypothesis had arrived on the scene, well-seasoned, long-clarified truths that had been hashed through 1,000 times could now suddenly be dispatched as a liberating message with all the force of the new, to chosen addressees, in the center as on the periphery. One might be liberated from Jewish law on the one hand, and even more liberated in relation to the world of the Romans and their *religio*-disguised realism. Because the end is near, one might bear witness to truths that catapult us out of the self-affirming realism of the untenable world and lend us the wisdom to live uncomfortably *here* for a little while longer, in order to celebrate *there* all the more.

The "mystical" experience would have to have been of a different quality, at which Paul merely hinted, while unmistakably alluding to himself: he knows "a person in Christ" who 14 years ago was caught up to the third heaven – whether in the body or in mind or spirit God alone knows.[8] Although an expression like "third heaven" in no way speaks for itself, its suprematist sense cannot be misunderstood. Whoever claims to have been "raptured" there can only mean a transitory initiation into the sphere of ultimate secrets. Whether the experience was based on a grand mal seizure, as is sometimes conjectured, plays no role in the religious-historical consequences of the episode.

When one notes that the holy books of the people of Israel recognize rapture, or the heavenward journey, as an almost stereotypical motif in accounts of being called to prophetic office (as in Isaiah, Jeremiah, and Ezekiel, who in turn follow Elijah), Paul's statements appear in a different light: because the letter writer wanted to showcase, before the dissident part of the Corinthian community, his authority as an apostle – as a "servant" (*doulos*) and medium of Christ – the reference to an experience of rapture is also to be understood as part of his strategy of legitimation with regard to local skeptics. Even though, as residents of a Greek city, they may not have been much acquainted with figures of Jewish prophetism, there may have been some Jewish "Christians" there as well. Accordingly, Paul would have invoked "religious experiences" in order to emphasize his primacy over the parishioners who did not have such, or who had them only in lesser degree. In any case, he did not place himself on the same level as recipients of common charisms such as prophecy, poetry, speaking in tongues, or spiritual healing.[9] It should not be overlooked that the Prophet Muhammad is likewise said to have mastered, *summa cum laude*, the Jewish program of making a heavenly sojourn.

William James gave us the insight that, as a rule, belief for individuals in modern cultures is not based on simple acquiescence to authoritatively proclaimed doctrines; instead, with adults, it is inherently invested with the structure of a will to believe.[10] This in turn presupposes a belief in the paramount value of belief, through which everything else is evaluated. When it comes to their belief in belief, their faith in faith, James notes with pointed pen that most apologists for their life-guiding convictions fall into dogmatic speech: "when left to their instincts, they dogmatize like infallible popes."[11]

In no religioid act is the will to believe manifested more overtly than in asceticism. It forms the matrix of exaggerations that aim at the sanctification of existence as a whole. With their help, inner states of exception are generated that open access to "religious experience." When the ascetic subject – whether as an athlete, as a monk, or more recently as a radical artist – renounces its undisciplined former existence in everyday life, it enters a space for self-cultivation, the limits of which one does not at first recognize. Whether one interprets its dimensionality as height or depth or breadth does not initially matter for what follows. It supplies existential content for the rhetorical figure of hyperbole (literally: that which is cast upward), of exaggeration. In his textbook for oratory, Quintilian defined hyperbole as an "appropriate exaggeration of the truth"[12] (*decens veri superiectio*) and derived its propriety from human nature: everyone has a natural desire (*cupiditas*) to exaggerate or to minimize things, and no one is satisfied with "the truth." Teachers of asceticism in the context of *religio* attribute the necessity of extreme practices to the corruption of human nature – while teachers of artists and trainers of athletes elucidate compulsory exercises with reference to the highest attainments in the art and the state of peak performances in the event.

For Quintilian, exaggeration is a legitimate, appropriate, and effective stylistic device when "the thing about which we have to speak transcends the ordinary limits of nature."[13] In such circumstances, it is better to go too far than not to go far enough. Since the ascetic masters, with early Christian ascetics leading the way, disallow a "limit of nature" with regard to human corruption, in their eyes there can be no exaggeration that would go too far. The asceticism of atonement takes its measure from sinful corruption: if, as in the view of many theologians before and after Augustine, the corruption of mankind is monstrous, then there can be no limit to atonement, unless old Adam himself were to be entirely effaced. Those who admit to having disappointed God can never go too far in their acts of contrition.

The exercises in atonement practiced by the early anchorites and cenobites (from: *koinos bios*, common life) consistently showed – provided they followed fixed rules – an invasive endo-rhetorical and endo-poietic component. These stemmed from the application of hyperbolic figures of speech and poetic metaphors to the moral and physical existence of the practitioner. In particular, expressions such as mortification, expiration, perplexity, purification, retreat, seclusion, ascension, and resurrection were tested for their exaggerability. The result was that they met the highest expectations of their excess potential.

The fact that hyperbolic speech in the Christosphere enjoys an ancient right of domicile is proven by numerous statements attributed to Jesus and compiled in the Gospel of Matthew, in which a quiet humor of exaggeration is occasionally expressed – a humor without a smile, often misunderstood literally: God is able from these stones to raise up children to Abraham; in his prophecy, even the hairs of your head are all counted; if anyone strikes you on the right cheek, turn the other also (requiring the slapper to be ambidextrous, striking first with the left hand in order to hit the right cheek, then striking with the right hand); if anyone wants to sue you and take your coat, give your cloak as well. Mark casts further paradoxical light on the hyperbole: it is easier for a camel to go through the eye of a needle than for someone who is rich to enter the kingdom of God; whoever wishes to be first among you must be the slave of all.[14] The prophet who speaks in such a way is allied with a rebellion of proportions; like satire, parables are allowed to do anything.

A book by one of the founders of Middle Eastern monastic culture, Evagrius Ponticus (345–99 CE), *Talking Back*, or the *Antirhetikus*, gives a clear view of the endo-rhetorical procedures of the monks. In accordance with the author's doctrine of the eight evil thoughts, which served for centuries as a breviary of self-contempt, Evagrius sets before his reader the primary demons exciting the more debauched thoughts of monastics – gluttony, fornication, love of money, sadness, anger, listlessness, vainglory, and cursed pride. In order to give a complete account of spiritual corruption, which invariably begins with hearkening to demonically induced inner voices, the author stints no effort in setting down nearly 500 such tempting thoughts, divided into 8 books, a whole compass rose of perdition. For every wicked thought, he administers – half psychagogue, half pharmacist – an antidote in the form of a quotation from the Hebrew Bible or the New Testament. From this it follows that monastic life must excite the opposite of tranquility, however much tranquility be praised. The more simply existence wanted to be led, the more it relied upon exacting stylizations; the more conscientiously the ascetic shunned all exchange with worldly persons, the more dependent the ascetic became on the perpetual self-persuasion that guided the objectives of the exercise. Those who shunned the din of the world without were compelled to notice how loud, confused, and disingenuous was the world within.

The most radical and, at the same time, most dubious innovation in the poetry of excess is displayed in the determination of early Christian preachers to involve dying and death itself in an intensification from which a morbid superlative was to emerge. Readers will want to decide for themselves whether they have the fortitude to learn more about this or else would rather skip over the next few pages.

That there are unpleasant alternatives to gently "slipping away" and "resting in peace" – to use common metaphors of dying and death[15] – has been always known among witnesses to the prolonged agonies that sometimes conclude a serious illness. The differences between easy and difficult modes of passing away are stored in the tacit knowledge of cultures. In the phobocratic empires of antiquity, they were combined with torture, taken up by kings, and espoused by counselors, judges, and executioners, in order to deter adversaries and evildoers by developing extended and extremely humiliating methods of execution. If one generally starts from the premise that delinquents would rather hasten to the end of the process, executioners (and their assistants) are given the license – even the imperative – to exercise their leisure from the start.

The constellation of being and time, elaborated by Martin Heidegger, does not come from the experience of the trenches of the First World War, where one could have learned to practice antici- pating or "running toward one's own death,"[16] as was sometimes claimed, beneath the hail of fire. Insofar as this constellation springs from any empirical prototype, it would surely come from the places of execution in the old world. In the executions of classical antiquity, the running toward death that the philosopher felt would provide seriousness to "authentic exist-ing" was forced – and at the same time impeded – by procedures of excruciating gradualness. Thus, for as long as physically possible, the horror of execution barred any escape to the end. Torture and executions thereby engendered horrific images of dying, traumatically burned into the imaginations of the bystanding populations. Roman crucifixions, for example, usually lasted several days (it was half a day on the Cross for Jesus because he was weakened from his earlier flagellation); executions on late medieval breaking wheels dragged on for hours, with the arms and legs of the criminal smashed into fragments with iron bars until they could be woven like ropes through the spokes of a wagon wheel;[17] in the infamous Chinese *lingchi* (banned officially only in 1905), individual limbs, organs, and muscle groups were very slowly sliced from the body of the naked criminal on the stake: perhaps hundreds of small, minimally bloody cuts, until, at the end of the day, the mutilated criminal's head might look down in an ecstasy of pain at his exposed skeleton – it remained uncertain whether he experienced his beheading as part of the torment or as the beginning of liberation. Such scenes, beheld by eyewitnesses and passed on through hearsay, propagated evidence supporting the idea that the threshold to salvation through powerlessness might be raised to extreme heights. It formed the hardest certainty of faith in the phobocratic age, the onset of which dates to the early empires.

If one understands prolonged executions as a comparative of the difficult death, intensification and escalation to the utmost degree of severity would be attained as soon as the prolonged dying under torment could be extended over and beyond death itself. Christianity recycled old Iranian motifs to realize and institutionalize this extension of torment beyond death in the imaginary of hell, with its never-extinguished fire – an achievement that Islam, as a religion of rigid duality, would eagerly appropriate for itself.[18] Islam, like Christianity before the invention of purgatory, was a religion without intermediate solutions.[19] There is a dictum attributed to Karol Wojtyła and formulated with bitter priestly humor: *speriamo che l'inferno sia vuoto* ("let us hope that hell is empty"); this hope may be a [theological] assumption – but, whether it is or it isn't, it seems ill suited to nullify a psychopolitics of horror that has been practiced for 2,000 years.[20] In Nietzsche's judgment, this was based on a "psychical cruelty" in which "there resides a kind of madness of the will, which is absolutely unexampled."[21]

Transition from the comparative to the superlative of suffering can take place as soon as one grants feasibility to the conception of the soul as both capable of suffering and also preserved over and beyond death. The superlative trait finds its expression in the Christian doctrine of Last Things, which, for its part, depends on the suggestive metaphysical doctrine of the inextinguishable being of the soul. With neo-Catholic and neo-conservative aggression, Hugo Ball articulated the secret common to both disciplines in a 1923 essay[22] celebrating John Climacus (*c.* 579–649), the author of the spiritually momentous text *Ladder of Divine Ascent* (*Scala paradisi*) and temporary abbot of St. Catherine's Monastery on Mount Sinai: "The superlative of health is immortality."[23] This statement poses the impossibility of escaping from being – but it brings forward the bright side of an ambivalent insight. Just as individuals cannot escape their skin during their lifetime, individual souls post mortem cannot deny their substantiality. There would be nothing to object to if healthy immortals were to be gathered around God – whatever the preposition "around" might mean in such a context. The flipside of everlastingness is likewise indicated, however, as comparative dying under torture is postulated as prolongable into the superlative of perpetual dying in an other-worldly fire. "For there is no greater or more grievous death than when death itself does not die."[24] As deathless invalids, the candidates for this possibility populate an underworld of darkly glowing prisons. They constitute the "city of woe" described by Dante, in which no one ever leaves their quarters. Hell means a perpetual lockdown: it warehouses souls capable of suffering, who discover too late that death offers no way out.[25]

In the thought of John Climacus, intensification and escalation constituted more than just a grammatical mode. With the teacher of Christian extremism in the mode of gradualness, they unfurled into the form of existence in general. What is intensified is the effort to expel worldly reality and its inner agent, the profane ego, which is relentlessly attested to be far removed from God. The procedure brought to prominence by John Climacus involves a path with 30 steps, leading over 29 comparatives to an ultimate superlative – namely: to the actually existing impossible. It is said of this that it can and should come to pass in consummate holiness, in this life, this body, this soul. The high number of comparatives is necessary because flight from the world, which begins with entry into the monastery, turns out to be a protracted undertaking and vulnerable to setbacks and paradoxical turns. In the reclusion, the obsession of those who flee the world becomes concretely manifest through mundane things. Monastics, who have set out for an angelic life, discover that the world pursues them into their cells, their dreams, the tenor of their prayers, and the vocabulary of their inner monologues and dialogues. It shows its power through the socialized I, trained to be a human among humans, which cannot stop wanting to please itself and the human world around it – and any posture of selflessness would constitute just such a stoppage. Just as analysands in psychoanalysis often exploit the treatment to serve their neuroses, not a few monastics used asceticism as a pretext for the aggrandizement of their egos. The masters of desert psychology did not escape this embarrassment, which is why they complicated the way through proliferating the harassments that needed to be suffered.

In order to shake off the tiresome being-pursued-by-the-world, the rungs of the sacred ladder, up to the twenty-fourth, work to overcome the vices that cling to the socialized soul, whether in the world or in the hermitage; only very late in the ascent can one speak of Christian virtues – and then only circumspectly. A relapse into *superbia*, into pride or excessive self-esteem, remains a menace to the last – all the more so the higher one ascends the ladder. Only with the highest rung has one left behind the virtual 29-times iterable distinction between arrogance and submission. Only then would the practitioner have become an illuminant, beyond emptiness and plenitude. Those involved were not astonished to find that the procedure could take 40 years – as with John Climacus himself, most of whose time was spent as a hermit in the desert. In incessant endo-rhetorical response to the capital Other, the designer of the Ladder of Divine Ascent had transformed himself into a post-human work of art.

The instructions of John Climacus show how the synthesis of comparatives and hyperbole is achieved. One presupposition was the poetry of the deferred Second Coming of the Lord. After it had become evident in the first Christian generations that the *kyrios*, the Lord, would not so soon come again in glory to separate the goats from the sheep, the hopeful had to make post-apocalyptic compromises by organizing themselves in the world against the world. The Lord was expected; but what actually came to pass was the episcopal church – and, at its edges, an expectation of the imminent eschaton would flare up every now and again. Consciousness of a truly authentic time characterized by its limited duration and the deferral of its end, and figured in terms of a historical extension of the *parousia*, of the Second Coming – all this was first left behind only in the Enlightenment.

The desert saints, who appeared sporadically from the third century on, and in larger numbers from the fourth century on, voiced the reservation that the church should not be more than a provisional, interim arrangement, else it risked ossifying into a waiting hall in the absurd. They were quietly discontent with the deferral of the *parousia*. By devoting themselves to practices of sanctification, they sought to compel the return of Christ in the consummate monk. If the Second Coming of the Lord in his *doxa* (Luther: "glory") was no longer likely, it should manifest itself, even so, in the luminousness of the perfectly mortified and vivified ascetic. Almost half a millennium after the Resurrection, monastic extremism drew its corollary from the non-return of Christ: it strove for the *parousia* in the actually existing saint. If Christ does not want to appear triumphant in the clouds surrounded by heavenly hosts, he will be drawn to hothouses of renunciation under the Sinai sun. In the West, this arcanum of Eastern Christianity was replicated only once, unconcealed: in the phenomenon of Francis of Assisi.

The fact that the majority church could not follow this path proceeds from the elitist character of ascetic extremism. The church had to back simpler procedures for the return of the Lord, so it invested the essential part of its ritual-strategic energy in the establishment of the sacrament of the Eucharist. In this way, the return of Christ was to be achieved in every celebration of the Mass without the individual having to go into the desert in search of transfiguration.[26] Those who receive the host – the bread that represented the sacrificial meat (lamb) and that was later replaced by the wafer – let themselves be consumed by what they received. The incorporation is intended to reverse the relationship between the container and the contained, according to the schema of the change of subject. Whoever receives the wafer is received by it, as if by an auratic envelope. If Christ were to take up the notion of appearing not in the form of the host, but in real fleshly presence – say, as a wanderer through the villages of Spain – the church established in his name would be forced to act against him as the worst heretic – as Dostoevsky proposed in the parable of the Grand Inquisitor, from his novel *The Brothers Karamazov* (1879–80). The tale ends, as is well known, when Jesus *redivivus* kisses the cold lips of the religious realpolitician, who has advocated Jesus' cause on earth with such tragic cynicism and who releases the returnee from his dungeon, but with the stipulation that he agree to never return again.

The highest achievement of Christian theopoetry in the liturgical-theatrical realm consisted in the repurposing of the term *sacramentum*, which among the Romans had denoted the soldier's oath of loyalty, the civil servant's oath of office, and a pledge or bond held as surety by a court.[27] As definitively articulated by the Council of Trent (1545–63), the term was recast into the system of seven "sacraments," necessary for salvation and organized around baptism and Holy Communion. The *sacra*, to which Roman soldiers were sworn *per sacramentum*, was the *aquila*, the eagle standard carried by each Roman legion, which was thought to have salvific power, which symbolically integrated the troops, and in which the command (*imperium*) of the Augusti and Caesares asserted a numinous presence. In baptism, Christians were sworn into service in the army of peace, under the command of Christ. One of the most occulted trade secrets of western civilization is the fact of the Christian will to recast the paradoxical – really the perverse – synthesis of a spiritual devotion to peace and a soldierly willingness to kill as a professional calling, a synthesis accomplished in the *miles christianus*, the soldier of Christ. The enthusiasm which the French Middle Ages showed for the sainted figure of Martin of Tours (317–97 CE), the merciful soldier, attests to the collective sensitivity with regard to the fundamental contradiction of western culture (now rightly so called). The second secret – execration of the Jews – was, like the first, hidden on the surface of the religion that preached love. Its signature is the hostile acquisition of the Hebrew Bible, whose reserves of meaning are recast in a pirate reading.

Since transfiguration does not happen overnight, the levels of the detailed ladder-comparative are worked out as exercise tasks and units of time. To seek to skim over individual steps would constitute evidence of ambition; ambition, be it said, betrays impatience, and impatience pride. Those who are impatient do not take sufficient time to mourn their own depravity; they do not go all the way in the attempt to "slaughter ambition with the fury of obedience."[28]

Ephrem the Syrian (*c.* 306–73) was the lyric poet among the doctors of the church, who also intensively worked the genre of polemics *contra Judaeos*; he was born in Nisibis and lived later in Edessa (northern Mesopotamia, today southeastern Turkey). In a speech attributed to him, one finds a detailed explanation as to why those who desire salvation should never resign themselves to a personal inability to mourn. It provides an introduction to the poetry of dismay at oneself:

> Well then, sinner, let's cry here, so that we don't have to cry there!... Who would be capable of describing the ordeal that came upon Job? He sat among the ashes for a whole week of the year. How many tears … must his eyes have shed when he saw the worms gnaw away his flesh ...? … The soul slain by sin is in need of pain, lamentation, tears, grief, and sighs of lament over the godlessness which has corrupted and ruined it. Because it is removed from God, therefore lament, weep, and sigh for it and thus bring it back closer to God.... When the pelican seeks to kill itself out of grief at the fate of its brood, the Creator takes pity and awakens its young from death. When, however, a soul perishes through godlessness and is separated from God, then God grieves even more about the likeness separated from him. So weep over your soul … ; let tears flow down upon it and thereby bring it back to life! … You are dead, and yet you do not cry from your soul's separation from you! … The tears that fall on a corpse no longer bring the dead body to life; but if they flow down upon the soul, they will awaken it and make it arise once more.[29]

One would hardly go too far in claiming that, up to the fall of Constantinople in 1453 and the eve of the Reformation – and in the sphere of the Orthodox Churches even into the nineteenth century – the literature of spiritual instruction in the Greek East, as well as the Latin West, consisted of paraphrases from Ephrem's doctrines. His praise of tears proceeds from the Christian appropriation of the Aristotelian doctrine of catharsis – with the nuance that what is at stake is no longer the theatre-goer lamenting the fate of the hero entangled in aporias, but rather fallen persons on the path of self-examination lamenting their own wretchedness. Ephrem's work clarifies the schema of poetry about poetry such that the secondary poetic character of the "true *religio*," and the secondary literary status of its theology, become irrevocably comprehensible – provided, from the outset, that one refuses to ignore it.

Taking the oath pledged by Roman soldiers and civil servants and recasting it into the sacraments was the most liturgically significant operation of Christian theopoetry; existentially, however, its most momentous semantic maneuver arose from the transposition of the everyday conceptual terms of life and death – the figure of the spiritual revaluation of all things established in the writings of Paul and John the Evangelist has already become common sense in Ephrem's oratorical elan. Only with this can the hyperbolic character of the Christian-intensified concept of sin become quite evident. "Sin" does not quite refer to minor or major inconstancies which befall individuals in the course of their acting, wishing, and dreaming life, nor to the delinquencies or crimes they consciously commit, however reprehensible. Sin, in the absolute singular, means nothing more and nothing less than the ontologically and morally relevant "fact" that humanity, as such, exists first and foremost as beings who at some point fell away from God and who subsequently remained separate. The fact of being-separated is attributed to those who have been separated by their own act and sequence of acts, with the point of the story being that the sin committed by the first person, the *peccatum originale*, is unavoidably repeated in the sin proper to the descendants.

Not by chance was it Augustine who insisted that humanity was already born in sin – as if the child in the confines of the birth canal not only struggled to free itself from the mother's body, but at the same moment assumed the consequences of its own proper participation in turning away from God. "Existence" as isolated human being is thus sin and a consequence of sin per se, as an act and as a condition. As a result, the way is cleared for the most existentially consequential symbolic operation in the Christian vocabulary: we are "cast" into a dead mode of being, into an evil existentiality outside of God. Even so, in the *sacramentum* of baptism, we can encounter a graciously offered opportunity, in spite of our being primarily turned away from God (which amounts to "actual death"), a belated opportunity to pledge allegiance to his kingdom to come. We are born as living dead and followers of Satan, but, through the baptismal inauguration, we are brought into life – or, more precisely: into a life revived. The Catholic baptismal priest is, in this matter, a life-saver who sacramentally reanimates the infant in the days after the birth.[30] Because the initial effect of baptism fades in adolescents, they must all their lives be warned against the resurgence of their sinful disposition. When the baptismal effect weakens, the Eucharist helps one along.

The inversion of the meanings of life and death forms the mainstay of the construction that Paul called the *ekklesia* – the parish that constitutes an anti-*polis*, an *oikos* where God governs as host and master of the house. After divine service, those who stepped forth from the church, the *oikos tou theou*, whether considered as a building or as a spiritual commune, could verify that they were really "inside," if the feeling presented itself to them that they were among the few truly alive amid a crowd of the wandering dead.

The most important implication of the recasting of ordinary life into death was revealed in the change of meaning in the Resurrection. Certainly, this must be defined as a post-mortem event, but now its point in time has been displaced forward into "this life," inasmuch as the return to true life is consummated under the forms of conversion, baptism, and Eucharist. The pre-dating of death suggests that the Resurrection be likewise brought forward in time. The meaning of the operation could be paraphrased with the formula "immortality now." Effects of this extend into German Idealism, manifest most clearly in the popular writings of Johann Gottlieb Fichte – notably, *The Way Towards the Blessed Life* (1806), which involves nothing less than an autogenous art of resurrection. This work explicitly executes the conceptual division of life into true life and illusory life, and it identifies illusory life with death – fully in harmony, in the author's own view, with the teachings of Christianity properly understood and as can be found in the Gospel of John.

By inducing the meditator's disidentification with embodied existence, East Asia has developed its own version of the Christian doctrine of the pre-dated resurrection. The spirit striving for emancipation aims to arrive, at length, at a state in which it does not feel affected by birth and its consequences, lingering in the blessed silence of unbornness which both precedes and follows the episode of existence. If the early Christian believer is an *athanasios* (a deathless one), the early East Asian counterpart might be called an *atokos* (an unborn one).

Ephrem's reflections on the indispensability of tears found a strong echo almost 300 years later, on the lower sections of the Ladder of Divine Ascent, which John Climacus dedicated to the "detention cell," a parade ground of shame and self-humiliation, on which one must drill extensively in order to have any hope of forgiveness for apostasy. In the fashion of a penal colony, the place was located a mile outside the monastery. Here the penitents, embittered against themselves, staged the utmost extremities in the metaphorical meanings of separation, severing, depravity, and self-contempt. Hugo Ball aptly described as "athletes of mourning" those brothers who, under the blazing sun and with their feet bound to a stake, accused themselves of all sins committed and not committed.[31] In fact, at that time monasteries were also called "asceteria" – places of training (from Greek: *askein*, to practice). In them, monastics competed as "athletes of Christ" for the reward of self-humiliation. Those seeking salvation must be able to despise themselves; happy are those who succeed in repudiating themselves; happiest are those fugitives from the corrupt self who win the gift of tears. Early monastic psychology discovered what Kafka later grasped once again in his own way: guilt follows upon the heels of punishment.[32]

The poetry of Christian excess was grounded in a metaphysical topology that exhibited a rift running through the created world, with the divide running straight through the human interior. The ego in its vulgar sinfulness must be classified with the everyday world, while the integral core of the soul constitutes an elsewhere that many have never sought to find; it is, as it were, an outpost of heaven that glows as an eternal spark beneath the ashes of profane self-consciousness. It glimmers forth with the withdrawal into interiorized composure. When the monastics of the East, and later those of the West, secluded themselves, they followed, mostly without knowing it, Plato's suggestion that the human being devoted to truth was *ho eso anthropos*, the inner human being. The young Augustine translated this, indirectly following Paul (2 Corinthians 4:16: *qui intus est*), directly with *homo interior*: "Don't head outward; return to your inward self. Truth dwells in the inner man."[33] The figure of the "inner human being" indicates that, among educated people of middle and late antiquity, conventional conditionings for obedience no longer sufficed to generate social and religious conformity – they were to be superseded by an inner-directed obedience operating according to insight into oneself, with the risk that the principle of insight might trigger a chain reaction of insubordinate doubt.

If the outer human being is accustomed to dwell in houses, the inner one is itself inhabited, however dubious the guests may be. Pre-Platonic Greeks spoke of good or bad demons keeping company with the self. It is known that Socrates consorted with a *daimonion* of a higher level, a divinity beyond the gods of the people. Later, it is said, without further ado, that "God" dwells in the inner human being. Augustine stated it more precisely, addressing the Most High: you are *interior intimo meo* – closer to me than I could be to myself. "The human being" in everyday life prefers to drift further outward. Martin Heidegger: "The human being is the path."

Between the third and fourth centuries, the hermitages of the Egyptian and Syrian meditators established prototypes for simple spaces and chambers for individuals on retreat, whether as primitive huts or as cavities in dry cliffs; abandoned buildings in the desert, even empty graves, were occupied as places for prayer and self-examination – for example, in the case of Anthony the Great (c. 251–356), canonized soon after his death. His reputation was based on the descriptions he made of his never-ending vision-struggles against the evil demonic invaders of his dwelling and its interior. If his visions had not consisted of unobservable inner images, Anthony would have been regarded as the father of fantasy fiction – beside being the patriarch of psychopornography. The winged and toothed vulva that tore at him will have been frightening to the afflicted; worse was the parade of heretics, who talked incessantly to him and were always right. His very great age lends credence to the legend that he was victorious over all temptations.

The earliest monastery was built by Anthony's disciples barely five years after the patriarch's death at an oasis 500 kilometers south of Alexandria. Soon after the first monasteries were founded, the monastic creation of space also arrived at the point where the mandate to provide housing for the needs of *Homo interior* could be fulfilled through architectural means – as, for example, common dormitories were divided into separate rooms, generally through the use of wooden partitions. The principle of the monastery – isolation from the "outside world" (hence *claustrum*: an enclosed place) – found new application within the building as a place of retreat for the individual monk. John Cassian (c. 360–c. 435) was able to declare with some justification that *Cella facit monachum*: the cell makes the monk. Each cell was to become a *palaestra* for the monk's pentathlon. His disciplines consisted of wrestling and overcoming superfluous seeing, overcurious hearing, empty speaking, impure desire, and secret resentment against obedience, which is almost never completely extinguished. In the cell, a limit was set for the "never dwelling anywhere"[34] that is characteristic of everyday, self-evasive existence.

The course of architectural individualism in the West began in monastic Egypt, when it endorsed the schema of "one person, one room," which, in the modern poetics of space, has since come to be taken as the norm.[35] In terms of building technique, the cell principle has survived in the essence of the penal system – as well as in biology, which adopted the cell metaphor with reference to the architecture of the late medieval monastery, once microscopes had revealed regular patterns in organic matter in the seventeenth century. The motif of seclusion from the world sometimes also manifested itself in the re-dedications of former monasteries. Clairvaux Abbey, for example, founded by Bernard of Clairvaux in 1115, was converted into a prison during the Napoleonic era, the largest institution of its kind in France, and one with the worst conditions of detention: for the most wretched of the prisoners, confinement was intensified in iron cages, recalling the heretic cages of St. Lambert's Church, Münster, and anticipating the terrorist cages of Guantánamo. Victor Hugo located his story "Claude Gueux" (1834) at this place of punitive terror – a preparatory exercise, in the view of literary historians, for his epoch-making, sociopolitical romantic novel *Les misérables* (1862). Since 1803, the Michaelsberg Abbey overlooking Siegburg, founded in 1064, has been a lunatic asylum, a penitentiary, a military hospital, a hotel, and a conference center.

The western monastic system, based on the solitary desert fathers of the old East, led to its excessive intensification through the establishment of the practice of reclusion or enclosure, also known as anchoritism. The desert was made transportable and was brought into the culture of western religious orders as a space for retreat and sensory deprivation. Residents of an anchorhold were walled up in a cell while holding a hybrid funeral Mass; supply access to and from the cell was provided by a window-like hatch and there was also sometimes a hagioscope with a narrow view into the church sanctuary. Entrance into the cell was conditioned upon a vow of life-long isolation. In late medieval Cologne alone, at the time of the young Luther, there are said to have been 18 anchorholds; they were typically built as additions to monastery churches, city churches, and occasionally also city walls. Enclosure was, above all, a female domain; among the best-known anchoresses were Wiborada of St. Gall (tenth century) and Julian of Norwich (fourteenth century). The young Hildegard von Bingen (1098–1179) also lived – under the influence of her teacher Jutta von Sponheim – in "enclosure" for several years.

Nowhere else in western monasticism did the hyberbolic violence of sealing oneself off from the world manifest itself with such vehemence. Here, the metaphors of separation (*anachoresis*), of taking leave from outer life, of expatriation and migration into the sphere of *Homo interior* were enacted with austere consistency. It must have been an unsettling idea for passers-by at that time that, behind the walled-up entrance to the enclosure, a living cell nucleus was hidden away in mystical immersion. In view of the tradition of enclosures, an aphorism from Franz Kafka suggests itself: "A cage went in search of a bird."

From the fifth century onward, only the mountainous Syrian wilds of Cilicia, north of Aleppo, boasted similarly unbelievable phenomena, when it was covered in a forest of pillars whose tops were inhabited by meditating monks, precursors of verticalism. They were all erected in the wake of Simeon Stylites the Elder (*c*. 389–459), of whom it is said that he spent 37 years on platforms atop pillars of increasing height, finally on a pillar 18 meters high, in constant prayer, with extreme fasting and an almost complete refusal to sleep. What Simeon and many other men performed on the pillars, in view of the public, were the idioms "come closer to heaven," "raise yourself to God in prayer," and "leave the world behind," supplemented with additional miraculousness attested by the permanent victory over the human *physis*. At the foot of Simeon's pillar, it is said that there gathered not only the curious from Antioch, two days' walk away, but also the wonder-seeking masses from farther away; Simeon's reputation reached as far as Gaul, even Britain, and just as far eastward. In a village not far from the scene of the extreme ascesis on the pillar, multi-story pilgrims' homes sprang up, whose ruins remind modern tourists in Syria that curiosity and spiritual lasciviousness were reasons enough to travel even 1,000 years ago. The emperor of Byzantium, Theodosius II (401–50), was among Simeon's visitors; he insisted on climbing up himself to the man praying on the platform, seeking spiritual and political advice; perhaps he saw himself as a *confrère* of the stylite, since he too was called to sit atop a towering superhuman pillar, the Augustus throne of Byzantium, surrounded by invisible hostility, ethereal intrigues, and woven into the murmur of spiritual whisperers.

The asceticisms of unremitting prayer and pillar-dwelling operated at the extreme end of the spectrum of discomfort; to the extent that they were attended with self-abomination, learned and mastered, they involved the practitioner in a heightened agony of the soul. Their motifs, consistently found in intensified endo-rhetorical and endo-poetic procedures, were translated into chronic psychophysical exertion. In this context, prayer, whether formulary or freely articulated, formed variants that were easier for the inexperienced to understand. Where depressives of modern times will experience an amorphous self-devaluation, formerly, with penitential exercises, crises of this kind had a meaningful form available to them. On the other hand, it was precisely the monasteries that were breeding grounds for monastic *acedia*, a malady of listless apathy in which a lack of drive was indistinguishable from the feeling of having been forsaken by God and the world. Monastics afflicted with such emptiness might reflect, however, that even burnout was a stage on the path to salvation. The ever-present assumption typical of this milieu was that the world was a place in which it would be senseless – indeed harmful – to feel oneself at home.

It is in the nature of things that ascetic dispositions are susceptible to tendencies of self-harm, especially when their exercises are stimulated by a spirit of competition. In the ever more perfect repudiation of the self, someone will advance the most quickly – and why should it not be me? The forced renunciation of the ego, cultivated just so, flows into the asceticism of dolorism. Those who seek agony feel more acutely; those who feel more acutely have better reason to renounce their selves. It was in view of phenomena of this kind that Nietzsche called the earth the "ascetic planet," inhabited by disgruntled creatures for whom self-inflicted pain serves as probably their only pleasure.[36] With practicing dolorists, metaphors from the field of meaning – the thorny, the searing, the biting, the stinging, the scourging, the burning, the piercing – are put into action with the aid of applicable instruments. Those possessed of a nervous system can make themselves suffer as they seek participation in non-trivial communions. The reward for pain consists in the idea of joining the community of saintly sufferers. Those aspiring to reach the heights might imagine themselves as partaking of the suffering of the Lord.

Often enough, primitive self-punishment reflexes stand at the origin of an excess. One of the desert fathers is said to have thrown himself into a thorny hedge during a fit of sensuousness and wallowed about there until the venereal demon fled. Frenzied elite formations in dolorism retain their notoriety to this day: droves of penitents in the High Middle Ages swarmed about the countryside, thrashing themselves with whips and barbed scourges and shouting terms of abuse against temporal and spiritual authorities; it took a papal bull to put an end to flagellant anarchism in the later fourteenth century. From ancient times, hermits and monks wore coarse robes to discourage any thought that one was in the world in order to feel comfortable in one's own skin. The Catholic organization called Opus Dei was founded in 1928 and was initially close to "Spanish-style Fascism," until these ties went underground, submerged after Franco in decanted right-wing extremism; members who place themselves fully in the service of Opus Dei, called numeraries, are still obliged to undergo regular exercises with a penitential cilice, in the form of a spiked garter made of braided wire and looped around the thigh. As with the desert fathers of the Near East, the rule applies: "Discomfort engenders commitment." Some practitioners seek to assure the public that the practice is easy to abide by – that it signifies nothing more than a small token of mortification.

Those who have been opiated on God, in Spain and elsewhere, are at liberty to increase their dosage as they wish. Much the same is reported from various other ascetic orders.

Resolute dolorists took much more literally the injunction to overcome the outer person within themselves than did the moderate practitioners who took active repentance as a metaphor for a transaction in the market for redeemable debts. The dolorists, by contrast, looked to punitive pain as the great medicine of existence. From their circles, there emerged experts who distinguished themselves from the rest of the world as carriers of "religious experience" – Max Weber called them, with precise irony, the "religious virtuosos." The aptness of the formulation is manifest in that those so designated often seemed to have access to ecstatic states that they could call up like pieces on a musical instrument of their choice. The apparently paradoxical expression "ecstatic technique" suggests the possibility of evoking, through an act of will, exceptional psychospiritual situations. After a 40-day fast, many things are possible that cannot be done under normal metabolic functioning. Long-term sleep deprivation, severe self-imposed pain, intense fasting, endless repetitive movements, and other practices that prompt the organism to switch to complex, archaic alarm- and hallucination-programs[37] – these techniques not uncommonly arouse inner states on a scale ranging from disintegration to epiphany.

Even the utmost extremity seems to be "integrable," so long as it can be framed by a spiritual doctrine. Consciously induced suffering retains the quality of an accomplished act. The strong attributes of the technical – repeatability and transformation of force – are expressed in religioid psycho-physical exercises. Transformation of force takes place insofar as an expenditure at one location is compensated by a gain elsewhere in the system; Arnold Gehlen formulated this precisely with his theorem of "relief" or discharge.[38] Such heterogeneous concepts as priestly celibacy, grants and opportunities promoting gifted students, acrobatics, extreme sports – all are based on a transformation of force. So far as repetition is concerned, it is the universal weapon of spiritual exercises in service to projects of self-fashioning. It is not only the cell, it is also repetition that makes the monk, as it likewise makes the musician, the athlete, the tightrope walker, the hasid – and occasionally the scholar.

Even when they exhibit no aspect of ecstatic technique, acts of *imitatio Christi* do sometimes lead to a longing for the ultimate passion: on May 23, 1498, when the reformist Dominican preacher Girolamo Savonarola and two other members of his order were to be executed on the Piazza della Signoria in Florence on accusations of heresy and schism – executed by hanging, but with subsequent incineration of the hanging corpses – his *confrère* Fra Domenico da Pescia petitioned the judges, requesting the favor of being burned alive, so that he might suffer for the Lord and with the Lord. Obviously he had taken up the idea, which had spread since the days of Francis of Assisi, that the true believer attains *conformitas* with Christ through the Passion[39] – which suggests that "conformism" started as extremism. His request was refused by the judges and disapproved by his Dominican superior. Even so, he is said to have approached the gallows as if full of joy.

Ignatius of Antioch (d. second century CE) could have been among his models: an early doctor of the church, who aroused displeasure as a religious dissident, he was under escort from the East to Rome, where he was to suffer his condemnation *ad bestias*; en route, he wrote to his local Christian friends that they should make no effort to save him – he was, he said, longing with feverish excitement for the day when, as the wheat of God, he would be ground into "pure bread" by the teeth of wild animals. To those who would follow such candidates for the slaughter, the Sacred-Heart mystic Marguerite-Marie Alacoque (1647–90) offered a maxim pointing the way: "The highest suffering consists in not suffering enough."

Down to the present day, passion plays and imitative crucifixions have become firmly established as part of local folklore in Catholic locales from Bavaria to the Philippines. It is unnecessary here to go into analogous rituals of suffering in various religious cultures, regardless of whether they be in India, Spain, Russia, or Iran. Whatever the case, their effects are to be attributed to blunting, refinement, or a compound of both; in all of them, there is the endocrinological paradox to be reckoned with – namely, that pain can manifest itself as a psychotropic drug and as an autonarcotic. In religion, as in sport and in other exercise-intensive disciplines, the same motto applies: no pain, no gain.[40]

It belongs to the motives, as well as to the consequences, of the Reformations in the sixteenth century that the Protestant churches rejected the memory of extreme asceticism. What they retained in "inner-worldly asceticism," to take up Max Weber's expression, were as a rule moderated disciplines in the conduct of life. They always took form from tracings of religious literature in everyday existence. What remained left over from asceticism was the methodical regulation of daily routine. It was to this that the boundless *how-to* journalism of the early modern period addressed itself, including handbooks for the courtier, books of etiquette, household literature, to say nothing of almanacs filled with quotations from the Bible, and the calendars with their wisdom of the day.

Where sacred hysteria once flourished, monocultures of tempered compulsivity arose in its place. In this respect, one could rightly say that it was Protestantism – if one might so blithely use the singular – that excised the East from Western Christianity.

In fact, the Christianized *vita activa* has reabsorbed contemplation and integrated it into the motor activity of successful urban life. Whether that has led to a new affirmation of the world or else resulted in a permanent flight from the world – this is one of the questions that modernity must ask of itself, regardless of whether its motivations are Protestant or post-Christian. The fact that the young Martin Luther did not find his solutions without serious crisis is part of general education in the West; from the eastern perspective of a John Climacus, Luther would be regarded as a scarcely half-finished monk who, on the tables of spiritual progression, bowed out at the dungeon level. Just as faith gave Luther consolation in his youthful near-desperation (*prope desperatio*, in thesis 16 of his 1517 disputation), his autotherapeutic secret was to remain secret, notwithstanding the abundant journalism of the Reformation.

It is understandable why the circuit through Rome was something that countless Lutherans and Calvinists wanted to spare themselves – the princes of the northern countries, in particular. There was a certain aspiration, between the sixteenth and eighteenth centuries, and at all levels of seriousness between Puritanism and Latitudinarianism, to discreetly cloister bourgeois life in a kind of open prison. It was impossible for these reformers to foresee that this could be no more than an interim solution. In any case, mindful of the primal Protestant image that following Christ could now also be endured in the arms of the minister's wife, many pupils of the Reformation concluded that it was more plausible to seek proximity to the Most High in natural surroundings.

An unsettling insight into elaborate strategies for wearing down the self in the service of spiritual transformation is afforded by some Buddhist-inspired systems of practice, at home in Japan and elsewhere. Of these, the extremist school of *kaihōgyō*, practiced by monks of the Tendai sect, has recently also attracted some attention in the West. In its longest version, this ascetic practice of "circling the mountain" consists of a sequence of 1,000 long-distance treks stretched over a 7-year period, at 30, then 60, and, near the end, 84 kilometers per day in length. Along a walking path marked by 260 prayer sites, the monks circle Mount Hiei overlooking Kyoto, 100 nights in a row for the early years, then 200 nights in a row in later years, wearing out a great number of waraji sandals during these runs. Notwithstanding the brevity of their sleep times, the monks undergoing this training are also obliged to take part in the regular daily prayers of the monastery. The ritual is traced back to a monk named Sōō Oshō, who lived on the monastery mountain at the turn of the ninth to the tenth century – at the height of the Tendai sect, there are said to have been around 3,000 places of refuge and retreat there. The excess within the excess is a 9-day phase at the end of the fifth cycle of the course, which involves complete fasting, resolute sleeplessness, and incessant walking up and down in a temple vestibule with the strictest prohibition against lying down – the subject has two helpers constantly by his side to support his struggle against the temptation to let go. At the end of this hyperascesis, visions from the imaginarium of the Buddhist pantheon appear to be inevitable – among others, the appearance of the popular Buddha Amida and the esoteric Fudō Myōō. If, after the 101st day, a monk wanted to forsake his attempt, a knife was made available to him with which he could kill himself.

The mortifications of Buddhist priests who resolved to enter nirvana through self-mummification passed into the completely incomprehensible. The procedure is known as *sokushinbutsu* and it was practiced mainly in monasteries of the esoteric school of Shingon-shu in northern Japan, having been introduced there by a monk in the ninth century. It involved three phases of 1,000 days each, the first two of which dictated a radical diet with the aim of complete fat loss and self-desiccation, until the individual was almost literally left with only skin-covered bone; bathing in icy waterfalls for hours was also part of the procedure. In the second phase, the monk consumed only small amounts of tree bark and roots, as what remained of his body was semi-pickled from the inside by drinking poisonous teas; in this way, it was to have been made resistant to attack from bacteria and maggots. The one striving for nirvana vomited frequently and suffered from severe pain; in dying off, his nervous system, which was actually hardly needed anymore, produced absurd peaks of pain. The Buddhist dictum *sarvam dukham* – all existence is suffering – at this point reached a hellish literality. Because the meditator knew he was on a path benefitting the salvation of many, he did not hasten to cease breathing. Indeed, since at that point he existed only as a savior, he remained alive for an inconceivably long time.

Finally, for the third 1,000 days, the practitioner was enclosed, in the lotus position, in a narrow vault connected to the outside world only by an air duct and a bell; the man who passed over subsisted on only air. When, after a time, the bell-ringing from inside the vault came to an end, priests on the outside would seal the tomb until the end of the third 1,000-day phase, whereupon they would open it

up again: now it would be seen whether the victor over himself had
started to decompose – which indeed happened quite often. That
of itself was no cause for disdain, for the monk had undertaken the
most extreme venture. The occasional success of the magnum opus
was noted with the greatest awe. From the last half-millennium,
there are reports of about 25 cases in which the monk accomplished
his dying off under the condition of successfully preserving his self-
desiccated and disinfected "body."

Upon recovery of his relics, the one who had passed on came
to be venerated as a "living Buddha." In its own way, then, the
East also knows that life–death inversion, without which Christian
theopoetry, up to its extreme radicalizations, would not have become
effective. In some places, the prevailing belief was that the mummies
were still alive in some subtle sense and they were credited with a
salvific spiritual presence. Occasionally, one such body would be
displayed in shrines to serve as an object of meditation for pilgrims;
in some cases, the self-mummified body would be encased within
a gilded figure of Buddha. Adorers approaching such an object
must have sensed that, standing before them, hidden within the
Buddha-morphic figure, was the absolute Non-object, a presence
from which a subtle radiance emanated, something beyond being
and nothingness.[41]

Similar procedures, possibly less cruel, are known from Thailand
and Mongolia; some mummified monks in Tibet have caused a stir
because their preservation evidently proceeded from neither the
Japanese nor the Egyptian methods. Perhaps the most recent case
of mummification in a living person is reported to have occurred in
1973 on Ko Samui, an island off the east coast of Thailand. There,
the almost 80-year-old abbot of Wat Khunaram temple passed
away in meditative pose. He had urged the brothers at the temple
to display his corpse, in the event of its non-corruption, in order
to remind his fellow beings of the teachings of the Buddha; his
body being largely well preserved and the condition of the request
fulfilled, the monks granted his request. Stylish sunglasses placed
on the corpse conceal its empty eye sockets, but leave the casual
impression that a prominent tourist might be resting incognito in
front of the temple.

It is beyond all question that these asceticisms are based on
physical adaptations of endo-rhetorical metaphors and poetic
verbs – such as those of extinguishing, leaving something behind,
fading, emptying out, and passing over. What must be extinguished
from the ground up are thirst and fire, both understood in the
ultimate figurative sense. What must be left behind is the incen-
diary craving at the bottom of the addiction to prestige, position,

and self-propagation. The multifarious and exorbitant practices were varied ways of coming to terms with the shedding of one's willfulness. They served the autopoiesis of the void.

In the eyes of western observers, such procedures appear as prolonged suicides which, in view of the extension of the agonies involved, arouse disconcert and horror; this impression is accompanied by the suspicion that there must be a misunderstanding of the metaphors of enlightenment in the sacred scriptures of the Far East. It is largely forgotten, in such instances, that the West knew its own fascination with mummies, especially around the religious orders and in the Orthodox churches, where a connection between perfect holiness and the incorruptibility of mortal remains was sometimes asserted and celebrated; a rumor might circulate, for example, that an unearthly fragrance emanated from the body of a saint. Soviet propaganda of the 1920s was compelled to take action against "popular superstition" by disseminating images of common instances of the undecayed dead: a counterfeiter from the time of the tsars, desiccated by frost, and the photo of a dead frog, perfectly dehydrated where it had been trapped in an exhaust duct, were cited as testimonials to the truth of materialism.[42] The Buddhist cult participants, however, enthusiastic about salvation through extinguishment, considered the "living Buddhas" to be nothing less than the most sublime calligraphies of nothingness.

18

KERYGMA, PROPAGANDA, SUPPLY-SIDE OFFENSE, OR, WHEN FICTION IS NOT TO BE TRIFLED WITH

In the discussions of the sociologists of religion who came to prominence after the Second World War, Peter L. Berger foremost among them, it has become customary to describe the broad field in which many religious systems operate side by side as a "market-place," in which vendors promote their products among consumers in a modern or postmodern society. Some will ironically term it a bazaar or a supermarket; others, in something of a tone of disappointment, call it a clearance sale, or a competition in the packaging of basically similar content. Dismissive judgment intensifies into contempt, as soon as one labels religioid phenomena as mere fashions.

Those who judge in this way neglect the possible subtlety of the concept of fashion, which, as "mode," initially referred to nothing more than the fleeting imitation of a temporarily attractive "model." In "Dialogue between Fashion and Death" (1824), included among his *Small Moral Works*, Giacomo Leopardi demonstrated how contempt for fashion often succumbs to a conventional fallacy. He had the younger (Fashion) call out to the older, "Madam Death, Madam Death!" – whereupon Death replied: "Wait until your time comes, and then I will appear without being called by you." To which Fashion replies, "As if I were not immortal! ... I am Fashion, your sister.... Do you not remember we are both born of Decay? ... I recollect it and I know also that we both equally profit by the incessant change and destruction of things here below, although you do so in one way, and I in another."[1]

Following Gabriel Tarde's work *The Laws of Imitation* (1890), fashion, "mode" – also in lexical and factual proximity to the concept of the "modern" – can be understood as an epidemic imitation of the contemporary and unproven – accompanied by an awareness of the volatility of *imitandum* and *imitat*. It stands in markedly light-footed contrast to the continuation of tradition as an imitation of the old, of the classic, of what has been proven and approved by the "morality of custom" – to recall Nietzsche's formula, which emphasized in custom the coercive effect of settled conventions which enforce conformity through the threat or imposition of some kind of penalty.

Traditional cults have practiced a "conservatism" understood as the cultivation of the traditional; this has been so, at least implicitly, from time immemorial. In more recent (i.e., post-Revolutionary) days, this conservatism has been made more or less explicit. In such cases, one sees the *imitandum* transposed to such lofty heights that one also sees why the older imitation intrinsically demanded a distance of humility and strictly forbade parody. But the imitation of the contemporary and the imitation of the traditional are both equally daughters of innovation – to use modernism's term for the productive aspect of the ephemeral. One covers long chains of repetitions and variations, the other varies with the least change in the wind.

In the pejorative use of the concept of fashion, it is generally overlooked that everything that later looks like a venerable tradition, even in religious matters, must initially have been the uncertain imitation of a novelty, whose future was not decided *in situ*. If the first imitations had not related to innovations that could only be adopted by taking up a "fashion" – after all, even a new doctrine of salvation is initially unproven, like a fashion newly launched – then the imitators would have had nothing at hand that would appear worthy of carrying forward. It is not by chance that the oldest conversion metaphor in the Mediterranean cultural sphere was to "put on the Lord Jesus Christ" – in the sense of clothing oneself in a new garment; its author is Paul of Tarsus, a man whose expertise in matters of fabric and fit cannot be denied.[2] By the time of Paul, the figure of vesture had already gone through a long prehistory in the sacred language games of Indo-Aryan cults. Clothes create identities; it is unsurprising, then, that real changes of costume were adopted by Christian hermits, clergy, people in religious orders, and professors – until the Reformation, the Enlightenment, and modernity arranged for the separation of religion, dress code, and social status.

The crystallization of a tradition results from imitations of the imitations that impressed contemporaries (and their descendants) under the aspect of their still-potent imitation value. The brevity of human life entails the consequence that even relatively new ritual, doctrinal, and anecdotal content, when passed on to the third or fourth generation, crosses the 100-year threshold and thus, especially in cultures of oral transmission, evokes an impression of the immemorial. "Memo activity is the fitness of the gods" – and, to continue further with Heiner Mühlmann, the eternity effect follows from a "misjudgment of the slow."[3] What is remembered for 100 years and more comes to be provisionally regarded as venerable, perhaps even immortal.

Speculation about imitability did sometimes produce results; one finds evidence of this in the case of a spiritual instruction book published anonymously around the year 1418 under the title *Imitatio Christi – The Imitation of Christ* – and attributed to a Dutch Augustinian canon named Thomas à Kempis. This *opusculum*, with around 3,000 editions, became the most widely distributed book in Europe after the Bible. Between the fifty-fifth and seventieth generations *post Christum natum* (1450–1750), it attained a quasi-ubiquity among the literate of the Old World, with the dawn of the Gutenberg era fueling its exploding circulation. The first printed editions appeared in the 1480s: in Augsburg in 1486 and in Toulouse in 1488 – a fact which offers evidence for the aura surrounding "modern" Dutch devotional thoughts in the cities of the south.

From the sixteenth century onward, its half edifying, half dolor-istic tendencies allowed readers of all denominations to flesh out *The Imitation of Christ* with images, formulas, and associations from the store of their private exercises in piety. Wherever there was existential suffering, the analogy of the crucifixion suggested itself. Louis Capet, erstwhile King Louis XVI of France, is said to have read the book in the days of his captivity in the Temple prison before his beheading. The upgrading of the concept of "imitation" to "discipleship" can be discerned in its German title, *Nachfolge Christi*. The word betrays the impulse to move from the imitation of a model to the internalized espousal of one's modus vivendi. It is only one step from mode to the martyrium, from fashion to the shrine of martyrs. For a quarter of a millennium, the *imitatio* stood for the guarantee, desperately in demand in early bourgeois circles on account of anxieties about the afterlife stoked by the church, that the way to salvation could be found even outside the monastery walls – notwithstanding the fact that the book was written by one cleric, and intended for others like himself. The rest attended to the analogy of agonies: even if most deaths had little in common with crucifixion, the execution of the Lord allowed for a fraternal comparison with the often shatteringly painful struggles at the end of a human life.

So long as the imitations play out within a generation and within a region with a relatively homogeneous population, no judgment can be made about their character as fashion or about their potential to found a longer-term series. It is when a collective's chain of imitation oversteps the generational threshold, or when it steps beyond the *Lebensraum* of the instigating cultural group, that it becomes decidable whether discrete bundles or continuous currents spring from the primary rays of imitation (Gabriel Tarde's *rayons imitatifs*), and whether institutions with internal rules, system-specific classical scripture, and learnable functional roles will emerge from the flux of the current. That such crossovers are possible becomes evident as soon as influencers appear on the scene who champion their brand with everything they have, are, and know – and who, if necessary, are prepared to die for their product.

Among the former cult fashions that have successfully advanced into the top flight of cross-generational and expansive *religio* traditions, Christianity and Islam undeniably stand forth – the first as a disruptive split from Judaism with initially uncertain future prospects; the latter as a secondary split from Jewish and Christian models. After a brief phase of flirting with elitist spiritual secession, they became demonstrably determined to conjoin armed persuasion with non-violent recruitment for acceptance of the faith. Both have adopted from Judaism a shared convergence of divine law and holy book. Through their compulsive devotion to the book, their cult innovations were able to break through the imitation radius typically compassing the scope of virtual, non-scriptural fashions; their readability supported repeatability in times when there would no longer be an imitator of the first generation among the living. Already for Jews of Jesus' era, literacy was an ancient legacy; a returning Jesus could not have been surprised to see written traces of his first appearance in circulation – the circumstances of his departure from the earthly stage were supposed to occasion extreme memoactive effects. For Arabs in the milieu of the Prophet, the world of writing was a more recent acquirement – indeed, with the appearance of the Quran, it almost seemed as if Allah had not only revealed instructions for how to live properly, he had also included the art of writing together with them. Pre-Islamic poems, inasmuch as they had been written down, had to suffer being set aside as testimonials from the "Age of Ignorance" (*jahiliyyah*).

The transition to writing brings with it the emancipation of the spoken word from the listeners who had been present at the initial event. The rest follows from the ordeal of its history of reception.

Until the scriptures are set down, it is listeners at first, second, and third hand who decide what they have heard. After the first textualization, there was, within just a few decades, no one left alive who could attest to having heard it *this* way and not otherwise; even the oaths of old witnesses do not override the propensity of the pious ear to omit, to reformulate, and to creatively supplement what they have rightly heard.

Legibility is not, by itself, sufficient to generate a historically durable chain of repetition; this is clearly visible in the case of attempts to establish cults that failed to produce later generations sufficiently attracted to sustain the project. Notably, it befell the faith project of the Mesopotamian-born religious founder Mani (216–77 CE), which, after strong initial success, stagnated due to the withdrawal of favor on the part of the Sasanian king, and died down after four or five halfway successful transfers to subsequent generations – leaving aside scattered islands of survival, as among the Uyghurs and others in China, where Manichaeism persisted into the fourteenth century. The memory of Mani's system – the first construct of this kind explicitly put into the world as a "religion" and put into writing by the founder himself – lived on in Catholic polemics and in the youth of the church father Augustine of Hippo – persisting, moreover, in the structure of his thought, which was marked by dualistic intensification. It also haunts a language game of the vulgar enlightenment, which, at the very first sharp-edged either–or binary, finds itself tempted to cry out "Manichaean." For the later course of the old European culture of rationality, the suppression of Manichaeism resulted in a grave loss of differentiation. Its premature extinction left lacunae for a logically immature, morally inflexible, pre-dialectical half-Manichaeism in Christian clothing. Almost without a fight, it consigned the earthly realm to the devil – formerly Ahriman – as the "prince of this world" and, amid the *opus diaboli*, it reserved only an enclave for an earthly bridgehead of the *civitas Dei* – even as the sophisticates noticed early on that the devil can be found prowling inside church walls too, roaring like a lion "looking for someone to devour."[4] The haunting of the spiritual and intellectual sphere – then christened the "Church," later renamed "Culture" – was carried forward against the earthly state into the dualistic spiritual wars of the twentieth century, when vulgar materialists and pseudo-idealists made war upon each other with words and sometimes weapons. A mature Manichaeism would undoubtedly have left behind the growing pains of dualism and have developed a ternary or polyvalent logic; it would have grasped the mixture of good and bad as a basic feature of reality, and taught their always problematic disentanglement as a conundrum for practice.

The Hellenistic designer cult of Serapis was synthesized from fragments of the cults of Isis and Zeus, and promoted around 285 BCE under Ptolemy I Soter for the Greeks of Alexandria. For a good half a millennium, it puttered along, too sterile to grow larger, too hardy to die a quick death. It was capable of reproducing itself in small circles up to the fourth century CE; with a few places of worship scattered across the Aegean Sea – including a temple in Rome, whose construction and maintenance were tolerated due to the imperial policy of cult coexistence – the Serapis religion embodied one of the melancholy copy-and-paste religions of late antiquity.[5] Its most important temple, the Serapeum of Alexandria, was destroyed in 391 CE in the course of the Christian persecution of pagans, after Constantine the Great had already demanded its closure.

Bábism, by contrast, originated around 1844 with the teachings of the Báb, a preacher active in Shiraz, in Qajar Iran, and it spread very rapidly. It was extinguished within a few years, however, by the Shiite orthodoxy of the country in a spasm of massive violence, in which tens of thousands of Báb's followers were tortured and killed. The Báb had proclaimed the imminent arrival of the twelfth Imam, and intimated a little later that this was none other than himself. In the event, the Bábi movement did not survive the execution of its leader. If one compares the events of 1850 with those after 1979, one notes that the clericalist Persian theocracy has remained true to itself, with the nuance that, since March 21, 1935, Persia has returned to calling itself Iran – the land of the Aryan peoples.

One thing Christianity and Islam have in common is the critical interval between the prophetic interventions of the founding innovators and the textualization of their messages. Jesus had appeared in public for scarcely 3 years; Muhammad's preaching and leadership activity is said to have spanned around 22 years. It was probably about the same span of time before the Quran was codified under Uthman, the third Caliph (d. 656). One had to wait at least 100 years for the creation of a text that could be read more or less independently of oral tradition – with instructions for pronunciation and the meaning of the consonantal marks. The notion of self-contained reading may of course be a postulate imposed from the modern West – as is, likewise, the idea of a historical-critical edition of the Quran, currently under way with a superbly credentialled international scholarly workshop in Berlin. However imperative it appears, however conducive to irenic clarification, it represents a gesture of "Occidentalism," an anachronism in the sense of extreme belatedness, and an act of philological condescension to the textual traces of a constellation of attitudes and ways of thinking characteristic of late antiquity – in short, a project provoking suspicions of blasphemy among ultra-conservative Muslims.

With regard to the understanding of early Christian documents, questions of dating cannot be separated from questions of meaning: the earliest of the four Gospels, the Gospel according to Mark, is dated to around 65 to 70 CE, which implies a gap of 35 or 40 years from the Golgotha event. Luke and Matthew followed about 10 and 20 years later, and John, according to the preponderance of expert opinion, probably another 20 years after that.[6] For the attribution of the author's name to writings initially copied anonymously, claims appear only after 130 or 180 CE. Who wrote (or redacted) what – and why, and against whom – can no longer be authentically ascertained retrospectively; the scant testimonial evidence is scattered over a problem area of 150 years. The margin for misattribution and misunderstanding is greater than modern experts in the interpretation of the 360 canonized documents of the New Covenant would prefer. Then again, as long as almost nothing is really clear – thanks to the fragments that still sporadically emerge from the soil of Syria, Palestine, and Egypt – thousands upon thousands of experts around the world are allowed to keep their professorships and their market segments in Bible-study sensationalism.

One circumstance is not to be misunderstood: the sermons of the first instigators were filled with the certainty that their testimonies would not be quickly dispersed by the winds of change. The proclaimers proceeded on the assumption that their message would spread from first-hand listeners to reach new ones. For such transmission, Christian imitation early on offered the term *kerygma*, meaning proclamation, and the temporal horizon for this activity stretched no further than until the end of the living generation. It would be preposterous to assume that the first followers of Jesus wanted to fulfill (or felt they were commissioned to fulfill) a "universal" "mission." Matthew writes in the Olivet discourse of the "end of the world" – more precisely, the passing of the age (*aionos*). Later interpreters might schedule this end however they liked, but in the understanding of the speaker and the hearers *in situ* – if there ever was such a situation – it applied to an imminent event. At first, one reckoned in weeks and months; at the outside, in years – then, God willing, in decades. Hence the insistent admonition to spend the remainder of one's life waiting in the posture of wakeful watchfulness; the end could come to pass in the blink of an eye. The best-known figure of apocalyptic abruptness is found in the Parable of the Ten Bridesmaids from Matthew 25:1–13: the five foolish ones who had not prepared their lamps for the path through the darkness find the gate to the kingdom of heaven already closed – the bridegroom had come too precipitously from the point of view of the careless. Just a few hours might make the difference between salvation and disaster; catastrophe is right around the corner. "Woe to those who are pregnant and to those who are nursing infants in those days!" declaims Jesus in Mark 13's speech of impending doom. As it is all over for the women, at that point, so it is all over for those whom they carry. It is further urged: "Pray that it may not be in winter."

The episode of the sleeping disciples on the eve of the Passion was inserted with literary chutzpah into the events of the day later called Holy Thursday, or Maundy Thursday.[7] The inability of the disciples to keep wakeful watch for even one night anticipates the indolence of the post-paschal times and, early on, dampens the optimism and energy for setting out over the "still existing" world, in view of its imminent end. If the children of the world are allowed to assert an unassailable claim upon sleep, and if, within the short period presumably remaining, Christ does not return as judge and avenger upon the vast majority who are unconverted, then one has probably misunderstood something essential. Whereupon every word has to be rethought. All years *post Christum resurrectum* are years of rewriting[8] and of a continual re-dating of the last things. Not a century has gone by without zealots being seized by the conviction that the end times had begun – one thinks, for example, of the Seventh-day Adventist Church, founded in 1863 and the largest end-time church of the present era, with 16 million baptized members.[9] In this respect, they are close to the Jehovah's Witnesses, who have called themselves this since 1931 and who, over the course of the twentieth century, calculated dates for the end of the world several times. Instead of feeling themselves refuted by the non-appearance of the event, they adhere more than ever to their scripturally based conviction of the end-time character of every present.

One of the birth defects of Christianism is its apparently ineradicable misunderstanding of universalism. It was laid out by Paul of Tarsus (or was credited to him) and was then soon adopted into the accounts by the composers of the Gospels. Paul – presuming the letters in his name don't trace back to some subsequent imposture[10] – seems to have lived in the certainty that time was nearly up; consequently, it was no great leap to expect that most would be lost. John went as far as pronouncing the leitmotif of divine tragedy in the prologue of his Gospel. The Logos came down into a world that had been created by him, and the world did not recognize him: "He came to what was his own [*eis ta idia*], and his own people [*hoi idioi*] did not accept him."[11] But to the few who took him in, he gave the commission to become the children of God (*tekna theou*).

Nobody could have been unclear about the fact that only a small minority of the living would be among the elect – although being Greek, being a slave, being a woman could no longer count as grounds for being excluded from the elect of the second order.[12] Even wealth offers no hindrance shortly before the end of all things, since one might have wealth as if one did not have it; likewise, being married can no longer be held as grounds for exclusion, since one might have a spouse as if one had none. "For the present form of this world [*schema tou kosmou*] is passing away."[13] Procreation becomes pointless. Here apocalyptic irony takes on the contours that appear, even in the present day, every time radical groups refuse respect to "this world" on account of its supposed untenability. Skepticism with regard to the world and its deceptions, a skepticism inherent in every apocalypticism, forms the matrix of conspiracy theories.

The misinterpretation of the appeal to all while acquiescing to the fact that few will follow was compulsively propagated after Justin Martyr (100–65 CE) inaugurated the translation of Jesuism and its message into the terminology of Platonizing theologians. It culminated in the adventurously perverse thesis heard in the nineteenth century, more still in the twentieth, and heard even with Karl Jaspers, to the effect that the Enlightenment – which actually oriented itself on the motif of "truth for all," to the extent that intellectual maturity allowed for the annulment and sublation of the esoteric clauses – was, paradoxically, the often anti-Christian coded continuation of Christianity by secular means. Anyone seriously interested in the Enlightenment should have noted the fact that, to begin with, it could be nothing other than the revenge, deferred for a millennium and a half, of ancient pluralistic humanism upon Christian theocentrism and its barely concealed salvific elitism, something transparently articulated by both Augustine and Calvin. Through the pragmatic awareness of time, history, and processes of the West, the Enlightenment makes a place on the agenda for the rectification of oriental apocalypticism and its hysteroid end-time tendencies of thought.

In the nascent Islam of the Medina period (after 622), an imperative for expansion became apparent – a fact soon materialized in the military recovery of Mecca in 630. Like any other awakening expansionism, it found it could adopt the language games of universalism in pretty short order. The collection of transcripts to the revelations shared by the Prophet, and their canonization under the title of *al-Qur'an* – that is: the "Reading," "Recitation," originally perhaps "Liturgy" – brought into the world an acute obligation to imitate. This did not refer to the Prophet himself – to imitate him *ex officio* would have been a blasphemy. Rather, it entailed the task of replicating a self-citing book, one that is itself rapturing away every doubt. Still more, it entailed replicating the pattern of pious existence outlined in it, as, so to speak, an Arabic repetition of the Mosaic exodus as election under the word of God.

The obligation to imitate that emanated from the "work of reading," or the liturgical book, had the peculiarity that Islam – after Mani's failed attempt to combine Buddhist, Christian, and Platonic elements in a carefully coded doctrine – constituted the first synthetically founded "religion" with enduring success. Muhammad may not have known the Roman term *religio*, but the phenomenon of "religion in power" will have presented itself to him as a virtual model one might strive for. The mode of prophetic, putatively logocratic speech, if not familiar from the beginning, must have been easily accessible in the milieu of Mecca and Medina. The scraps of Persian, Judeo-Aramaic, and Christian-Caesaropapist speech cultures in their local adaptations must have dictated only patchy opportunities for illiterate recipients to hear and internalize authoritative spoken messages. Even before the appearance of the prophetic subject, it is invariably the case that the spiritual field, with its favored tone and vocabulary, is already active. Prophets will have the sound of their God in their ear before they step forth to utter their first word.

Logocratic speech – having originated in ancient Mesopotamian cult, elaborated in the directives of the Persian king of kings, replicated in the aspirations of Judean theocracy, and copied with high pragmatic efficiency in the edicts of the Roman imperial chancelleries – reached its historical peak in the Near East of the seventh and eighth centuries. It organized armies of charging horsemen, hitherto lacking in orientation, and almost worldless young men, now unexpectedly breathing the air of conquest. It drafted wandering border lines onto as yet unmapped expanses of Arab, Egyptian, Syrian, Persian, and North African zones – soon reaching as far as the Pyrenees, later to Sicily and to the borders of China. From what the Stoic grammarians had called the imperative, the metaphysics of command, in a military sense, arose like a genie from its bottle.

Logocratic speech rose again to similar heights only in the twentieth century when dictator-generals, who considered themselves prophets and envoys of History with a capital H, submitted whole continents to their edicts for a reorganization of the world. One may refer here to the forgotten comrade Stalin, whose now forgotten treatise on language, published in *Pravda* in 1950, advocated the thesis, much to the astonishment of those around him, that language is by no means a mere "superstructural phenomenon" – here contesting the doctrines of the Marr School.[14] He knew from experience that with half a sentence – spoken in the dominant language – he, the Georgian who had adopted Russian, could decide the life of classes and peoples, either annihilating them or granting their survival. From this it follows: when it comes to setting reality into motion, the command assured of execution in no way lags behind economic activities, labor, and manufacture. Thus, language – especially with its imperatives, vocatives, appellatives, and interrogatives in a given national coding – does not reflect a pre-existing basis of being; rather, it is itself involved in the creation or destruction of what it is talking about.

The century following the death of Muhammad in 632 proved that the task of imitation in his case was by no means fashionable and "of one generation," to recall an expression [*einaltrig*] coined by Eugen Rosenstock-Huessy – the most important philosopher of language of the twentieth century, who for the time being is concealed in the blind spot of the linguistic turn, analytic autism, and academic hermeneutics. Right from the outset, Islam carried within itself a space-claiming, virulent, cross-generational dynamic. Nevertheless, early Muslims must have been surprised by their successes, as if they had discovered a method to be followed, commissioned for nearly a century: *Be amazing!* They performed a part in a play the likes of which the historically turbulent world had not seen since Alexander the Great. What was brought to the stage was an interpenetration of martial and religious dramas, whose ethnogenic, character-forming, and dynastic consequences continue to have effects up to the present day. At first, the drama of Islam was intoxicated by the divine judgment implied in the constantly renewed victory; it spread terror through the translation of sacred verse into martial effects. In the Islam of the seventh century, the thesis about Christianity promulgated by the church father Tertullian came into its fulfillment – it was the *militia Christi*.[15]

One should take account of the religious-political predicate that was articulated at the beginning of this style. Appeasement-minded theologians from various confessional and ideological faculties like to minimize the polemogenic implications of radical monotheistic collective formations, but the debut of Islam up to the middle of the eighth century makes the facts of the matter plain to see. It embodies the only variant of monotheism that was founded as a violently determined, elite movement – to be sure, it only became expansively oriented in a second phase, but it was already thoroughly endowed with the distinguishing feature of an arabophonic afterlife. An Islam capable of coexistence with non-Muslims without a unilaterally imposed "peace" (i.e., demands of submission) could only emerge if one might put bold secondary formulations about Islam and non-Islam into the mouth of the Prophet. One could best locate such formulations among the hadith which, with casual retrospection, decompose the life of the Prophet into an array of anecdotes. Naturally, Muslim anecdotage nowhere reaches the intensity of the passion story of Jesuism. Even so, it has the potential to turn Muhammad into a wise man who, without constant threats of hell, would have sought approval for ethical visions which are easily acceptable, all things considered, and only need to be corrected for their noxious sexism. Work on such a secondary formulation falls to Muslim theologians who are willing to learn, and who have not been lacking since the eighteenth century.

The term "secondary" here, *nota bene*, belongs to the vocabulary of New Testament scholars: at least since Rudolf Bultmann in his study of the Synoptic Gospels (published in 1921), many of the "Lord's words" ascribed to Jesus by the community in Jerusalem, alleged "quotations" from the Q source of Jesus' sayings (*logia*), as well as some fictional elements of the narrative plotting from Bethlehem to Golgotha, have been designated as "secondary formulations." In this expression, the originally more poetizing function of imitation claimed its philological approval. Putting words into someone's mouth (*in ore ponere*) is one of the privileges of recipients who have been captivated and get carried away. They can avail themselves of it so long as there is no supervisory authority to oversee the written word. Each ear-witness quotation brings into play a personal syntactic–semantic contribution of the guarantor who has been called to the stand. The fact that every sentence of the Quran should have been sworn to by two ear-witnesses "of that time" – sworn as heard in this way and not otherwise – documents the effort undertaken to achieve an authentic wording; at the same time, it also illustrates how the adventure of quoting precedes the fixing of a holy scripture.

From this, it follows that critical philology observes the properties of letters or phonemes and graphemes on written carriers as precisely as physics observes the doings and sufferings of elementary particles in colliders; before its seat of judgment, not a single word in the New Testament or the Quran can be regarded as absolutely certain, so far as the statements of Jesus or the recitations and sayings of Muhammad are concerned. The most that can be achieved is an acceptable probability. But doesn't believing mean, from the outset, living in approximations as if they were certainties? Tradition cannot prove anything in this field, except that it has nothing better to show than what it says and does. The copyist and compilation pathways were too long in both cases, too susceptible to error, too vulnerable with respect to omissions and additions. The only thing entirely certain, although often intangible as such (save in the more brazen forgeries[16]), is the co-poetic activity of the mediators who have contributed their part to the resulting shape of the holy books.

It does not matter for present purposes that, through the veil of secondary – perhaps primary – formulations, the Gospels identify Jesus as a superior parable poet and preacher-performer; in the framework of the thesis presented here, concerning the poetic nature of religions, it should also play no role that the Quran, in its edited form, constitutes a great and sonorous poem in rhymed prose, one in which the relative freedom of the verse-line lengths and the restrictions of the compulsory rhyme make flexible compromises. Rather, the question lies elsewhere: given writings of a character that is plainly quoted and compiled, with undisguised poetic imagery and features that emerged out of the incorporation of earlier poetry and were refreshed in performative new enactments of older liturgies – how, in such a context, did it become possible that there could arise society-forming, civilization-determining, soul-shaping absolutes that succeeded in making their poetic, fictional, or mythical character invisible? Wherever one opens the holy books, one finds oneself in the midst of paraphrases; with each sentence, one enters into the sphere of an excited intermonotheistic, inter-zealotic, interfictional quotation.

The hypothesis advanced a few years ago, to the effect that the Quran might be better judged from a Syro-Aramaic dialect base than from the premises of Classical Arabic studies,[17] remains controversial now as ever, but it is far from having been completely refuted, especially since the considerable presence of Aramaicisms in the sacred text is not disputed by anyone. Its approach rests on the conjecture that Classical Arabic is a consequence of the reception of the Quran, but that the Quran itself was not formulated purely in the Arabic that it made classical. This could explain why one can only guess the precise meaning of a good fifth of the traditional text, rather than simply deciphering it according to the rules of the art.

The reading from Syro-Aramaic, which is not accessible to many scholars, could at least offer some significant illuminations – for example, that the martyr-warrior is gratified in the hereafter not by 72 ever-available virgins, but by the same number of white grapes – which in this case would constitute a plausible correction, revising distorted notions of the hereafter as a sham joy house for sexually frustrated young men. Moreover, there might ensue a momentous rectification of the controversial "headscarf" verse of Sura 24:31: a Syro-Aramaic reading suggests that it does not speak of a head covering, but rather of a belt or girdle – something of a complication for those young women of the Islamosphere for whom wearing a headscarf has recently served as a signifier to buttress their identity. One seems to sense, at the very least, that fashion has some unfinished business to settle with custom. Those who consider fashion to be more important than tradition are committed to modernity. The state in which headscarf designers vie with hairdressers is fundamentally modern.

If the Syro-Aramaic hypothesis has inspired any changes in the art of Quranic exegesis as a whole, it has not been sufficient to provoke philological battles with their heavy artillery. In the community of experts in the field, the author, appearing under a pseudonym, was far from being warmly received. An observer not materially involved can hardly avoid the impression that leading scholars in Riyadh, Cairo, Berlin, and Paris would prefer to dismiss all guidance from minor fields of study.

The imitation of imitation transitions into a crisis of cultural education, when the excited ones of the earliest days must begin to confer their spiritual vibration not just upon easily inflamed followers, but also upon their families and neighborhoods. As soon as children get caught up in the slipstream of such processes, the door is opened to the transgenerational incorporation of poetry, regardless of whether the input is imparted from parents to their children or whether older mentors address themselves to youths in order to teach them and form them, in the spirit of a Christian or Islamic *paideia*. In principle, this applies to every religioid tradition that addresses the problem of children.

One can assume that, in the geopolitically explosive phase of Islam, the practice of the new cultic regime advanced more through the recruitment of young men available for an eventful life on the perpetual offensive than through the impregnation of Arab tribal communities with the rules of the then-new modus vivendi. A hundred years later, at the latest by the middle of the eighth century, once the frenzy of conquest had abated (and also amid disputes over the legitimate succession to Muhammad), the new Quran-inspired way of life had been diffused somewhat more sustainably among the populations around the Near and Middle East, as well as across North Africa and in southern Spain. What the Islamic modus vivendi imposed was no longer the call for campaigns full of enthusiasm and plunder – which had led to the establishment of clan-male camp cities in the conquered areas. The agenda was now dictated by the process of a movement becoming a culture that strove ever more for the fulfillment of its existence as a whole. Initially inspired by masculinism, the impulse henceforth extended to the world of women and the sphere of offspring. The impingement on children transformed the hypomanic wave into something fixed in place: a didactically oriented discipline. Accordingly, it had to shift emphasis from mobilizing allies and young men to enculturating offspring, whose introduction to the hard world made its mark upon them by way of beatings and irresistibly melodic liturgies.[18] The early believers, who were now gradually beginning to call themselves Muslims, felt the general embarrassment of higher cultures in locating the fine line between proper upbringing and child abuse. There can be no refined culture without the attempt to transform the impossible into the everyday.

When an innovative–charismatic movement is ripe for becoming a civilization, the mobilization of religious warriors recedes into secondary importance; full-time workers in divine eristic are now needed less than teachers who can convey the mental basics of a religion on its way to routinization. One might argue the virtues of the organization of Christianity, but it is striking that Islam has not given rise to a formal clergy, despite its propensity to invade all areas of its adherents' life. From a social-evolutionary point of view, this means that for Islam, unlike for Christianity, there was no imitable imperial bureaucracy ahead of it.

The relative pacification of the Islamized territories gave rise to the moment when jihad patterns of action could be directed inward; it prompted the thought that the pious should be called to campaign against the unconverted remnants in their own hearts – as happens in a *religio* in the stage of internalizing intensification and endopoetic deepening. There is relatively little talk of jihad in Islam during the millennium of its cultural consolidation. The expression is cited from the late eleventh century onward as a call to fight against the invading armies of Christian knights encamped before Jerusalem; it also plays a role when it comes to denouncing Muslim rivals as infidels in order to present an internecine quarrel as, instead, a holy battle to be fought for the sake of Allah. In Sufism, on the other hand, the holy struggle has throughout assumed a spiritual meaning, in the sense of a psychomachy or a conflict of the soul, and this is how it is interpreted today by many of the Islamic scholars who are inclined to enlightenment ideas.

The re-externalization of the struggle, as it has become manifest since the eighteenth century in the combustion points of a puritanical, restorative proclamation of Islam on the Arabian Peninsula, broke fresh ground in the last third of the twentieth century – driven not least by the humiliation caused by the technical and political superiority of the West and the offense of its imperial demeanor. The illiberal Sunni "sects" of Wahhabism and the Salafi movement are, in their current generations, to be blamed for the fact that, worldwide, the terms "Islamism" and "terrorism" have become synonymous in recent decades. This should not be misinterpreted as evidence of Samuel Huntington's thesis concerning a so-called "clash of civilizations." Concerning terror, one can find more competent interpreters of the most varied stripes among the readers of Friedrich Nietzsche and René Girard, who supplied powerful instruments for deciphering jealous imitations and the projections of resentment on the world political scene.

Comparable dynamics should be taken into consideration with respect to the Christian spheres in the period stretching from the first communities to the Byzantine emperors of the fourth century. In the beginning, the operative elements were "fashion," initial contagion, excitement, and consternation among the principals of the early times; over time, what took charge were enculturation, neighborhood life, pedagogy, and everyday communal life. The stabilization was now and then disturbed by tidings of local persecutions and executions of their co-religionists at the hands of the Roman authorities. It now became apparent that Christianity, like Judaism, worked as a "religion of good memory" – to take up a formulation by Manès Sperber who sought to give the phenomenon of *ressentiment* a positive meaning. Cruel incidents could be collected as exempla and etched into the institutional memory to enrich the sacred treasury, beginning with the early martyrologies and the first registers of the saints. After Christianity was elevated to an imperial religion in 380, and all the more so after 391, when the ban on "pagan" cults was enacted, "the churches were flooded with nominal Christians.... Christianity became the fashion,"[19] writes Ruth A. Tucker in her study on the "missionary" history of Christianity. The author does not trouble herself with the fact that the term "mission" did not appear until the sixteenth century, when European seafarers had brought testimonial evidence that there were more members of the human race on earth than had been supposed in Rome,

Byzantium, Wittenberg, and Geneva. In the second stage of fashion, Christianity offered many of its new followers the feeling that they were members of the right club.[20]

The popularizing routinization of the Christian cult could only be achieved at the cost of forming a hierarchy that had not been provided for in its original constitution – its precondition was profoundly rewriting or repoetizing the original legacy of Jesuism's doctrines. The central figure of the cult, whether understood as identical or as similar to God, was a childless unmarried man in his early thirties, with no fixed address and without concrete earthly perspectives – today we might describe him as an attachment-refusenik who typically preferred to surround himself with followers rather than relatives. It was only by inverting the key signature, then, that his later veneration in ecclesiastical forms could be made culturally compatible and suitable for the people. The maneuver required a reversal of direction from Jesuism to patrocentric modes of living and patrophiliac language games – popes, abbots, fathers, abbés, desert fathers, church fathers, and various other professors of patrology. The agents and partisans of restored fatherhood practiced an acquired infirmity of reading which helped them shunt a not easily misunderstood admonition from Jesus into a blind spot of the church: "you have one teacher, and you are all students. And call no one your father on earth, for you have one Father – the one in heaven [*ouranios*]."[21] Where "secondary formulations" had come to dominate, tertiary ones were not long in arriving. The practice of putting words into someone else's mouth had its best times yet to come.

Beside the change in figuration from brotherhood and sisterhood to a re-erected paternity, one finds a noteworthy re-stylization effect in the gradual reinterpretation of Christian militancy,[22] up to its complete conformity with the requirements of Roman military service – in the language of today's public relations, one might speak of reshaping the narrative. Hence the emergence of the figure of the *miles christianus*, whose sequel in the Middle Ages was the "Christian knight" or the "crusader" (*croisé*). Until the third century, the Christian *religio* had been considered largely incompatible with military service, which is why soldiers who refused to renounce Christ were occasionally executed. From the fourth century onward, by contrast, in the east and the west of the empire, "there was established a perfect concordance between the army and the Christian Religion," as Harnack observes. The church had come to understand itself as the victorious *militia Christi*; whoever could not or did not want to serve in it was contemptuously referred to as a civilian (*paganus*).

The two most successful cult creations of the middle and late classical period – which, substantively, one might more properly designate not as religions, but rather as syncretistic systems of discipline and exercise for unremarkable, pious mediocrities – were characterized by their kerygmatic (proclamation-demanding) or Quranic (reading-demanding) dynamic. It is due to this specific dynamic that they form the prototypes of a purely supply-side religion.[23] They were diffused throughout their communities accompanied by demands requiring that the faithful recite the basic poems every day, even many times a day, together with specific body-language gestures. Their addressees were populations, for whose want of salvation they claimed to have available precisely the right remedies. For this purpose, Christianity had to securely integrate into its message the doctrine of the a priori sinfulness of all human beings, which Augustine had formulated to the end; for its dissemination, however, it did not need to wait for the ingenious mother's son and the theologian from North Africa, who with advancing age was becoming increasingly gloomy in his outlook.[24] Supplying the offer of salvation made an explicit, early assertion of its own exclusive necessity – beyond anything that could be achieved through traditional tribal and ethnic theotherapies. This effort found success by propagating and fostering a corresponding awareness of one's insufficiency and consequent jeopardy. It draws from a burgeoning discontent with regard to being-in-the-world that arose among people of various times and places, a discontent itself arising from both a general awareness of mortality and from the basic psychological disorders acquired in the years of early childhood and widespread since the formation of the Bronze Age empires. Early on, aggressive "monotheism," whether coded as Old Iranian, Jewish, Christian, or Islamic, certainly preached specifically to the rulers who wanted to procure legitimacy from the heavens – and they obtained it at the price of their followers joining the new faith; it likewise sent a message to pillagers who sought plunder without remorse – of whom there were quite a few among Muhammad's (later apostate) allies from the Arab tribes, to say nothing of the baptized warrior chiefs between Clovis I and Charlemagne. When it called God the Merciful, aggressive monotheism spoke most of all to the damned and the wretched of the earth, and to those plagued by the never fully healed wound of the unloved. These people justify Marx's dictum that religion is "the heart of a heartless world." It casts a spell over the troubled and the burdened as soon as they feel that, in a pitiless, unbrotherly world doomed to ruin, faith could mean being able to feel there was nonetheless a chance, an opportunity, in spite of it all. For Arabs in the era of Muhammad, the

sermon of the eternal good life with Allah was an inspirational alternative to traditional resignation in the face of the transience of all
things; and when the Quranic doctrine of omnipotence ultimately
resulted in a recoding of fatalism, it brought a light from above into
the existences of people beyond count.

The Islamic analogue of post-Augustinian Christianity's burden
of original sin manifested itself with respect to the ignorance of
non-Muslims, which had become punishable since the formulation
of the Quran came into view. Those who did not hasten to make a
profession of faith to Allah and his Prophet were guilty of a reprehensible will to ignorance. It was not for nothing that the pre-Islamic
era was called the "Age of Ignorance" in Arabic historical rhetoric.
There was a conditional indulgence extended to it, but anyone who
willfully persisted in such ignorance was to be properly regarded
as unrighteous. The evangelist John proposed something similar
when he let Jesus reason that the unbelievers among his people no
longer had an excuse for their stubborn refusal, since he had come,
preached, and authenticated himself through miracles.[25]

From the point of view of those aggressively offering and
supplying a religion, anything can be forgiven – anything except
the haughty, repudiating sentiment that one has no need of what
is on offer. Therein lies the "blasphemy against the Spirit";[26] thence
springs the fatal skepticism against "signs." What is confessed is
forgiven. From the first hour, however, the calm and self-confident,
the undaunted, the balanced and hysteria-averse, those who were
disinclined to quick confessions of sin and collapse-like admissions of one's failings – these attracted the attention of threatening
polemics, of which Jesus had already given a gloomy specimen. The
author of the Johannine Apocalypse escalated all enthusiasm for
maximalist threat in his imagistic flights of annihilation-psychotic
intensity. It was thanks to the intransigence of Bishop Athanasius
of Alexandria (c. 300–73) that the writing of the so-called John of
Patmos was incorporated around the year 370 as the final book
in the New Testament canon – rightly, perhaps, in the objective
sense that the future-oriented New Covenant would have remained
incomplete without a document that goes beyond the Gospels and
focuses on the Last Things; wrongly, because the Apocalypse of
John disavows the concept of revelation by engaging it in a psychotic
flight of images and in the eruption of a language of annihilation
that is adverse to culture.[27] During his Medina years, corrupted as
they were by "political" struggles for success, Muhammad, too,
sometimes escalated the intensity of his threatening speech to
alienating extremes (and on occasion to parafanatical viciousness).

Motifs of this type were exposed and highlighted by Nietzsche in his critical writings on religion in the 1880s, even if he also overstates his case when he construes the attractiveness of Christian doctrine in terms of a moral substitute for slaves, small-minded people, and those lusting for vengeance. Nietzsche underestimated the Janus-like ability of metaphysicalized Christianity to articulate itself as at once both a religion of the masters and a religion of the people.

Christianity and Islam occasioned a household cleavage in the consciousness of peoples, one that produced not only divisions among the living, but also between the living and the dead – divisions that early proclaimers mostly just hinted at, but without being able to think them through to the end. The status of those knowing nothing of the proclamation of salvation – up to the fatal day of their encounter with it – consisted not just in their "disbelief" or their "alternate beliefs," nor in their worldly unconcern about their otherworldly fates. The awkward embarrassment they repre-sented, from the point of view of the new religious suppliers, proceeded from the fact that, in the event of their non-conversion, they risked sinking into the hitherto unknown zone of the awful state of being-the-past. One had to constantly remind them that their previous existence, in unreflecting forms of life dominated by inferior demons, necessitated a revolutionary revision, reconsider-ation, and conversion. By disclosing itself, the new wants to be also the first and the original. The expression "See: I'll make everything new" implies a second sentence: "Understand this: I'll set everything right!"

Since tidings of the highest level of truth, pronounced in their moment, brought with them epochal interruptions, they had to embed their own advent within the surrounding histories, roughly following the schema of "in the fullness of time." This had, in the strong sense of the word, fateful consequences for everything that had happened on earth in older times, before the descent of the Logos or the holy book. When the eternal breaks into the hitherto existing, what had formerly appeared to be forever valid is summoned before the judgment of the newly proclaimed. The false Old must tremble before the true New – the New, however, presents itself as if only there does what truly flows from the origin continue to flow. The truth would thus possess the form of a river delta, in which only a few currents reach the sea, while most of them stagnate in the meanders of an oxbow lake.

In promising eternal life to their believers – subject to the caveat of judgment – the new tidings pronounced, mostly implicitly, but sometimes explicitly, a retrospective spiritual death sentence on those who died before the era of salvation. In order to make a place in memory and consciousness for this particular implication of the new proclamation, it became necessary to make special provisions for a number of eminent figures from the earlier epoch: the righteous few, before Christ as before Muhammad, were to benefit from the fact that, in them, the spirit of truth had been at work in advance. In such accounts, Jesus was not idle on the "Harrowing of Hell," his descent to the Limbo of the Patriarchs; there he roused the few good ones from earlier times to the Resurrection. But the retroactive deliverance of only an elite among the pious could not altogether eliminate the awkward embarrassment engendered by the proclamation and the cleavage it created between the living and the dead. That Abraham should belong in an Islamic heaven was self-evident, of course, for those who claimed descent from Ishmael, Abraham's older son, who had been overshadowed in the Jewish account in favor of Isaac; likewise, Islam could not deny that Jesus himself had been sent forth in advance of Muhammad – even if Islam could not approve of his deification by the mad Christian–Platonic doctors of the church. For both Jews and Christians, it came as a surprise to be told that Abraham and Jesus were Muslims *avant la lettre*. For their part, Muslims have difficulty understanding the role they play in the script of Muhammad-Knows-Better-Than-the-Descendants-of-Abraham-and-the-Successors-of-Jesus. Which Muslim scholars have ever accepted that they were participating in the piratical appropriation of the pre-Muslim past?

The new doctrines of faith brought a profound embarrassment into the world: who would want to affiliate oneself with a salvific movement whose preachers decreed that the antecedents of new believers would not normally be granted retrospective incorporation into the newly revealed space of salvation; indeed, they might count their blessings if they were settled in Limbo, a mildly climate-conditioned zone of the underworld.

Conceived as a drastically winnowing religion of election – "For many are called, but few are chosen" (Matthew 22:14) – Christianity, to say nothing of Islam, cannot forever hide the fact that it invites present and future generations to weaken or abandon their solidarity with past generations: "Follow me, and let the dead bury their own dead!" (Matthew 8:22). The human world is traditionally understood as a community of the living and the dead, right up to depositing ancestral relics like skulls into tribal houses, but once such a pronouncement has been made, the human world comes to be fissured by two movements that operate to dismantle this capacious sense of solidarity. The first separates, among those who died in earlier epochs, the recuperable few from the myriad masses of second-class dead, who cannot be helped even afterward. The second splits the world population of the living into those believers who can be saved and those who at the lapse of their time are even today struck from the books of life because they did not find the path of salvation or, although it had been made known to them, they did not wish to walk its path.

One comes up against a characteristic trait here which brings to light the self-contradiction of universalism crossed with election. The turn to everyone supposes a latent conviction that not everyone will follow. The Mormon movement, founded in the United States in the early nineteenth century (and since then splintered into many dozens of denominations), and otherwise so rich in strangenesses, betrays a profound aspect[28] in that it not only advocated the baptism of the deceased, it also declared the possibility of the retroactive redemption of members of previous generations.

With his characteristic clarity of vision, Paul of Tarsus mulled a preliminary stage of the underlying dilemma:

Everyone who calls on the name of the Lord shall be saved. But how are they to call on one in whom they have not believed? And how are they to believe in one of whom they have never heard? And how are they to hear without someone to proclaim him? And how are they to proclaim him unless they are sent?[29]

So Paul comes along – why else? – to speak of one's own role in the event of salvation. The existential-metaphysical premise of the evangelical enterprise is no longer something he needs to elucidate in greater detail: those who associate their own person with the motif of needing salvation will straightaway understand that their cause is being negotiated here; those who do not feel it regard salvation as a topic of the religious feuilleton, something that, for the time being, concerns only those who find that sort of thing interesting. The third possibility is seldom if ever considered – even though, outside of excited revival speeches, it should be the "normal" one among mortals: that individuals neither refuse nor aspire to the idea of salvation because what they want in life, and what is expected of them, are, if not identical, not too far apart either. For great civilizations, it seems characteristic that that specific "normality" becomes an exceptional case that applies only to primitives and those blessed with unusually good fortune.

At the same time, the not-interested, the damned of then and now, are indispensable for motivating the aggressive tone in which the proclamation is offered and supplied: the proclamation gains vigor so long as it contends with expected refusal. If the mission were to encounter no resistance at all, it would resolve itself through its very success. Even the very obstacle of denial proves to the proclaimers that their message is based on the unconditional. If everyone effortlessly endorsed the tidings, then heaven and hell would follow roughly the same course – no one would fall into the eternal fire. It must, to the contrary, be possible to confidently assume that very many, if not most, are not to be included, such that the choice between believing and non-believing results in the difference for everything.

The speculative meditating on refusal[30] is to be maintained right up to the visions of the Last Judgment: else, on the day of reckoning, one might look for the damned near and far, but all in vain. If the threats were not carried through, then all the zealots' work on the refuseniks would represent wasted effort.[31] This concern was already mitigated by the early Christian ecstatics, who, on their journeys to heaven and in their dreams of the afterlife, saw doubters, deniers, and sinners cast into the eternal fires.[32] On the second part of his Night Journey, Muhammad received similar indications of the densely populated pit in the wasteland (*Sijjin*), where the wicked are confined until Judgment Day.

It is characteristic of sharply defined supply-side systems that, as soon as their proclamation has begun, they beget an either–or that cannot at first be mitigated. They found a poetry of the wager for all or nothing. The virtues of such sharp definitions become apparent when the existence of believers is wrested from indifference, discouragement, and the downward slide. As the cell makes the monk, so one-sided partiality makes the convert.

Ideas of religious election encounter their inner limit as soon as they have to resolve the tension between the formal universalism of their doctrines and their regional and particular embodiment. Sooner or later, willingly or unwillingly, those of the elect and those sent as messengers must admit that they too are not merely sinners – that is, chronically deficient partners in the covenant with God; they are also particularly positioned, self-contradicting universalists.

The bottleneck logic of the apocalyptic situation meant that, to "everyone who calls on Christ," Paul was only able to give assurance of salvation on the horizon of the scant "time that remains": the few who have been saved will have reason to be happy because they heard and accepted the good news in time; while the numberless lost are also included, this is only in the sense that, ever thereafter, they would be certain of their lostness.

Among the lost, the manifest naysayers form the core group, but the vast majority consist of those who never got a chance to hear the message in time for the Lord's return. One finds here the nucleus of the Christian idea of history as the postponement of the Last Day:[33] for the sake of the many, it would be desirable for the Lord to defer his return, together with his judgment, until everyone living on earth was so fortunate as to hear his message – even if this took 2,000 years and more.

The idea of expanding the Acts of the Apostles into the history of world salvation sounds at first like a concession to the sense of metaphysical fairness; the curtain on the world as a whole should not close before access to the good news is available to everyone under the heavens. In all this time, all across the still unmissioned globe, people continue to die unredeemed deaths under false heavens; this fact, however, would play only a minor role in Christian versions of world history as the story of the spread of its message. In the third millennium after the death and non-return of Christ, the history of salvation, understood as a global fishing expedition for salvageable souls adrift on the ocean of the world, is largely still like the voyage of a small fleet of rescue ships on an ocean of unholy disaster.

The complete impossibility of a real Christian universalism without hidden barbs becomes visible in the mystical literature of the seventeenth century, where, especially in French, there appear on the scene authors who constrict the circle of spiritual communication to an almost impassable point, even as their claim to validity remains unsurpassably universal. Thus, François Malaval stated in his treatise *Pratique facile pour élever l'Ame à la contemplation* (1670): "I write only for persons capable of inner things, those who have been fully mortified with respect to the external senses and all passion, fully drawn to God by his pure love and fully detached from all that has been created."[34] More than 30 years earlier, in his *Discourse on the Method* (1637), René Descartes had deployed the Christian-derived approach of withering away all worldly, non-religious things; he did this so that, even from his residence in the large, foreign city of Amsterdam, he might win the advantage of a solitary and withdrawn life, as if he lived in a desert wasteland, intending nothing other than "the pure truth." Without the desert, there is no focus of the will. New constructions of truth are to be erected in the desert from evidence that suffices for itself. Although the gates to this new construction are open to all, only a very few will be billeted there. Christianity's universalism has this in common with epistemological and philosophical universalism: it is accessible only to a self-appointed and self-selecting elite.

From a religious-economic point of view, supply-side oriented cult- and belief-systems constitute behavioral patterns that ought to arouse, in their addressees, a keen sense for the appeal of buying in. Not least because of the suggestive, occasionally turbulent, mode of their transmission, they come close to supplying one of those infamous offers that cannot be refused.

There is no reason to assume suppliers did not generally want to make the best possible message available bona fide to their potential co-religionists, but the certain conviction that they were delivering truly good news did give the messengers license to be forceful. Indeed, it seldom stopped at the threshold of pushiness, and it crossed that threshold without scruple when, as a result of the strategically targeted conversion of rulers, whole peoples were netted like incidental bycatch for the Roman Catholic Church – the paradigmatic example being the baptism of the Merovingian warlord Clovis around the year 498. Through this event, the *praedicatio gentium* (preaching among the peoples) or the *conversio infidelium* (conversion of the infidels) succeeded with one of their most consequential moves. It is almost needless to note that Clovis, like Constantine on a smaller scale, believed he recognized in Christ a god who offered assurance of victory – for who, if not Christ, had stood with him against the Alemanni in the Battle of Tolbiac (*c.* 496 CE, near Zülpich, southwest of Cologne)? Thanks to the Frankish adoption of Nicene Christianity, there came to be established, on "western" (later European) soil, a set of collective cultic transformations originating from the East: the victory cult and the imperium cult reshaping the passion cult and the charitable primary proclamation addressed to the individual. At the provisional end of this appropriative reshaping, one finds groups such as the German Christians who pledged themselves to Adolf Hitler's program, and the American evangelicals who have enjoyed open doors at the White House for more than half a century (and not only at the National Prayer Breakfast).

The expansion histories of supply-side driven "religions" cannot be treated here in detail. The *promulgatio evangelii*, also known as *propagatio fidei* (propagating the faith) or *peregrinatio propter Christum* (peregrinations for the sake of Christ), came to terms with itself, after one and a half thousand years, when, shortly after the founding of their order in the second half of the sixteenth century, the Jesuits began to circulate the term "mission" (*mission*: sending, transmitting). It has been readily projected back onto the history of Christianity by European historians; soon enough, even the hurried movements of the tentmaker Paul between Jerusalem, Damascus, Antioch, Athens, and Rome came to be described as "missionary journeys," even though in his day that type of activity was simply odd – indeed, not even articulable as such. Tradesmen and craftsmen were familiar with travels along the trade routes of the inhabited Mediterranean world and supplemented them with correspondence between distant interested parties and recipients of instructions from the centers of power. There is some evidence that Paul initially wandered the streets of the empire as a craftsman available for hire.[35] In the course of this activity, he may have found enough time to disseminate his colorful ideas concerning the relationship between law and grace, the Cross and the flesh, *agape* and the ordering of life before the end – though it is also possible that the majority of the Pauline letters, like so much else from that heyday of pseudoepigraphy, came from later fabrications.

The driving force of Paul's haste was a consequence of the evident short-term nature of early-Christian expectations of the world. It would be an anachronism to apply the modern concept of "mission" to his travels. Paul would have wanted to save those who could be saved, but his view of the world and the shortness of the time remaining allowed him to set aside the unsavable – and to do so without sentimentality. The parable of the potter from the Epistle to the Romans suggests that the clay has no right to complain if the potter has not seen fit to mold it into a well-formed vessel. For the apostle, the shapeless clay and the spiritually unreachable masses had much the same status. When Augustine of Hippo wrote, 350 years later, of the *massa perditionis*, the lump of perdition, he was still making use of the Pauline equation of ruined vessels and failed existences. That did not hinder him from offering his remarks in a tone seemingly intended for all.

If the term "mission" was coined by the Jesuits, it nevertheless obtained its lasting meaning through its potential for projecting forth. It was not by chance that it was conceived on the threshold of the modern age. The arc of the mission, thought through to the end, conceals what would be called "world history" from the eighteenth century onward. The economic interplay of missionary history and world history arose from the circumstance that the explorers, conquerors, and emissaries, the natural scientists and overseas traders from the sea-faring nations of Europe, were from the beginning provided with clergy. As the Europeans came to realize that there were peoples of color beyond number, these clergy responded to the expansion of empirical humanity with a planetary expansion of their missionary consciousness. Columbus (Colón) is said to have assigned himself apostolic tasks: after the discovery of the New World, he resolved to read his first name

Cristoforo (Christóbal) programmatically and he set himself the task of carrying the savior once more across a body of water.

Whereas, barely 200 years after the Reformation, Europe would open up to the twilight of religion through the Enlightenment, Iberian overseas trade from the now so-called Old World supported the first intense waves of proselytizing upon other continents, starting with the New Worlds of North and South America, followed by destinations in Asia and Africa. After the discovery of the Americas, the new four-continent worldview became authoritative for the oceangoing centers of power in Europe. The "Age of Discovery" allowed an abundance of geopoetries to emerge from out of European theopoetry. With the "Age of the World Picture," it was picture worlds that began to proliferate.

The expansions of the early European nation-states liberated psychological and physical energies that were literally mighty; they flowed into a character type that was, all at once, strong-willed, resolutely faithful, flexible, and useful in the field – a type that could shape itself as required into a seafarer, a conquistador, a colonial governor, the administrator of an estate, a soldier, a planter and overseas trader, and finally a missionary. With the Catholic missionaries, a variant of activist mystic made its entrance upon the stage of history. The ecclesiastical agents – at first mainly graduates of the Jesuit school of the will – went about their tasks with zest, as if they wanted to win Alexander's campaigns in cassocks. One might have thought that the forces mobilized in the inward-directed campaigns of the Egyptian and Syrian desert monks had resumed as an outward offensive following a moratorium of nearly 1,200 years. Europeans at the start of the twenty-first century can hardly conceive what the missionaries undertook in order to proclaim the sublime absurdities of a belief that was nearly untranslatable but, thank God, easy enough to simplify – and to do so in the most adverse environments: among the indigenous peoples of Canada, the denizens of the Middle Kingdom, the Patagonian clans, on the islands of Japan, and among African tribes.

They would have been hardly capable of this feat had they not carried within themselves the motives that gave impetus to European expansion since the sixteenth century – in the first place, the compulsive quest for meaning embraced by second, third, and fourth sons of large Iberian families, who held fast to the scripts that were just emerging for the age of the Catholic opening-up of the world;[36] then the para-anthropological doctrine of the ecclesiastical writer Tertullian, according to which the human soul naturally conforms to Christianity, *anima naturaliter christiana*. One who truly thought in this way might travel among strangers, perhaps as a well-intending meddler, but never as an exploiter and a rapist. In their expansions, the emissaries of Europe mostly left open whether they had in mind a visit to far-flung family relatives or whether they were guided by the project of submitting the "rest of" humanity, alias "the rest of the world," to "Judeo-Christian" concepts.

In order to understand from a distance the vigor of the Christian world mission, the endo-rhetorical and endo-poetic self-regulation of the missionaries must be addressed. It followed from daily mental training in the form of prayers, readings, sermons, and other acts of faith-strengthening fitness, which enabled the clergy to work amid the cultural circumstances of an alien people and yet preserve their apostolic identity – even if, like the Jesuits in India, they operated in the garb of Brahmins or, as in China, they dressed like mandarins, until, following a lengthy dispute, assimilation to local customs and rites was definitively forbidden by the bulls of the Holy See in 1742 and 1744. For the apostles in the field, as for all high achievers in advanced civilizations, it was evidence, to be renewed each day, that believing, working, and keeping fit amount to the same thing.

Looking back over almost half a millennium from 1492 to 1945, it is impossible to avoid the impression that it was the Age of Imposition, to give it the mildest possible expression. Its most violent actions were brought about by political-economic projects and religious colonization enterprises whose sources of transmission lay in the national empires of Europe and their sacramental monarchies. The ultimate wellspring of the "missions" remained, at first formally (then later also substantially), situated at the Holy See – although there, for more than a century, the Iberian kingships had been given the privilege of protecting and expanding the "missions"; it formed part of their right to take possession of the world, according to the apportionment set forth in the Treaty of Tordesillas in 1494 – which, in an unprecedented act of sacred diplomatic piracy, awarded one half of the globe to the Spaniards and the other half to the Portuguese.

The concept of a world religion gained its first precise articulation in Rome. On January 6, 1622, a new agency was instituted under Pope Gregory XV, which described itself with unembarrassed simplicity as the Sacra Congregatio de Propaganda Fide. It was established to reclaim for the Vatican unequivocal responsibility for questions of the diffusion of the faith – not just formally, as hitherto, but now also in practice. It was equivalent to an ideological second strike, after Catholic and imperial troops defeated the Protestant princes in the Battle of White Mountain on November 8, 1620, in the first major battle of what would later be called the Thirty Years' War. The term *propagatio fidei* initially referred more to European horizons of papal concern than to overseas projects. The most urgent priority, in the view of the Holy See, was to regain the territories that had been lost to Protestantism in the years since 1517. The fact that Catholic polemics occasionally caricatured Luther as a Turk betrays the intertwining of an unrest on the internal front and an armed struggle on the external front. The caricature exhausted its right to rudeness (and worse) when it portrayed Luther, the writer of a "Military Sermon against the Turks" (1530) and other anti-Ottoman treatises, as if he were himself a hateful Oriental consumed by delusional beliefs; in other engravings of the age, the Reformer was presented as the Beast of the Apocalypse – while Luther, for his part, also tending toward apocalyptic moods in the face of increasing resistance, interpreted the Turks as the fourth horn of the Beast. Nonetheless, he appealed to the city council of Basel to release the scholar Theodore Bibliander (1506–64), who had been incarcerated in 1542 for his project to publish the Quran in Latin. The Reformer wrote a foreword to Bibliander's splendid three-volume edition of the Quran in 1543, because he was convinced that there was no keener weapon against the Turks than unobscured insight into the "lies and fables" of Muhammad.

Two months after the establishment of the Sacred Congregation for the Propagation of the Faith, Francesco Ingoli, its secretary, organized the world map into thirteen zones, each to be assigned a cardinal and a nuncio – the propaganda agency's resolutely geopolitical style of thinking was there from the start. "Globalization" as a denominational-polemical concept, availed itself of the new medium of cartography to depict the world as a sphere of influence – that is, as the sum of possible destinations for Rome-based missionary mandates. In *Relazione delle quattro parti del mondo* (1631) – his first report of results, and based on reports from the missionaries in his agency – Ingoli observed that Christianity was often perceived by the new peoples as attending violent European expansions, while Islam enjoyed the advantages of a peaceful proclamation spread by traders. The canonization of Francis Xavier, the Apostle of Asia, was squarely on the agenda for the new agency in March 1622; his arm, weary from the blessing of tens of thousands, had been moved to Rome several years earlier.[37]

The later history of the meaning of the term "propaganda" demonstrates how the Catholic Church lost control of its signification. In 1790, it was appropriated by a group of Jacobins who wanted to popularize their ideas; they knew what analogy they conjured up when they spoke in affirmative tones of *propagande*

– every zealotry cites a different one. One might apply Paul Valéry's remark to these founders of militancy in the political ("the political," *nota bene*, was anti-militant, having emerged from the discovery of neutrality and the Third Way): "We cannot act without moving toward a phantom."[38]

The interchangeability of phantoms is part of the basic experience of modernity. In the twentieth century, the concept of "propaganda" has come to stand for the permanent degradation of collective intelligence through its reduction to conditioned semantic reflexes by means of monotonously repeated stimulus words and stimulus images. In the war of slogans and suggestions, campaigns were organized to stimulate the flow of salivary streams and their mental equivalents in the conditioned masses of opinion followers, in accordance with Pavlov's findings on dogs. Ivan Petrovich Pavlov (1849–1936) himself later turned to sociological themes and tried to show that "cultures" represent complex aggregates of conditioned reflexes; his notion was that cultures take the general biological automaton of the association between stimuli and reactions and develop it into culture-specific automatisms of the association between signs and mental reactions. In his reflections, Pavlov placed the accent on the reaction-directing stimulus-quality of exogenously placed signs, whereas Sigmund Freud had emphasized their quality as symptoms in relation to "neurotic" tensions of endogenous origin. In the social-psychological field, Pavlov's intuitions far surpassed Freud's hypotheses inasmuch as it can hardly be doubted that, in all modern cultures, the political tone of the crowd is regulated by the strategic manipulation of signs, while the enlightening use of language, image, and figures in the semiospheres of the masses plays a subordinate role. Agitations are indeed always preceded by conditioning, and they have conditioning effects themselves. Just as some asthmatics will suffer an attack of breathlessness at the sight of plastic roses, well-conditioned comrades, when they read *Pravda* and analogous organs of western journalism, are seized with abomination the moment they encounter words such as "capitalism" in an article. Given preparation suited to the purpose, an abstract expression such as "the existent" or "the status quo" might come to generate strongly adverse reactions, while stimulus words such as "creativity" and midlife mobility clichés such as "reinventing oneself" might come to trigger intense appetitive reflexes. Pavlov lived a long life, but he died too early to be able to observe how his cultural-physiological conjectures were realized in the consumerist nations of the West after 1950. Aldous Huxley's *Brave New World* (1932) is already thoroughly shaped by the application of Pavlovian concepts, including those of a satirical nature such as "hypnopædia," which gives the students of the happy western European world a nightly brainwashing in the form of the thousand-fold repetition of progressive platitudes such as "Every one belongs to every one else."

At the same time, the praxis of propaganda, now under the name of "public relations," contains the seed of technically planned manipulation of collective opinions and moods in the media age. In an apparently neutral political context, it takes on the sense of democracy-compatible consensus fabrication. At first, this may appear to be a purely secular business; on closer inspection, however, it bears unmistakable family resemblance to procedures for generating conformity developed by the Roman Catholic Church, the Jacobin Club, Joseph Goebbels, and various Leninist and Maoist directorates.[39]

Theopoetries in the age of national-imperial transmission were launched by the Catholics – especially by way of the Franciscan, Dominican, and Jesuit orders – and later also by the central offices of various Protestant missionary societies, to say nothing of those who accompanied the Dutch and British East India trade around the globe; in this way, all across the globe, they developed and showcased the portrait of a cosmically competent, expansive, community-building God who was at the same time intimately intertwined with every single soul. This project's strongest trait consisted in its evident ability to absorb older images of otherworldly powers, so that, almost unnoticed, compact local gods were refigured into the one heavenly, super-heavenly, worldless transcendent; which is why the word "God" took on as many colors as there were local gods and communal spirits. Roman Catholic images of heavens and hells were hybridized in a variety of ways after having been crossed with regional images of the afterlife, much as, under regional circumstances, the veneration of saints was spliced together with earlier polytheistic ideas – most impressively in the case of Brazilian and Caribbean slave cults such as Macumba, Candomblé, Vodou, and Santería. Moreover, the theology of the Trinity, impenetrable for the logics of foreign peoples (and, indeed, little different in the case of rationality closer to home), left it to the discretion of the converts to decide whether they would rather affiliate with the Father, the Son, or the Holy Spirit. The current triumph of Pentecostal Christianity in South America and Africa speaks for the attractiveness of the third option.

What was evident after the worldwide transmission of the image of a God so keenly interested in his own dissemination was that such a God would not be satisfied with leaving in peace those newly won to his cause, unperturbed in the places where his message had found them. Just as, for 3,000 years, YHWH had been most closely bound to the Jews as a partner in blessing and in punishment, the God of the new peoples was soon likewise to demonstrate his non-indifference with respect to their fates.

That God had special plans in mind for the Americans was already expounded for them by one of their prophetic authors at the turn of the seventeenth to the eighteenth century: they could take it from the book *Magnalia Christi Americana* – in essence: the glorious works of Christ in America, accomplished through the instrument of the new chosen people,[40] written by Cotton Mather (1663–1726), New England's master thinker of puritanically inspired exceptionalism. Why shouldn't Boston's experiment succeed just as brilliantly as what had been accomplished in Rome, in Wittenberg, and in Geneva? The modern world was initially nothing more than a network of fast-breeder reactors for ideas of election. Its basic figure is Pauline: "And how are they to proclaim him unless they are sent?"[41] On American soil, the question of the original mission was made explicit; closely on its heels, there followed the further question of the possible degree of self-election and self-appointment to the mission. The historian Leopold von Ranke had sound intuition when he asserted that John Calvin was the true founder of the United States; Walt Whitman declared more or less directly that the United States was itself the greatest poem – had he instead affirmed it as the greatest active fiction, it would be even easier to share his view. The rest of the world learned what it needed to know on April 6, 1917, at the latest, when the USA entered the First World War.

Heaven could be made to speak only against the backdrop of a theology that had little respect for distinctions between insistence and intrusiveness, where inhabitants of the earth could not finally determine with certainty the properties of this heaven – apart from its unremitting ambivalence, which from time immemorial had prefigured itself in the perpetual heavenly alternation of day and night. Even the super-attribute "all-powerful" is unable to permanently mask its brittleness. Considered from a present-day perspective, an attribute such as all-frail might seem rather more plausible; learned specialists might for their part consider whether "all-resilient" could be a theologically meaningful expression. None of God's qualities can be regarded as ultimately justified and free from contradiction, save for the one demonstrated in the book of Job – that God is able to interrupt and make interventions in the course of a life lived seemingly straight. One has to accept that God shares this ability in common with luck, which is proverbial for its dumbness.

Motifs of what we have called "supply-side religions" reached their twentieth-century apex in the work of the Lithuanian-born philosopher Emmanuel Levinas (1906–95). One would do no injustice to Levinas if, due to his family background and his deliberate choice of themes, one wanted to see him more as a rabbi than as a philosophical thinker, notwithstanding his proximity to Husserl and Heidegger. One has Levinas to thank for intensifying the "supply-side religion" approach to the thesis of the absolute priority of "the Other" – by way of which there appear the most important declensions of otherness: the stranger, the person in need, and God. In the world of Levinas, it is not the Almighty who solicits the self-involved subject to enter his community and there learn some measure of humility; what happens, rather to the contrary, is that a fragile being sends out its cry of suffering into the surrounding world and provokes a response or a non-response. The world is split into those who, perhaps despite themselves, allow themselves to be captured by the appeal for help, and those who, engrossed by other priorities, prefer to ignore the voice of need.

Levinas's special role was to have interpreted the essence of supply-side religion in terms of the force of the appeal of the Other, something attested by way of the human face. As a philosophizing theologian of the twentieth century compelled to respond to an event like the Holocaust, he achieved what no one could have expected: he took the outdated Augustinian doctrine of original sin and translated it into a contemporary, continuously updated dimension. He described humanity as an increasing crowd amid which the appeal for help rarely finds an adequate response. The appeal issues from the face of a life suffering infringement. One who is amenable to hearing the appeal will minister to the forlorn child, the victim of mishap, the displaced person, the suffering creature in any form.

The Levinasian paradox is based on the fact that the face of the suffering Other necessarily makes its address in close proximity, while the appeal as such straddles a far greater distance. The collapse of the distant into the proximate thus animates sin as an inevitable sin of omission. Accordingly, a sinner would be someone who fails to suffer and act in solidarity with those who suffer.

Radicalized original sin intensifies the importunity of the message into something like coercion. It forcibly imposes itself in the moment that the ethical subject is suddenly overcome by responsibility for the helpless Other. Some will refuse to recognize that a situation is serious enough that an appeal for help imposes a captivating claim upon the ethical subject; such persons comport themselves like unbelievers. The real *peccatum originale* is not inherited like a common genetic trait. Augustine's error could not be greater – original sin always comes to pass anew because, from case to case, even when locally operative, compassion lags behind the adversity it would redress for the Other. It resembles what Karl Jaspers, somewhat unhappily, called "metaphysical guilt" in 1946 – by which he intended to designate a finally insuperable solidarity deficit among finite beings.[42] Max Weber, admired by Jaspers, spoke more plainly of the "world domination of unfraternity." In the twentieth century, a darting flame of sin committed ever anew flared up when the Holy See in Rome was aware of the planned physical annihilation of the European Jews through the politics of German National Socialism, and yet it failed, for whatever reasons, to say early enough what needed to be said.

If expressions typical of aggressive religions could be arrayed in a ranking of unbelievability, the term "original sin" would appear high on the list – surpassed, it may be, only by "immaculate conception" and "ascension," and certainly ahead of expressions such as "verbal inspiration" or "the closing of the gates." Such a scale would formally display what has long been evident to ordinary intuition: that it is sometimes only a step from local surrealism to a "world religion."

19

ON THE PROSE AND POETRY
OF THE SEARCH

Proponents of the thesis that proclivity to religion is an element of human nature, and thus an innate disposition, will not fruitfully be countered by making appeals to visible exceptions. When making assertions about human disposition, one has to accept the equation between normality and the mean so long as deviations from the majority view can be interpreted as dispositions as yet unactivated. After all, a religious blank slate might deploy its psychobiologically preinstalled *anima naturaliter christiana* only upon being set in motion by an activation code.

Moreover, from a pragmatic point of view, there is no such thing as "unbelief" in individuals able to cope with life. The capacity to operate under everyday pressures implies that a posture toward existence is supported by guiding convictions, whether they remain unspoken or else emerge in articulated confessions. In all the world, no one is more devout than a mother raising three young sons by herself, knowing that her children rely on her to see them through to adulthood.

Whether or not convictions (technically speaking: syncrasies, or commixtures of energy reserves with values and objectives) are determined as "religious" statements is a secondary question in view of the vagueness of the concept of religion. Convictions that can be formulated float on the surface of the conscious mind like icebergs – the greater part of them belongs to the sphere of non-declarative imprintings and the preconscious habitus. To be sure, Tertullian found it necessary to remark that Jesus said he was truth, not custom or habit, but almost all religious statements, impulses, and feelings are based on the foundation of a habitus.[1] And whether one defines religions with Salomon Reinach as systems of scruples, or paradoxically as a construct of functioning absurdity, or existentially as a revolt against the scandal of senselessness, or in conformity with the latest neuroanthropological research as an extension of empathy to invisible agencies, or economically as systems for the mobilization of gifts, or in terms of critical ideology as a ceremonious complement to the false world – i.e., as the opium of the people – none of this plays an appreciable role for an external prospect upon the map and the territory of those who are religious. Paul Valéry conceptualizes theopoetics' contribution to the *fait humain* by way of a question: "What should we be without the help of that which does not exist?"[2] Conversely, what would heaven be without the anticipating ear of those to whom it speaks?

In his 1896 lecture, "The Will to Believe," William James outlined the decisive factors. His reflections suggest that the primary difference in questions of religion does not concern differences between rival beliefs, as when orthodox believers will sometimes, and with the most intense hostility, denounce alternate beliefs as disbelief – in the way that the orthodox of the three largest monotheisms will refer to non-Jews as *goyim*, to non-Muslims as *kuffar*, while Christians will determinedly malign non-Christians as *pagani* (heathens, people from the countryside, members of the "peoples"). James was enough of a psychologist to assert his observation that, insofar as belief is unprompted and not just the result of early and lifelong enculturation, it is, especially among the educated, first and foremost about a personal contribution of the adult believer. He calls this contribution, this capacity, the "will to believe" – notwithstanding the traditional thesis among theologians that faith as such is a grace already granted from above. Like every recourse to grace, this one aims to bring a halt to reflections that would otherwise tend to dissolve their object – allowed to range freely, thinking would nonetheless recur to grace by disclosing a will or readiness to *accept* the gift of grace as grace's own precondition. In order to be allowed to insist on the precedence of the gift, a second grace is necessary: the grace of the will to accept the gift of faith. In its contest against the will, grace can only succeed when the will is prevailed upon to suspend its prerogatives.

It was the English poet and literary critic Samuel Taylor Coleridge (1772–1834) who coined the phrase "the willing suspension of disbelief,"[3] to describe the momentary calm of the will in the reception of aesthetic fictions. One could also speak of allowing oneself to be convinced, hypothetically, by intense improbabilities. The discovery of the willing suspension of disbelief might be applied even more aptly to religious behavior, especially when the belief in miracles and the work of invisible agents comes into play. Of course, it is mostly involuntarily that believers enter into the suspension of disbelief, as when an irreversible impregnation with the contents of a belief has pre-empted the impulses of disbelief. One might say that believers of this type lack the courage to disbelieve.

With the turn to the will, reception came to take precedence over proclamation – in economic language: demand came to take precedence over supply. This expresses an experience that found its first explicit articulation among the Americans. Cotton Mather had not preached in vain – even if his hopes in matters of faith were disappointed by later developments in the American way of life. Over the course of the nineteenth century, it became ever more apparent that, in a nation composed of the pooling runoff of peoples,[4] being born into a religious community did not necessarily imply the formation of durable bonds. In Calvinist language, this means that the grace of faith can be revoked; perhaps the benevolence of heaven might be manifest in altered denominational form.

In a "nation" based on immigration, the multilingualism of heaven is one of the moral facts that precede the constitution of anything national – on the same level with acquired collective traits such as restlessness, mobility, and compulsive extroversion. As soon as people in the New World left home, especially in the milieu of the Second Great Awakening (1790–1840), a profusion of messages from inspired religious campaigners would din in their ears. When citizens would embrace a new creed, those around them would suppose that heaven had found a way to speak to them in a new idiom. If one disbelieved, the heavens were thought to have turned away for a time. Real atheism could be conceived only as a kind of hunger strike against the beyond, which sooner or later would have to be tackled with a well-meaning force-feeding.

From the view of market formation, belief cannot be separated from choosing a religious product. The basic form of choosing a faith (as with choosing a self) is a choice between remaining with an existing community, or else entering into a new one and adopting its symbolic system – including the possibility that the new group is one that rejects religious statements. Ordinarily, irreligious people do not regard themselves as belonging together as a group, since – rightly – they do not regard the shared lack of a religious characteristic as sufficient grounds for the formation of a community, so they are generally assigned to the group of those who refuse to form a group. The existence of staid and stuffy atheist associations in the nineteenth century shows, however, that even unbelief might sometimes aspire to flourish where statutes protect voluntary associations. In Germany, what were called egoist societies (with reference to Max Stirner) ensured that even insisting on one's own uniqueness might find an organized accompaniment.[5] The choice to believe is also colored among the moderns by modern trends in religiosity: from visibility to invisibility, from open profession to reserved. My faith is my unspeakable *secretum*.

William James's clear-sightedness was manifest in the way that, from a transatlantic distance, he conceptualized the mental consequences of the European Reformations: without will, no choice; without choice, no faith. Those who consent after the fact to the advance acceptance effected through socialization make the decision to stay with what they have practiced, be it in the spirit of conventionalism or of renewal; those who wish to make a break with what has come down to them are free to devote their inclinations to other plausibilities. This element of freedom had become recognizable in northern Europe in the fifteenth century through the mystically tinged *devotio moderna*; in the sixteenth century, through the affiliation of innumerable individuals to the theses of Luther, Calvin, Zwingli, and other Reformers; in the seventeenth century, through the merging of mystical circles with the group reading of edifying literature; and in the eighteenth century (and thereafter), with the freedom of private choice in reading. Where there was once a congregation, an audience or a reading public would come to flourish. The tendency was intensified in the American experiment, which turned confessions into sects and – on account of the disreputable aura of the word – the sects begat "denominations" and dissident-conformist free-churches, the number of which runs into the thousands. Believers on the American side of the Atlantic had left behind not only Europe (which had become the Old World) – not infrequently, they had also left behind the creed of their parents who had emigrated. They came close to the figure of the religious wanderer en route to the formless.

In his lecture of 1896, William James intimated indirectly that, from a psychological point of view, *real* unbelievers most closely corresponded to depressives – that is, to persons who had succumbed to a collapse in their belief systems. Those who had suffered a mental breakdown received their clinical designations soon thereafter: in 1899, the sixth edition of Emil Kraepelin's textbook on psychiatry gave clinical definition to "manic-depressive insanity." In the years since, it has come to be renamed "bipolar disorder" to distinguish it from unipolar depression, which knows only the lows. This condition is characteristic of individuals who are unable to feel their life-guiding motifs clearly enough to orient their lives accordingly – and what is not felt is not obeyed. Just as those who suffer from mania believe more than would benefit them in the long run, so depressed persons believe less than would conduce to their flourishing.

Statistics can take little account of the ambiguities and degrees of belonging to a religious or denominational collective. Methodologically, they are compelled to set aside the fuzziness that spreads both between the continents of faith and within their populations. In the crude simplification that is their métier, statistics register that, of the 7.3 billion people who populated the earth in the year 2015, nearly 2.3 billion were Christians – but they have no way to contend with the fact that Christians today affiliate themselves with more than 30,000 different forms of legally autonomous church entities, including great numbers of them newly founded in recent years. Such churches flourish especially in the small indigenous structures of South America, Africa, and Asia, and so are hidden from the eyes of unsuspecting Europeans who have bought into the ideology of secularization – indeed, they are hidden more deeply in a universe of ignorance than are undiscovered fish species in the deepest seas. Muslims in 2015 were numbered at nearly 1.8 billion people – though they, too, are split up many ways into large groups analogous to denominations, with various sects tending toward militancy or else meditation, toward folklorization or indifference. Altogether, statistics suggest that "monotheists" make up more than half of the world's population. In addition, there were, in 2015, 1.1 billion Hindus and half a billion Buddhists, with 14.3 million Jews registered in the club of "world religions" more because of the antiquity of their traditions than because of the importance of their numbers. The old adage about "three rabbis, four opinions" reminds us how far statistical statements can be from the facts of the individualized life of conviction.

For atheists and the religiously indifferent, reliable numbers are hard to come by. The Pew Research Center lists them in its overviews as the "Unaffiliated" and numbers them, as of 2015, at slightly fewer than 1.2 billion.[6] One might conjecture that this group is in fact significantly more numerous, since a large number of them are presumably hidden under masks of formal affiliation to the large collectives. The irreligious, whether declared or undeclared, present a complicated challenge for statistics, since there seems to be a call for marking distinctions between unassuming atheists, the religiously indifferent, the religiously ambivalent, syncretists, avowed laicists, and missionary unbelievers. In total, they compose perhaps a fifth, or even a quarter, of the earth's population. From the perspective of those who theorize an innate religious predisposition common to all human beings, the existence of the religiously indifferent and the denier does not, of itself, constitute a valid objection to their thesis. The religiously indifferent and the denier could well be seekers of God who are still in the preliminary stage of their search. An orientation toward sex, money, and status might belong, in this view, to the preschool of faith, and so its proponents like to cite the old adage that man's extremity is God's opportunity.

Credible numbers are even more difficult to ascertain for animists. The clans and tribes that could authentically be called animist may indeed be numerous, but they are individually too small to play a role in global statistics. Animism's theopoetic trait is its extravagant use of the concepts of the ensouled, the animated, the imbued-with-intention; its adherents exist in the midst of a luxurious superabundance of soulfulness, next to which almost all other forms of belief appear as austerities. If one proceeds from Jean Piaget's theory of cognitive development, according to which young children go through an animistic stage in which the distinction between animate and inanimate is not yet firmly established, one is driven to the conclusion that there are at least 6 billion former animists on earth today. Presuming that most of them have no very acute likelihood of relapsing into the conceptions of early childhood, these ex-animists form an incalculable reserve army for the re-enchantment of the world.

The transformation of the religious "field" – to recall Pierre Bourdieu's paraphysical expression – into a marketplace for faith products necessitates corporatizing the churches both as a precondition and as a consequence. This in turn proved responsive to the rapid change in collective and individual religious receptivity in populations newly capable of reading and voting. What had once been figured as the hubris of understanding – requiring Šubši-mašrâ-Šakkan and Job, for example,[7] to be put in their places – becomes a normal situation in the biblical Gutenberg world, a normality pertaining previously only to the melting pot of Alexandria in late antiquity: those who can read will ask questions. Luther's intervention of October 31, 1517, initially concerned only his doubts as to whether there was Gospel warrant for the mountebank practice in which authorized brokers of the Roman Catholic Church would market and sell "letters of indulgence," with the suggestion that one could thereby buy relief, for oneself and one's relations, from the expiatory purification of purgatory. Viewed from a distance – and not only through a Protestant lens – the indulgence offered for sale was nothing more than a ruse exploiting anxieties about the rigors of purgatory; from the twelfth century onward, often making recourse to the figure of Pope Gregory I (papacy from 590 to 604), purgatory had been placed upstream from eternal hell in order to accommodate the demand of Christians who were anxious for alternatives to irretrievable damnation; to this day, Catholic catechism sustains the beautiful fiction of a post-mortem purification by way of discrete modifications.

As a phenomenon, the Reformation announced that, in matters of religion, the supply side is not everything. Although the universal Church had been divided both theologically and organizationally, since the East–West Schism of 1054, through intractable conflict between Rome and Constantinople, it was not until events of the sixteenth century that denominational conflict emerged, a state of affairs which operated on the Protestant side as a matrix for further differentiations. As soon as the Catholic supply-side monopoly was broken up, and through the centuries that followed, countless products poured into what came rightly to be called the religious marketplace – each better calculated than the last to respond to the voices of demand and the moods of the time and place. In contrast to the mainstream churches, with their inflexible supply-side commitments, didn't most of the more recent prophet-figures claim to have a clearer grasp on what the faithful wanted? Since the seventeenth century, the histories of churches, heretics, and sects, whether impartial or sectarian, concerned themselves much more with what people wanted to believe than with what the apostolic bloc tried to impose on them after the loss of its monopoly. Insofar as they remained bound to the Roman Catholic Church, the notion of purgatory served to ameliorate concerns of a worst-case afterlife. Lutheran Protestants and Calvinist Reformed churches turned their backs on the medieval concept of an intermediate hell;[8] for them, the hard either–or of the old doctrine, allowing for only two possible states, was made bearable by the fact that the believers invested all their energies in the autosuggestion that they themselves would be counted among the saved; on the sinking ship of the world, it's every man for himself and let the devil take the hindmost. Anyone seeking to understand the individualistic erosion of "world society" in the present era should not rest satisfied with neo-antiliberal diagnoses of the "spirit of capitalism." Competition for the scarce commodity of "election" reaches back to the age of the Reformations that shaped Europe – and still further back to the old metaphysical pharmacies of the Middle East.

Together with the will to believe, the wish for specific preferred beliefs enters the picture – and, first and foremost, this involved one's election to eternal life; this wish was bolstered by the supposition that earthly success would allow the successful to infer their election. Since then, the tide of modern practice has been moving as a sum of vectors of self-fulfilling wishful thinking.

The expansion of Pentecostal churches, which has made the leap in recent years from North America to Brazil, speaks very clearly: the strength of the movement derives from those making demands, while its designers import whatever is most in demand at the point of sale – and what is desired are rigid moral rules, simple dogmas, concrete prospects for social success, stable community, protection of children, the binding of men to the family, immunization against crime and drugs and, not least, enthusiastic communal celebrations. With the triad of jubilation, work, and structure, the growing Pentecostal and Evangelical churches of the Global South orient themselves toward the demand of populations who make no secret of their economic, social, cultural, and spiritual deficits. Their plainly expressed need for stability drives a pop culture of simple formulas.

In European modernity, the individual's stance with regard to religious demand followed the laws of miscellany and mixture more than those of orthodoxy. High-, late-, and post-modernity resemble Hellenistic antiquity in their syncretism. Where it was shaped by elements of higher education, modernity sympathized with doctrines coming from outside of the apparently exhausted traditions,[9] and it tended to be skeptical of dogmatism and the tone of pulpit discourse. For the moderns, unchurching and spiritual receptivity were not opposed terms. Abstract friendliness with regard to the strange and foreign was their distinguishing mark. The young Martin Buber hit upon their basic mood in his introductory remarks to his well-known collection *Ecstatic Confessions*: "We listen to our inmost selves – and do not know which sea we hear murmuring."[10]

Anyone in such a mood will find something elevated in literature, edifying in wisdom from the East, sublime in classical music, pathos-inspiring in state funerals, absurd in Kierkegaard, consolatory in the discretion of hospice chaplains, numinous in a wall of art by Anselm Kiefer, and redolent of the Most High looking out from Land's End upon the open sea. For educated persons of recent times, floating in ultimate groundlessness is a commodity dearly purchased. The avant-garde of the Old World had struggled for it since they learned, beginning with the thinkers of the High Middle Ages, to definitively articulate the indefinite.

The behavior of demand, explicitly articulated in terms of truth, meaning, and lifestyle – in elevated religious language: redemption, epiphany, liberation, unbornness – is on display in countless variants of the poetry of seeking. It belongs to the beginning of the age of existentially unsettled individuals breaking from the enclosures of tradition; it is manifest, for example, in the Indian legend of young Siddhārtha Gautama, the overprotected son of a genteel Kshatriya, a member of the warrior caste, who, on four excursions from his father's palace, discovered the negativity of existence. It appeared before his eyes in the form of a decrepit old man, a feverish patient suffering in agony, and a rotting corpse. According to one of the legends of the becoming of the Buddha, the gods presented the young Shakyamuni with the three sights by the wayside as something like test patterns in order to initiate shock therapy.[11] As in any case in which the utmost is transmitted, secondary formulations here also came into their own. On his fourth outing, the young man encountered a monk who drew his attention to the possibility of asceticism: only asceticism could liberate him from the universe of suffering. The fifth departure of the later Buddha opened into a search with no return: he left behind his wife, his son (named Rāhula: "fetter"), and "the world" itself.

The restless subject sallies forth into a specific way of being – the way of the wanderer, the seeker, the spiritual adventurer, the wayfaring hero. In the movements of the search, moments of propulsion through fear and dismay are bound together with those of a powerful current that catches the subject up in anticipations of future liberation that are equally intense and indeterminate. Within the seeker, the entanglement of aversive thrust and end-point attraction generates the structure of a radically subjectified time, forming the arc of a search, from first setting out, to the liberatory discovery. In this way, the essential time assumes its shape as a path: the time of the hero's journey, the time of struggle, the time of training, the time of sanctification, the time of detachment.[12] On this path, patience and impatience negotiate the next steps. It is the time in which the subject emerges as a moving singularity, occasionally with the result that it grasps itself as a non-subject, as a non-ego. As the substance "evolves" as a subject, the evolved subject cancels itself and sublates itself to become a figure of pure mediality – and thus also a teacher of the non-teachable. Those who teach the impossible can be role models for the inimitable.

The main features of the path include the encounter with an individual who points the way to the ascetic modus vivendi, the decision in favor of departure and farewell (Buddhist: "leaving the palace"; Christian: discipleship and *peregrinatio*; Hindu: *sannyasa*, or retreat into renunciation), a trial-and-error phase in the form of attaching oneself to various teachers and teachings – followed by profound disappointment, the great crisis – up to illness, depression and suicidal impulse, resignation and abandonment of the search, and, finally, the advent, the finding, and the epiphany.

In the myriad narratives of seekers, what predominates is the schema of the subject's change over the whole course of the specific path taken. What befell Paul of Tarsus in an almost exemplary manner – that the object of his pursuit seized him along the way and converted him from persecutor to proclaimer – comes to pass, in variants coarser or more refined, wherever seekers are changed by what they find. Where the way proves more rudimentary, what is found retains its object form, and the finder, having overcome certain obstacles, emerges from the search enriched after acquiring some kind of treasure or secret knowledge.

The image of an advanced student of the robust seeking-and-finding relationship can be found, for example, in the figure of the physician Thessalus of Tralles, who, before the turn of the first to the second century CE, was alleged to have been the author of *De virtutibus herbarum*, a treatise on the effects of medicinal herbs in relation to the influences of the stars, with a prefatory letter to Caesar Claudius (10 BCE–4 CE). In the apparently autobiographical preliminary report to his pharmacognostic opus, Thessalus tells of his desperate search for true and effective knowledge – desperate to the verge of suicide, as he tells it: he had spared no journey, however arduous, to gain knowledge. Finally, he reports, a high priest in the Egyptian temple city of Diospolis (Thebes) arranged for him, by aid of magic ritual, an audience with Asclepius, the Greek god of medicine, who revealed to him hitherto unsuspected knowledge about the synergies of stones, stars, and plants, and especially about the cosmically determined favorable moments for harvesting medicinal herbs.[13] Subsequent to his encounter with the god, the seeker considers himself to have achieved the goal he had set out for himself and he happily lauds himself now as a man possessed of both divine and practical knowledge. Thessalus thus claims his place in a line of succession from the early Greek *iatromantis*, in whom the roles of the singer, the healer, and the interpreter of signs were scarcely differentiated. When enlightened solutions are lacking, second-rate conjurers will surface to supply their own answers.

More subtle forms of quest and questioning effectively dissolved the symmetry of seeking and finding by figuring the object as opposed to the search. They made the object vanish before the eyes of the seeker, but without de-realizing it in the mode of "nihilism." As a result, the shift in the subject is actualized in such a way that the seeker is not enriched or aggrandized, but rather undergoes a metamorphosis as a result of the search. Thus, it comes to be said: those who seek shall be found. It is insofar as seekers allow themselves to be found that they undergo their transformation. The object of the search proves elusive and ungraspable, since it evades the ray of the seeker's regard, so to speak. This evasion has a method. So long as it is presented as objectively attainable, what is sought escapes all grasp. Only when the seeker resigns the search that had been envisioned, "forsaking all" (in the phrasing of the mystics), can what is sought present itself in the subject as its own locus of perception. What is sought is that which seeks. The great aspirations – truth, God, meaning, nature, happiness, wisdom, redemption, epiphany, etc. – lie outside the brain game of "attainment." They are located in the heart of the spontaneity and restlessness that set the search in motion. The ego, which reflects on itself in order to self-seekingly gain an image of itself, will sooner or later see that it has no further business here. Whatever is spontaneous in the subject cannot be the type of finding or discovery that would just fall into the hands of a seeker after a sufficiently patient search. There is an elan that forever pre-empts me. It is there inside me, wanting, but without saying what it would like.

In his late-period treatise *De venatione sapientiae* (*On the Pursuit of Wisdom*, 1463), Nicholas of Cusa mapped the landscapes of the attainable and the unattainable with a clarity for which there is no counterpart in modern thought. The point of the Cusanian equation of thought, life, and pursuit or hunt was illustrated a good 100 years later, through the allegory of the hunter Actaeon, in Giordano Bruno's work *De gli furori heroici* (*The Heroic Frenzies*, 1585). Here, the paradox of the search for truth comes to light even more clearly than with Nicholas of Cusa.

Actaeon is said to have accidentally surprised Diana while she was bathing naked in the woods, whereupon the goddess transformed the hunter into a stag, to be pursued, attacked, and torn to pieces by his own hounds. In Bruno's reading, the initially hidden purpose of the hunt is to turn the prey-maker into the prey, the hunter into the hunted. The hounds are the thoughts of the hero seeking after divine things; they devour Actaeon's physical and psychological existence so that he will no longer try to appropriate the image of the goddess Nature with a wishful eye. Since he was discovered by the one he sought, Actaeon is no longer the man that he had been; his individuality has been decomposed in order to reach his objective as part of the unity that courses through every limb and link of nature. The fate of Actaeon plainly forms a metaphor for death; it translates the about-turned hunt into a cognitive *Liebestod*. Is it that what is known from the realm of the senses shouldn't be possible in the realm of knowledge? It is notable here that Actaeon is not said to have gazed upon the naked goddess through the eyes of male desire; instead, his glance functions as source of a ray that strives for union without physical hindrance. The vision of Diana arouses nostalgia for the splendor of the divine as such; any supposition that there might be vaginal access to the same never enters into consideration.[14]

The poetry of the search is expressed in stories about the journey. The feature they share in common is that the movements of setting out and seeking can be narrated, whereas the condition of the seeker after arrival cannot. Since there is nothing to narrate concerning one whose discovery or finding has already been accomplished, it can subsequently be claimed that there was nothing to be found in the first place. When such claims circulate more widely, some will conclude that there is no need to set out in the first place – why, or to what purpose, does one tread a path, when the path itself is the objective? Why inquire into higher things, if, when all is said and done, everything runs its course on a single plane? The serenity of those devoted to train station-bookstore esoterica will smother all the poetry of the search.

In 1961, the American novelist Walker Percy depicted a modern variant of aimlessly searching consciousness with his figure of an apathetic young man from Louisiana named Binx Bolling, who passes his days at the cinema:

Neither my mother's family nor my father's family understand my search.

My mother's family think I have lost my faith and they pray for me to recover it. I don't know what they're talking about. Other people, so I have read, are pious as children and later become skeptical (or, as they say on This I Believe: "in time I outgrew the creeds and dogmas of organized religion"). Not I. My unbelief was invincible from the beginning. I could never make head or tail of God. The proofs of God's existence may have been true for all I know, but it didn't make the slightest difference. If God himself had appeared to me, it would have changed nothing. In fact, I have only to hear the word God and a curtain comes down in my head.

My father's family think that the world makes sense without God and that anyone but an idiot knows what the good life is and anyone but a scoundrel can lead it.

I don't know what either of them are talking about. Really I can't make head or tail of it. The best I can do is lie rigid as a stick under the cot, locked in a death grip with everydayness, sworn not to move a muscle until I advance another inch in my search....

The only possible starting point: the strange fact of one's own invincible apathy....

Abraham saw signs of God and believed. Now the only sign is that all the signs in the world make no difference.[15]

20

FREEDOM OF RELIGION

In Walker Percy's narrative, the young man from Louisiana involuntarily fulfills one definition of what an older tradition called negative theology. Its rule of the game was that the Most High should be kept free from all predicates; only as a name without qualities would it be sealed off from the encroachments of representational thinking. The very word "God," whether used as a noun or as a form of address, risks generating an excess that tarnishes the inexpressibility of what is designated.

"All the signs in the world make no difference." One can read this confession from Percy's hero as if he were searching for a truth that asked for neither evidence nor persuasion. For him, the time of signs and wonders is over and done with – in his eyes, a god who would traffic in that sort of thing would be like a used-car dealer seeking to direct the attention of customers away from hidden defects. The apathetic young man is convinced that, however he came to make his appearance in the world, his existence there was not purchased through any friendly clasp of hands.

"The strange fact of one's own invincible apathy" can be construed as a Louisiana cogito. It does not permit inferences to be made from a thinking in progress, to the existence of the one thinking; it points from an existence congealed here, to an enlivening sensed somewhere in the far distance. Apathy forms the starting point of a striving toward its own opposite. It expresses the revolt against automated existence, and the absence of any earnestly held conviction. By holding fast to his lack of motivation, the main character in Walker Percy's novel discovers, *ex negativo*, the "utopia of motivated life." To insist on the absence of any convictions that might give one purpose is tantamount to a negative confession: no axiom of belief prompts assent, no ritual act is deemed effective or true; the darkness in one's head spreads from the moment the word "God" is uttered. If there were gods today who tried to use traditional persuasive means to talk people into believing, it would provoke only compassionate skepticism – they would have nothing more to offer than a hand-me-down religiosity. Twenty years before Walker Percy's novel, Jean-Paul Sartre remarked, with reference to Nietzsche's well-known dictum, "He is dead: he used to speak to us and he has fallen silent.... Perhaps he has slipped out of the world to some other place, like a dead man's soul. Perhaps all this was merely a dream.... God is dead, but men have not, for all that, become atheists [athée]."[1]

Percy's moviegoer is not to be taken simply as a random witness to modern alienation. He is memorable because, in his out-of-the-way mystical quarter, he demonstrated that seeking is an impulse independent of the existence or non-existence of its aim. Persons engaged in the search reserve the right to non-belief – and would do so, even if God himself were to drag them by the hair in the direction of belief. Seeking insists on this prerogative: not being forced to find.

Leaving aside whatever might be advanced in favor of the state of being a seeker – patented mystics extol it as a dry bath in a tub-full of doubt – from a realistic point of view, it is at first nothing more than a variant of perplexity. People get into it when they are in over their heads, when there is an insufficiency in their internal faculties for navigating their external situation. Persons susceptible to perplexity include individuals who forsake their role models as well as collectives whose leaders confess (or let it be seen) that they no longer understand the world. Perplexity also characterizes times in which traditions are perceived as idle self-reference, lacking vital connection to the privations and excesses of the present day. Those who suffer perplexity experience freedom from its dark side. Freedom might be exalted to any height in a thousand speeches – but still, to individuals who are serious about it, it also exhibits itself as a confused indefiniteness, not infrequently as a noxious lack of connectedness, as having been cast without resource into a situation that is wildly beyond control. To suggest a psychological counterpart for an ontological formula, the "being-immersed in nothingness" evoked by the early Heidegger manifests itself in states of indecision, vacillation, and the collapse of ground from beneath one's feet. In the 1920s, such conditions became pandemic among Europeans – regardless of whether they fancied themselves among the winners or the losers of the First World War. There is a fiendish floating feeling – one knows it from dreams in which the agonizing indistinctness of a situation persists until one awakens out of it – a hovering sensation that arises from the feeling that one has come to be subjected to existence without having been briefed on its essentials. For the time being, work and any number of diversions will protect us against the awareness, the knowledge, of there being actually nothing to do.

From the point of view of philosophical anthropology, as it came to maturity in the twentieth century, "human being" represents more than just that entity distinguished by its "eccentric positionality," to use Helmuth Plessner's phrase; humans are fundamentally exposed to the risk of perplexity and indecision, compelled to act – "condemned to freedom" – even as, looking inward, one discerns an invariable insufficiency in the subject's grounds for action. *Homo anthropologicus* finds an under-motivated, under-inspired, under-determined existence – unless the subject has experienced, from childhood on, such stable imprintings that a single set of convictions will suffice for a lifetime. The underdisciplined subject will, furthermore, lack the crutch of routines to help with getting through the day. Ego-forming rituals are then suspended, and neither work nor structure will lead any further. It follows from this that, for many, the balance between doing and not doing remains tilted to the side of not-doing – it is the few who set the tone by doing, whether they do so out of conviction or from the joy of playing with unbound forces.

It would be a fallacy to conclude from this that the nature of *Homo sapiens* is essentially characterized by deficiency – and it remains a fallacy even when committed by authors such as Johann Gottfried Herder and Arnold Gehlen. "Human being" is not a deficient entity; it forms a section in the arc of elan that generates vague options and eligible aims. Freedom and scope of action grow in tandem with one another. From the outset, humans have been characterized by a luxury – they are the beings who, through a "body-liberation,"[2] through the de-specialization of their physical endowments, stumbled their way into the privileged embarrassment of openness to the world. Above all, they benefit from the freeing of hands for polyvalent grasping, and from the unlimited increase in their language gifts. More than by anything else, their luxuriant nature is denoted by the release of perception and awareness into a hovering, a floating, that is unfocused, unharnessed from intention, and far removed from alarm.

From attempts to resolve indeterminacy, remedy confusion, and reduce astonishment, all disciplines and instances of rational practice emerged in the course of cultural evolutions: oracles, the priestly arts of reading signs, medical theories of the nature of symptoms, the culture of debate, the judiciary, wisdom literature, astronoetics, philosophy, theorizing forms of the state – in sum, the basic manifestations of reason in its advisory, sedative, deliberative, and orienting forms. The common character of these disciplines is apparent in the fact that, almost without exception, they first appeared on the scene as woven into religioid, mythical, and cultic patterns. And yet: intertwinements of these kinds all subsequently proved to be extricable bonds. The ties that did prove impossible to disentangle were bound to written form, which – at different times, but first in Mesopotamia and Egypt – penetrated civilizations and made possible more complex structures of memory culture in the interplay of book and memory. The cultural evolutions of the past 3,000 years have demonstrated that every single one of these rational disciplines was able to emancipate itself from its symbiosis with the spheres of rites, sacrifice, and myths of the gods. The myth of the "Axial Age" was an inapt attempt – not without some measure of insight – to supply an umbrella term for the staggered beginnings of various emancipations in widely divergent cultures.

With regard to the phenomenon of "religion," these emancipations suggest that what "religion" means has always been a joint venture of otherworldly and this-worldly practices, often endowed with extravagant and theatrical features. No one knows why celebrants at a festival in honor of the ancestors in Melanesia wore heavy masks up to 10 meters high on their heads. It is understood that people around the world cultivate affiliation with their forebears, but the local arts of remembrance are self-governing. They don't solve a problem, they give shape to puzzles. Tribal comrades show their gratitude to the battered mask wearers by tending to the wounds on their shoulders after the festival.

To the extent that this-worldly practices crystallized into autonomous procedures that satisfied adherents through their immanent coherence, other-worldly practices were relegated to mere symbolic gestures of little consequence. When, at their inauguration ceremonies, presidents of the United States of America swear their oaths upon the Bible, they show the true state of affairs before the cameras of all the world – regardless of whether or not the person takes the oath uttering the formula *So help me God*. The oath may be sworn upon a Bible, the Bible may have been owned by Abraham Lincoln – but this matters as little for foreign policy as it does for public finances. For the duration of a minute, the other-worldly is bidden to the table in Washington; thereafter, as before, pragmatism is the sole determining factor in power, and it is only as potential coalition partners for a presidential election that transcendently composed sects find themselves of interest for the temporary residents of the White House.

The Enlightenment, which has been emanating from Europe since the seventeenth century, is grounded in a consent to processes that work toward the autonomy of this-world practices – science, the state together with its tax authorities, police, prison operations and the military, the judiciary, as well as local administration and the school system; to which one might add economics, mechanical engineering, transport and tourism, medicine, the art scene, sociability, neighborhood culture, communications and the media, social insurance practices, statistics, demography, birth control, future planning, environmental protection, etc. The consequence of this independence – "differentiation" in the technical language of systems theory – is shown in the fact that established religion (traditionally regarded as universally relevant), together with its morality, is now reduced to merely simulating the supercompetence in any and all domains that was once taken as its self-evident property. To assert religion's universal competence as if it were a fact is no longer in its power today, and lies for the most part far beyond the radius of its ambition. Exceptions might be asserted for some Islamic and Catholic countries, where it makes for the experience that religion interferes with almost everything.

In the incomplete Enlightenment, "religion" must confine itself to the field it can claim as its own. It does not, on its own authority, decide on the delimitation, since its field is defined as a residual domain within the structure of modern life practices – a residual field from which other applicants have withdrawn, or for which they are only half-heartedly competing. When German soldiers fall in Afghanistan, a minister of state will lead the ceremony, possibly with the assistance of denominational representatives. When a pandemic breaks out, churches, synagogues, and mosques are closed; virologists and ministers of health are the ones who interpret the situation.

Of all the determinations of the "religions" – whether they were called *therapeia theon* or *cultus deorum*, whether one sees in them systems of scruples or projections of intrinsic human powers upon the screen of the heavens, whether one interprets them as irradiations of the divine in the human spirit, or as traces of the resentment that the dead hold against the living, or as "the sigh of the oppressed creature," or quite simply as guilt feelings coupled to various holidays – essentially, only one statement remains valid within the horizon of a modernity that officiates as the current cohort of a humanity pressuring itself to learn: "religion" is composed of the remainder of worldviews originating in civilizations variously archaic and great – it is what is left over, once one has subtracted out those manifestations of life now replaced by pragmatic and secular forms.

Conceived as a vanishingly small but not further reducible remainder, religion would be nothing more than a manifestation of human freedom in face of the embarrassment of beings who are ill equipped in the world. If it were to have a function entirely and unconditionally its own – something inarguable, untranslatable, and indispensable – it would consist in suggesting a meaning, an effect, an aspiration, a relation to the "truth" of existence, which could not have appeared without the tension of existence as such, the exposure to a stream of events open to surprise.

Human beings are not merely the "animal with classics," as Ortega y Gasset put it; humans are the living beings in which "it" begins to speak. At some point, the power of speech led to utterances in which the heavens – the divine point of origin – addressed themselves to human beings by way of suitable intermediaries. Perhaps such conversations are nothing more than the mirages that occur when language disports itself. If this were the case, the addressees of great language events would have their parts to play too. They would have to adapt themselves in accordance with the sender. When the gods make their pronouncements, their human transmitters become mediums, mouthpieces, performers. The fact that such speech actually appeared on the scene from elsewhere, and was not just produced out of the everyday speech of collaborators playing their parts, shows this much: if the heavens could not be brought to speak for themselves, it was nevertheless possible to make language speak in ringing speeches of exalted quality. The occasionally attested shying-away of early singers, poets, and prophets, with respect to what language said in and through them, can be taken as evidence that the uncanny exists and dwells among us. Concrete religions are styles of the uncanny.

If one accepts the definition of religion as the remainder left over after subtracting everything that migrates into science, economics, the judiciary, medicine, general therapeutics, media theory, linguistics, ethnology, popular literature, political science, etc., then one retains a domain that can be designated – simply, if vaguely – as a comprehensive aid to the interpretation of existence, right up to the illumination of the inaccessible and the domestication of the uncanny. Even moral and legal groundings, which in the early Enlightenment were still considered within the domain of the religious – albeit preferably in the mode of "natural religion" and the religion of reason – have now long assumed independent standing and no longer require heavenly underpinnings.

Once this has been established, two things follow that have not hitherto been explicitly stated as such. The first says that religion or religiosity has become simply free in the present for the first time since it emerged from the fog of angst and intuition over Paleolithic landscapes – free in the sense of its complete release from all social functions; this, of course, only applies to parts of the world where, under the pretext of a modern "freedom of religion," there is no longer any evocation of tangible, coercive community affiliations, such as those persisting and politically promoted in Erdoğan's Turkey, notwithstanding its secular constitution. The freedom of religion, as it was articulated in the declarations of human rights at the end of the eighteenth century, thus no longer means just the entitlement of the individual to choose or eschew one or another cult community, or to articulate or conceal any conjectures and convictions concerning the transcendent – and to do so free from the prior censorship of any office of orthodox authority. Far more than that, freedom of religion implies the thesis that religion as a whole is released from the function of furnishing a political collective – a "community," a "society," a "people," a "nation" – with the pre-eminent motive for its current togetherness.

"Freedom of religion," grasped as a legally protected right that adheres inalienably to individuals at the age of majority, not only assures citizens of the unenforceability of denomination and cult participation, it means above all that there should be no state religion under any circumstance, including no state atheism, and that it is not as a religious project, even in part, that the citizenry of a given state should grasp their social synthesis – that is, the strong basis for their coexistence in the space of a regional entity, under common body of law, with a common language, and, if possible, with shared memory.[3] The state is not allowed to do what the sects are allowed to do. Those who speak of civil religion or consider one to be desirable (or necessary) participate in mostly regressive fictions;[4] such pronouncements are hardly better than the pretensions of the Catholic Church in 1864, which, through the mouth of the Pope, fundamentally rejected the idea of any freedom of religion.[5] A state believes in nothing except that it should exist to advance the interests of its members. Its citizens agree to its existence – that is to say, to its legally structured agency – and they do so without considering it a god, notwithstanding Thomas

Hobbes's wish to elevate it to a Leviathan in the context of his era of political strife and disunity.

In consequence of being released into the sphere of the socially useless, religion as such has become free. It is one of the achievements of modernity to have allowed religion (and religions) to make their exodus into virtual asociality. Asociality in matters of faith is the inviolable privilege of the individual; of these, each and every one is, in the first instance, alone with his and her sense and taste for the infinite – or whatever one wants to call the total X of Being. As may regard declared religious communities, they are de facto under the protection of the secular right of assembly and association, or under a civilized analogue tailored for churches, which are entitled to respect as corporations under public law; they acquire legal capacity according to the general provisions of civil code – even if they prefer to say of themselves that they are the Mystical Body of the Lord or the community of the Rightly Guided. The major churches today – the Roman Catholic Church above all – as "church tax churches" indulged (even caressed, dare one say) by the secular state, enjoy de facto benefits from a freedom that, until recently, they did everything they could to resist. Ever since they have come to seem powerless, they have been courting the sympathy of those who are no longer very much faithful. An authentically modern "society," that is, one animated entirely through the spirit of a self-imposed constitution, would have replaced all the socially relevant auxiliary services of religious tradition – from educating young people and building moral consensus, through charitable solidarism, to caring for the welfare of the sick, the weak, and the marginal – with system-specific institutions, but without hindering the continuing contributions to such tasks made by religious communities. The much-cited thesis known as the Böckenförde dilemma (1964) – to the effect that the liberal, secularized state lives by prerequisites which it cannot guarantee itself – applies to an era of transition from the contemporary state church system to the secular, religiously pluralistic situation. Once that has come to pass – at least in the context of western European conditions – social capital thenceforth derives to only a lesser extent from pre-secular traditions. It is composed of daily political sensitivities, civic engagements, historical and ethnic knowledge, as well as all forms of solidarism and their articulation in old and new media. Its regeneration through generational processes is increasingly taking on experimental features. Its fate will depend on the degree to which it succeeds in converting raw sentimentality out of fear, and *ressentiment* and trust, into informed empathy – a process formerly known as education.

The fact that "religion" in the present can for the first time be defined as quite simply free – notwithstanding conspicuous tendencies toward identitarian closure and defensive efforts to preserve the status quo – is essentially related to the second novelty, which follows from the reduction of the religious to a remnant in the midst of omnipresent, secular, mostly state-financed, but often also civic-minded substitute formations for its own former socially directed partial functions.

The second liberation of religion reveals its affinity with two intimate rivals. Liberated religious impulses are forced to concede that in their own field – the interpretation of existence in the context of its contingency, its finitude, its need for happiness, and its communicativity – two other forces are active at the same time: art and philosophy, insofar as the latter remains contemplative of wisdom. If it is true that liberated religion concerns itself with the interpretation of existence in its most general contexts, with the domestication of contingency, and with the shaping of mortality, then it is apparent why it finds itself in a rivalrous relationship in these areas with contemplative philosophy and freely creative art. As is well known, the arts, both linguistic and extra-linguistic, have only existed "as such" since they emancipated themselves from their servitude to religious cults; philosophy speaks on its own behalf only since quitting its position as a handmaid to theology. It was in keeping with the dynamism of both fields that, in the conquest of the useless – and in the liberation of their self-will – they were one epochal step ahead of religion. Religion – to persist with the fatal term – was only able to follow art and philosophy out into free and open spaces, once it had been denationalized, depoliticized, and completely relocated to the associative, or separate, life of individuals who were able to take care of themselves.

The sure sign of the fledgling freedom for religion is found in its surprising, uplifting, scandalous uselessness; it is superfluous, like music – and yet, as is said, "without music, life would be a mistake." Religion shares its luxurious character with the two other cultures of the interpretation of existence that have already broken through to their own independence. Since it no longer has to serve an external purpose, religion can draw parts of human experience to itself that would otherwise be at home, with individuals and with groups, in moments that are musical, meditative, sublime, lost, or devastating.

All other significant functions of a more official nature, previously assuming religious form – such as the cults of emperors and princes, the superelevation of the state, maintenance of the festival calendar, the blessings of armies and marriages, the education of youths, the consecration of buildings, the celebration of harvests, the security of oaths, the pastoral care of souls, management of sexuality, caring for the sick and the poor, psychagogic counseling, counsel with regard to last things, and the administration of rites of passage – all these subsequently prove to be secondary services which, as history shows, can be handed over to secular agencies, sometimes at a loss, but not infrequently with equal or better success. Even the contributions of religion to the formation of the ego and superego can, as has been observed since the eighteenth century, be supplied by substitute secular influences. The innumerable manifestations of contemporary mass culture in folk festivals, sporting events, and pop concerts are proof that modernity has likewise succeeded in secularizing collective elations.[6]

After subtracting out all that has proven to be replaceable by secular systems, it becomes apparent what, in the religious, cannot be replaced, except through the creative arts and reflective thought. The religious, now subtractively constituted, exhibits almost no similarities at all with the profiles of historical religions – which should not surprise anyone, when one considers the enslavement of the whole religious system, as formerly constituted, through the responsibility it had assumed for all aspects of social life before the differentiation of its sub-domains. What remains of the historical religions are writings, gestures, and soundscapes that occasionally still help the individual of our day to relate to the embarrassment and perplexity of their unique existence by way of formulas that are at once annulled and lifted up. The rest is composed of attachments of loyalty, together with a longing to participate.

The interpretation of existence, in its singularity and in its inter-weaving with other singularities, forms the manifestation and the irreducible nuclear function of religious and spiritual reflection – which it shares with the other two voices of the trio. Was there an archaic cult that wasn't also poetry, drama, and (first) music?[7] Didn't the first poetry already speak to the gods? And wasn't the first music, through its resounding and its fading away, an indication of the intense presence of serious and high-spirited powers?

It has long been clear to contemporaries in the present age that poetry, which was first declared to be creation, could not be brought to a standstill with the creation of man on the evening of the sixth day. Nobody rests any longer on the seventh day unless in a creative rest, preparing for the next days of genesis. And what should Sabbath and Sunday discourse be about, if not about dawnings that have yet to shine?

In lieu of an afterword

In §300 of *The Gay Science* (1882), Nietzsche plays with the idea that "the whole of *religion* might yet appear as a prelude and exercise to some distant age" – that is, as an indispensable preliminary training to be overcome for the heightening of self-awareness in individuals.[1] Prometheus was a forerunner of such great individuals when, fixed to his rock in the Caucasus, he fancied that, by being shackled there, he might atone for the theft of fire and light through which he had opened the door to human history. Prometheus could only have experienced his greatest moment, however, when he awoke from his delusion to discover that his whole history was his own work: "and that not only man but also the *god* was the work of his own hands and had been mere clay in his hands? All mere images of the maker – no less than the fancy, the theft, the Caucasus, the vulture, and the whole tragic *Prometheia* of all seekers after knowledge?"[2]

Is it possible to imagine that Paul of Tarsus could awaken from his apostolic dream at a later date? To discover the extent to which his undertaking, with all its incidents, was his own product: yes, that the journey to Damascus, his bedazzlement at the approach to the city, his hearing of the voice of Jesus, his conversion and everything that followed from it, all were his own creation, a creation that enveloped its own author – including the flash of light, the voice, and the fall to the hard ground of Syria, where he invented himself as a medium for his Lord, a medium that, since he had love, could speak in the tongues of mortals and of angels without becoming a noisy gong or a clanging cymbal – while his horse bowed its head to him, sharing in the wonderment of the event.

In 1918, Franz Kafka drafted a picture of thought that looks back to the ancient world and to the mythical antiquity that preceded it. It appeared posthumously in 1931 in a collection for which Max Brod and Hans-Joachim Schoeps edited as yet unpublished items from the poet's estate, under the title *The Great Wall of China*. I would call it "the entropic fable." It reports in lapidary style on the result of the metaphysical revolt:

Figure 2. Michelangelo Merisi da Caravaggio, *Conversion on the Way to Damascus* (1601), oil on canvas, Santa Maria del Popolo, Rome. Album / Alamy Stock Photo.

There are four legends concerning Prometheus:

According to the first he was clamped to a rock in the Caucasus for betraying the secrets of the gods to men, and the gods sent eagles to feed on his liver, which was perpetually renewed.

According to the second Prometheus, goaded by the pain of the tearing beaks, pressed himself deeper and deeper into the rock until he became one with it.

According to the third his treachery was forgotten in the course of thousands of years, forgotten by the gods, the eagles, forgotten by himself.

According to the fourth everyone grew weary of the meaningless affair. The gods grew weary, the eagles grew weary, the wound closed wearily.

There remained the inexplicable mass of rock. The legend tried to explain the inexplicable. As it came out of a substratum of truth it had in turn to end in the inexplicable.[3]

Notes

Acknowledgments

1 [Translator's note] See Johann Wolfgang von Goethe, *Correspondence between Schiller and Goethe: From 1794 to 1805*. Vol. II: *1798–1805*, trans. L. Dora Schmitz (London: George Bell and Sons, 1879): 182.

Preface

1 [Translator's note] See Heinrich Heine, "Germany: A Winter's Tale." Trans. Aaron Kramer. *Poetry and Prose*, ed. Jost Hermand and Robert C. Holub (New York: Continuum, 1982): 231–97.
2 [Translator's note] See Charles Baudelaire, "The Pot Lid." *The Flowers of Evil*, trans. James McGowan (Oxford University Press, 1993): 333–5.

1 The gods in the theatre

1 *Odyssey* I.64, trans. Richmond Lattimore (New York: HarperCollins, 2007).
2 Cf. Émile Durkheim, *The Elementary Forms of Religious Life* (1912), trans. Karen E. Field (New York: The Free Press, 1995): "The tribal high god is actually none other than an ancestral spirit that eventually won a prominent place" (299) – that is, one who comes to transcend the circle of the clan. Durkheim's statement refers to the cosmos of the Arunta tribe among the Australian aborigines.
3 Aristotle, *Rhetoric* 3.7.4, 1408a: http://data.perseus.org/citations/urn:cts:greekLit:tlg0086.tlg038.perseus-eng1:3.7.4.
4 Up to the ransom (*lytron*) that heaven pays to loosen the knot of sin in human beings or, from a different perspective, as a transfer fee to deliver humans, from being in service to the devil to existing in freedom under God.

5 Cf. Ludwig Feuerbach, *The Essence of Christianity* (1841), 2nd edn., trans. Marian Evans (London: Trübner & Co., 1881): "Darkness is the mother of religion" (193). A generalized concept of religion emerges after the sixteenth century as a hybrid of Enlightenment anthropology and the Christian world mission. The first concluded, from the universal fact of death, that religion must likewise be universal. The second assumed that all people on earth had been awaiting the gospel of a salvation that would overcome death. It is true that many people in many cultures buried their closest relatives with a certain amount of care (*religio*), occasionally with valuable grave goods – as attested, for example, by the Iron Age graves of princes and children; but this does not change the fact that, for a majority of people in a majority of cultures, a simple, cultically low-profile "corpse disposal" (Jörg Rüpke) had to suffice.

6 Jan Rohls, *Offenbarung, Vernunft und Religion: Ideengeschichte des Christentums*, Vol. I (Tübingen: Mohr Siebeck, 2012).

7 [Translator's note] The reference is to the opening lines of Hölderlin's hymn, "Patmos." See Friedrich Hölderlin, *Poems and Fragments*, 4th Bilingual edn., trans. Michael Hamburger (London: Anvil Press Poetry, 2004): 551–65.

8 In his work *Creation of the Sacred: Tracks of Biology in Early Religions* (Cambridge, MA: Harvard University Press, 1998), Walter Burkert explicates Protagoras' term *adelótes* (unclearness, nonevidence) as a defining feature of the religious sphere (5–6).

9 *Odyssey* VII.201–5.

10 In the literature of the twentieth century, the *locus classicus* of blasphemy committed at the level of affect is found at the end of the second part of Thomas Mann's tetralogy *Joseph and His Brothers*, when Jacob, in his grief over the supposed death of his favorite son Joseph, mounts an excess of lamentation, a fact which comes to distress him once his grief abates: "In silent embarrassment he recalled his reckless bickering and arguing with God in that first flowering of his sorrow and found it in no way an act of a God holding to His old ways, but rather regarded it as truly refined and holy of Him that He had not crushed him on the spot and instead in silent forbearance had let him sport with his misery" – Thomas Mann, *Joseph and His Brothers*, trans. John E. Woods (New York: Alfred A. Knopf, 2005): 538.

11 Adolf von Harnack, *Marcion: The Gospel of the Alien God*, trans. John E. Steely and Lyle D. Bierma (Eugene, OR: Wipf & Stock, 1990): 12.

12 [Translator's note] The reference is to Peter L. Berger and Thomas Luckmann, *The Social Construction of Reality: A Treatise in the Sociology of Knowledge* (New York: Anchor Books, 1966). See chapter 7 below.

13 In its own way, "ethnoastronomy" discovers the Saussurean arbitrariness of the sign – only, as it were, from the other side, as an arbitrariness of the signified: the constellation of the seven main stars, which the Greeks called the Great Bear, had the most various names among other peoples. The ancient Egyptians saw in it "the head of a procession, the ancient Romans seven plough oxen, the Arabs a coffin followed by three mourners, more recent North American Indians and

French a 'big dipper,' the English a plough, the Chinese a court official visited by supplicants, medieval Europeans the 'Great Wagon.'" Quoted from: Carsten Colpe, *Weltdeutungen im Widerstreit* (Berlin and New York: Walter de Gruyter, 1999): 119.

14 Matthew 16:3.

15 In his work *The Star of Redemption* (1921), Franz Rosenzweig undertook to de-astralize the motif of the heavenly sign in order to classify it, in a continuum of Jewish orientations, as an ethically transcendent model of human history beyond Babylon and Bethlehem.

16 Matthew 2:1–11.

17 Kai Trampedach, *Politische Mantik: Die Kommunikation über Götterzeichen und Orakel im klassischen Griechenland* (Heidelberg: Verlag Antike, 2015).

18 Virgil, *Aeneid* VI.850. The full sentence spoken by Anchises ("Roman, remember by your strength to rule Earth's peoples – for your arts are to be these: to pacify, to impose the rule of law, to spare the conquered, battle down the proud") is the key expression of Virgilian prophecy. It seeks a retrospective transfer of empire and happiness from Troy to Rome; even beforehand, it proves effective for the translations of the empire from Rome to Byzantium – and thence to Aachen, Vienna, Moscow, London, and Washington. See Rémi Brague's book *Eccentric Culture: A Theory of Western Civilization*, trans. Samuel Lester (South Bend, IN: St. Augustine's Press, 2002) for (among other things) a consideration of how the series of imperial transfers continued even after the Virgilian operation between Troy and Rome.

19 Exodus 31:18.

20 I-am statements in the mouths of gods belong to the theo-rhetorical conventions of Hellenism at the time when John was writing his Gospel (whether that writing is dated early or late); the best-known model is provided by the self-declaring aretalogy of Isis, which is presumed to have been ritually recited by a priestess of Isis at Cyme. See Jan Bergmann, *Ich bin Isis. Studien zum memphitischen Hintergrund der griechischen Isis-Aretalogien* (Uppsala: Almqvist & Wiksell, 1968).

21 There are, of course, disputes around the dating of the Gospel of John: whether to the early (and unlikely) year of 69 or 70, as suggested by Klaus Berger in his book *Im Anfang war Johannes: Datierung und Theologie des vierten Evangeliums* (Stuttgart: Quell, 1997), or else to a date around 100, as is more generally accepted. But, with all due respect for the flying sparks of philological argument on both sides, this debate claims little relevance from the point of view of the interpretation assigned retrospectively to the Passion. Whether the canonical evangelists copied from one another or not, and whether John got involved early or late in the interpretation process (if one accepts the trend toward early dating), they were all of them, almost half a century *post eventum*, scenarists and theopoets who shared a common interest in turning the Golgotha debacle into a programmatic act. The question of dating will be taken up again later, in chapter 18, in order to highlight the poetic contribution of witnesses who spoke later.

22 Seneca dedicated his essay *De clementia* (c. 55 CE) to the 18-year-old Nero with the notion of allowing the precocious murderer to contemplate the

mirror of an idealistic prince. Just 10 years later, Nero ordered Seneca to commit suicide.

23 *Epistulae morales ad Lucilium*, Letter 37.

24 When Caesar Augustus temporarily suspended the *missio*, he wanted to rescind the privilege that had been accorded to the sentimental mob – only the Caesar, he thought, should be entitled to grant reprieve.

25 On the classic theme of the evasion accomplished by drifting thoughtlessly through life, see Martin Heidegger, *Being and Time*, trans. Joan Stambaugh (Albany: State University of New York Press, 2010): §§51–2.

26 Georg Wilhelm Friedrich Hegel, *Lectures on the Philosophy of Religion*, Vol. III: *The Consummate Religion*, ed. Peter Hodgson (Berkeley: University of California Press, 1998): 305.

27 Georg Wilhelm Friedrich Hegel, *Lectures on the Philosophy of Religion*, Vol. I: *Introduction and The Concept of Religion*, ed. Peter Hodgson (Oxford: Clarendon Press, 2007): 329.

28 Frank Morison [Albert Henry Ross], *Who Moved the Stone?* (London: Faber & Faber, 1930).

29 In his novel *L'Évangile selon Pilate* (Paris: Albin Michel, 2000), Éric-Emmanuel Schmitt developed the criminological perspective on the disappearance of Jesus' body in order to convert Pontius Pilate, a skeptic, into the "first Christian," once alternate explanations are revealed as dead ends.

30 See First Epistle to the Corinthians 15:12–20.

31 Agnes Horvath and Arpad Szakolczai, *Walking into the Void: A Historical Sociology and Political Anthropology of Walking* (London and New York: Routledge, 2018): 149–60.

2 Plato's contestation

1 Plato used the concept only once, in *Republic*, Book II. There, however, we find it in an unspecific reference to "the patterns or norms of right speech about the gods" (379a). A more explicit equation of God (*to theos*) with the good (*agathon*) is made in the *Phaedrus* dialogue.

2 One might also ask how Jesus could have known of the existence of the Archons, Athens's city magistrates (later, the "rulers" more generally), chosen by lot.

3 A hint of this embarrassment can be found in the writings of Martin Luther, whose belief in the devil conformed to the orthodoxy of his day, and who notes in his interpretation of Psalm 117 from 1530: "I must grant the devil his hour of godliness and ascribe the Satanic to our God. But this is not the whole story."

3 Of the true religion

1 This is developed in a later chapter – chapter 17, "Poetry of exaggeration: religious virtuosos and their excesses."

2 Friedrich Nietzsche, *On the Genealogy of Morals*, "Third Essay: What

Is the Meaning of Ascetic Ideals?" §11, in *Basic Writings of Nietzsche*, trans. and ed. Walter Kaufmann (New York: Modern Library, 1968): 552–4.

3 "A Fond Note on Myth," in Paul Valéry, *The Outlook for Intelligence*, trans. Denise Folliot and Jackson Mathews (Princeton University Press, 1989): 39.

4 Adolf von Harnack, *History of Dogma*, Vol. I, trans. Neil Buchanan (Boston: Little, Brown, and Company, 1899): 243.

5 Max Scheler's section on "The Renewal of Religion," in his neo-Catholic opus *On the Eternal in Man*, trans. Bernard Noble (London: SCM Press Ltd, 1960), elaborates on an ontomasochistic structure of "primary religious experience": everything that makes up "the world" is simply too much for the subject because of its enormous breadth and diversity. Feeling supplies an answer (and objectivist ontology begins) with this figure of thought: next to the immeasurable, everything else is absolutely nothing. I am nothing, and what there is without me is everything. The masochistic turn ensues when feeling elevates Being to the status of the Lord, from whose hands feeling would welcome its own effacement.

6 [Translator's note] "Die religiös Musikalischen": a phrase originating with a formulation by the sociologist Max Weber, who described himself as "religiously unmusical" (i.e., constitutionally insusceptible to the enchantments offered by religion), but since echoed by philosophers Richard Rorty and Jürgen Habermas. See Willy Pfändtner, "Religiously (Un)musical, Musically (Un)religious" in *Diskus: The Journal of the British Association for the Study of Religions* 16.1 (2014): 3–11.

7 That early Christianity was not always a cult on its knees is indicated, among other things, in Canon 20 of the First Council of Nicaea (325 CE), which prescribes that, on the Lord's Day and in the days of Pentecost, prayer was be made to God while standing. Only a few years earlier, in 321, Constantine I had declared Sunday to be a binding national day of rest.

8 [Translator's note] Meister Eckhart, "The Talks of Instruction: 1. On True Obedience," in *Selected Writings*, trans. Oliver Davies (London: Penguin, 1994): ebook.

4 Representing God, being God: an Egyptian solution

1 Deviations from the rule did occasionally happen – as when, for example, anti-Egyptian sentiment caused the dismantling of the Roman temple of Serapis around 52 BCE. It was rebuilt when the more typical ecumenical mood had reasserted itself once more. Still, although Caesar Augustus remained suspicious of Egypticisms in the religious fashion of his time, in later imperial houses a veritable Egyptomania emerged, as in the House of Livia, wife of Augustus, on the Palatine Hill. Julia the Elder, daughter of Augustus, even surrounded herself in her villas with Egyptian-themed fresco images. These are visible still in the villa of Boscotrecase, on the slope of Vesuvius. The allure of Egypticism lay in its ability – later shared by Christianity – to delineate the idea of eternal life with vivid conceptions.

2 Robert N. Bellah, *Religion in Human Evolution: From the Paleolithic to the Axial Age* (Cambridge, MA: Harvard University Press, 2011): 231–46.
3 John A. Wilson, "Egypt," in H. and H. A. Frankfort, John A. Wilson, Thorkild Jacobsen, and Willian A. Irwin, *The Intellectual Adventure of Ancient Man: An Essay on Speculative Thought in the Ancient Near East* [1946] (University of Chicago Press, 1977): 66.
4 Nicholas of Cusa, Preface to *The Vision of God*, in *Selected Spiritual Writings*, trans. H. Lawrence Bond (New York: Paulist Press, 1997): 233–5. For further commentary, see Peter Sloterdijk, *Spheres I: Bubbles*, trans. Wieland Hoban (Semiotext(e), 2011): 570–83.
5 Helmuth Plessner, *Levels of Organic Life and the Human: An Introduction to Philosophical Anthropology*, trans. Millay Hyatt (New York: Fordham University Press, 2019).
6 Kai Strittmatter, *We Have Been Harmonized: Life in China's Surveillance State*, trans. Ruth Martin (New York: Custom House, 2020).
7 Jean Levi, *Les fonctionnaires divins: politique, despotisme et mystique en Chine ancienne* (Paris: Seuil, 1989).
8 [Translator's note] The reference is to ch. 61 of Robert Musil, *The Man without Qualities*, trans. Sophie Wilkins (New York: Alfred A. Knopf, 1995): 263–6.
9 On the motif of the wrathful God and the desire for justice as a transcendental compensation for suffering, see "The Wrathful God: The Discovery of the Metaphysical Revenge Bank," in Peter Sloterdijk, *Rage and Time: A Psychopolitical Investigation*, trans. Mario Wenning (New York: Columbia University Press, 2010): 111–82.
10 Hubert Roeder, *Mit dem Auge sehen. Studien zur Semantik der Herrschaft in den Toten- und Kulttexten* (Heidelberger Orientverlag, 1996).
11 In *Orpheus: A History of Religions*, trans. Florence Simmonds (New York: Horace Liveright, 1930), Salomon Reinach defined religion as "a sum of scruples which impede the free exercise of our faculties" (3). What Reinach calls "scruples" means, elsewhere, respect, reverential awe, and a keen attentiveness to the proper performance of ritual regulations.
   Ignatius of Loyola reinforced and refined this view when he remarked in the *Spiritual Exercises*, in his notes concerning scruples, that the enemy drives those of delicate conscience into exaggerated self-accusation, while he induces those of lax conscience to greater extremities of indifference, even if they be guilty of the most serious offense.
12 As dyadic jealousy that is averse to the independence of the other.
13 Bendt Alster, *Proverbs of Ancient Sumer: The World's Earliest Proverb Collections* (Bloomington: Indiana University Press, 1997): 324, quoted in Takayoshi Oshima, *Babylonian Poems of Pious Sufferers: Ludlul Bēl Nēmeqi and the Babylonian Theodicy* (Tübingen: Mohr Sieback, 2014): 59. The proverb as reported by Alster was found in a school exercise text.
14 Jan Assmann, *Death and Salvation in Ancient Egypt*, trans. David Lorton (Ithaca: Cornell University Press, 2005): 296.
15 [Translator's note] In the first half of the sentence, the quoted material refers to Aristotle's description of humanity as the animal who has *logos*; Sloterdijk has already referenced this in the opening pages of the

first chapter of the present book. In the second half of the sentence, the reference is to Faust's lines spoken to Gretchen in Martha's Garden: "Feeling is all; / the name is sound and smoke / beclouding Heaven's glow." See Goethe, *Faust I*, lines 3456–8.

16 *Epistulae morales ad Lucilium*, 41.1–2, in Seneca, *Epistles*, Vol. I: *Epistles 1–65*, trans. Richard M. Gummere (Cambridge, MA: Harvard University Press, 1917): 272–3.

17 Lecture VIII from Johann Gottlieb Fichte, "On the Nature of the Scholar and Its Manifestations: Lectures Delivered at Erlangen, 1805," in *Johann Gottlieb Fichte's Popular Works*, trans. William Smith (London: Trübner & Co., 1873): 204–11.

18 Ibid., 211.

5 On the best of all possible heaven dwellers

1 Friedrich Nietzsche, "The Greatest Advantage of Polytheism" §143, in *The Gay Science*, trans. Walter Kaufmann (New York: Vintage Books, 1974): 191–2.

2 See Dante Alighieri, *Divine Comedy: Paradiso*, Canto 33. For discussion of the "pure identity, formless whiteness" produced in the void of the absolute, see G. W. F. Hegel, *Phenomenology of Spirit*, trans. A. V. Miller (Oxford University Press, 1977): 31.

3 Nicholas of Cusa, *On Learned Ignorance (De Docta Ignorantia), Book I*, trans. Jasper Hopkins (Minneapolis: Arthur J. Banning Press, 1985): 10.

4 It is remarkable in Hans Urs von Balthasar's magisterial "experiment," *The Glory of the Lord: A Theological Aesthetics* (1961–7), that no special role is accorded to Plato's derivation of the beautiful (*kalon*) from the goodness of the intelligible circular form. For Balthasar, the beautiful is a form of the decay of the overwhelmingly glorious, which is religiously called the divine, philosophically the One (later, the absolute), aesthetically the sublime. "[W]here glory wanes, ordinary so-called 'beauty' emerges as a residual product": Hans Urs von Balthasar, *The Glory of the Lord: A Theological Aesthetics*, Vol. IV: *The Realm of Metaphysics in Antiquity*, ed. John Riches (Edinburgh: T&T Clark, 1989): 12.

On the ontology of the sphere, "Deus sive sphaera, Or: The Exploding Universal One," ch. 5 in Peter Sloterdijk, *Spheres II: Globes: Macrospherology*, trans. Wieland Hoban (South Pasadena, CA: Semiotext(e), 2014): 441–552.

5 Kurt Flasch, *Warum ich kein Christ bin: Bericht und Argumentation* (Munich: C. H. Beck, 2013): 157ff. See also Peter Sloterdijk, *God's Zeal: The Battle of the Three Monotheisms*, trans. Wieland Hoban (Cambridge: Polity, 2009).

6 [Translator's note] A possible reference to Friedrich Heer, *God's First Love: Christians and Jews over Two Thousand Years*, trans. Geoffrey Skelton (New York: Weybright and Talley, 1970), which catalogues 2,000 years of anti-Semitic abuse instituted by Christians.

7 Dante Alighieri, *Divine Comedy: Inferno*, Canto 3, lines 5–6: "fecemi la divina podestate, la somma sapïenza e 'l primo amore."

8 Hermann Schmitz, *Der Weg der europäischen Philosophie: Eine*

Gewissenserforschung, Vol. I: *Antike Philosophie* (Freiburg im Breisgau: Verlag Karl Alber, 2007): 139–58.

9 Pseudo-Dionysius the Areopagite, "The Divine Names," in *The Divine Names and The Mystical Theology*, trans. John D. Jones (Milwaukee: Marquette University Press, 1980).

10 The term "*Denkerei* [thinkery; think-shop; thinking-shop]" goes back to Ludwig Seeger's 1845 German translation of Aristophanes; Bazon Brock re-purposed it for his Berlin school, set up in 2012.

11 Charles de Secondat, Baron de Montesquieu, "Letter 57," in *Persian Letters*, trans. Margaret Mauldon (Oxford University Press, 2008): 78.

12 See the second book: François Arnaux, *Du Paradis et de ses merveilles* [*Of Paradise and Its Wonders*] (Lyon: Pierre Rigaud, 1614): 41. Quoted in Colleen McDannell and Bernhard Lang, *Heaven: A History*, 2nd edn. (New Haven: Yale University Press, 2001): 214.

13 See McDannell and Lang, *Heaven: A History*: 220.

14 Other examples of this can be found in the emergence of Mahāyāna Buddhism and in the reinvention of Judaism as a post-Christian rabbinical religion.

15 Plato, *Republic*, Book VII, in *The Collected Dialogues of Plato*, ed. Edith Hamilton and Huntington Cairns (Princeton University Press, 1963): 539b–540c.

6 Poetries of power

1 Henri Bergson, *The Two Sources of Morality and Religion*, trans. R. Ashley Audra and Cloudesley Brereton (New York: Henry Holt, 1935).

2 See Pascal Boyer, *Religion Explained: The Human Instincts That Fashion Gods, Spirits and Ancestors* (New York: Vintage, 2002). See also Michael Shermer, *The Believing Brain: From Ghosts and Gods to Politics and Conspiracies – How We Construct Beliefs and Reinforce Them as Truths* (New York: St. Martin's Griffin, 2012).

3 Matthew 6:10.

4 See Nicholas of Cusa, *Nicholas of Cusa on God as Not-other*, trans. Jasper Hopkins (Minneapolis: University of Minnesota Press, 1979): "Not-other is nothing other than not-other."

5 According to a source reported in Lucien Lévy-Bruhl, *How Natives Think*, trans. Lilian A. Clare (New York: Alfred A. Knopf, 1927): 73.

6 On the motif of "finger sacrifice" as a "part for whole" sacrifice, see Walter Burkert, *Creation of the Sacred: Tracks of Biology in Early Religions* (Cambridge, MA: Harvard University Press, 1998): 34–40. Institutionally ritualized offerings here form the human aspect of trans-actions with otherworldly entities. They follow the quid-pro-quo logic of the *do ut des*: "I give so that you may give," taking advantage of the gods' dependence on offerings.

Goethe's youthful poem "Prometheus" (1772/4) conceptualizes the venality of the otherworldly like this: "Meagerly you nourish / Your majesty / On levied offerings / And the breath of prayer / And would starve, were / Not children and beggars / Optimistic fools" [translated by Richard Stokes in *Oxford Lieder*, www.oxfordlieder.co.uk/song/1518].

To this state of affairs, the ancient Mesopotamian "Dialogue of Pessimism" offers a response: "Do not sacrifice, sir, do not sacrifice. / You can teach your god to run after you like a dog" – lines 59–60 quoted from Wilfred G. Lambert, *Babylonian Wisdom Literature* (Oxford University Press, 1963): 147–9.

7 G. W. F. Hegel, *Lectures on the Philosophy of Religion*, Vol. II: *Determinate Religion*, ed. Peter C. Hodgson (Berkeley: University of California Press, 1987): 467.

8 On the term "vertical tension," see Peter Sloterdijk, *You Must Change Your Life: On Anthropotechnics*, trans. Wieland Hoban (Cambridge: Polity, 2013).

9 Raffaele Pettazzoni, *The All-Knowing God: Researches into Early Religion and Culture*, trans. Herbert Jennings Rose (London: Methuen, 1956).

10 [Translator's note] See Johann Wolfgang von Goethe, *Faust: Part Two*, trans. David Luke (Oxford University Press, 1998): 93, lines 7488–9.

7 Dwelling in plausibilities

1 Blaise Pascal, *Pensées*, trans. A. J. Krailsheimer (Harmondsworth: Penguin Books, 1995): 35, §434.

2 [Translator's note] Friedrich Hölderlin, *Poems and Fragments*, 4th Bilingual edn., trans. Michael Hamburger (London: Anvil Press Poetry, 2004): 789.

3 Martin Heidegger, "... Poetically man dwells ...," in *Poetry, Language, Thought*, trans. Albert Hofstadter (New York: HarperCollins Publishers, 2001): 211–27.

4 Peter L. Berger and Thomas Luckmann, *The Social Construction of Reality: A Treatise in the Sociology of Knowledge* (New York: Anchor Books, 1966).

5 Albrecht Koschorke, Susanne Lüdemann, Thomas Frank, and Ethel Matala de Mazza, *Der fiktive Staat: Konstruktionen des politischen Körpers in der Geschichte Europas* (Frankfurt: Fischer, 2007). Concerning the "semiosphere" in connection with Yuri Lotman, see Albrecht Koschorke, *Fact and Fiction: Elements of a General Theory of Narrative*, trans. Joel Golb (Boston: De Gruyter, 2018): 90–107.

6 On August 23, 1914, four weeks after the outbreak of the First World War, Karl Barth gave a sermon to his parish at Safenwil, in the Swiss canton of Aargau, partly on the theme of "the selfish masses that we call nations": Karl Barth, *A Unique Time of God: Karl Barth's WWI Sermons*, trans. and ed. William Klempa (Louisville: Westminster John Knox Press, 2016): 91.

7 Dietmar Dath, *The Abolition of Species*, trans. Samuel P. Willcocks (London: Seagull Books, 2013).

8 Peter Schäfer, *Two Gods in Heaven: Jewish Concepts of God in Antiquity*, trans. Allison Brown (Princeton University Press, 2020).

9 Gisbert Greshake, *Der dreieine Gott: Eine trinitarische Theologie* (Freiburg: Herder, 1997).

10 Peter Sloterdijk, *God's Zeal: The Battle of the Three Monotheisms*, trans. Wieland Hoban (Cambridge: Polity, 2009): 40–9.

11 See Karl Eibl, *Karl Eibl, Animal poeta: Bausteine der biologischen Kultur- und Literaturtheorie* (Paderborn: Mentis Verlag, 2004).

12 Plato, *Laws*, Book X, in *The Collected Dialogues of Plato*, ed. Edith Hamilton and Huntington Cairns (Princeton University Press, 1963): 906c.

8 The theopoetical difference

1 Which is why, according to recent theology, it is only through a self-referral that one can get admitted to the place still, as traditionally, called hell.

2 Dante Alighieri, *Divine Comedy: Paradiso*, Canto 23, line 62. See also Kurt Flasch, *Einladung, Dante zu lesen* (Frankfurt: Fischer, 2011): 195.

3 Jörg Rüpke, *Antike Epik: Eine Einführung von Homer bis in die Spätantike* (Marbach: Tectum Verlag, 2012): 239–43.

4 Mircea Eliade, *A History of Religious Ideas*, Vol. I: *From the Stone Age to the Eleusinian Mysteries*, trans. Willard R. Trask (University of Chicago Press, 1978); Vol. II: *From Gautama Buddha to the Triumph of Christianity*, trans. Willard R. Trask (University of Chicago Press, 1982); Vol. III: *From Muhammad to the Age of Reforms*, trans. Alf Hiltebeitel and Diane Apostolos-Cappadona (University of Chicago Press, 1985).

5 Aurelius Augustinus, *Confessions X*, 27.

6 [Translator's note] Thomas Aquinas, *The Summa Theologica: Third Part (Supplement)*, trans. Fathers of the English Dominican Province (London: Burns Oates & Washbourne, 1922): 62.

7 It is quite some distance from Calvin's off-hand metal-pathological note to alchemical speculation concerning magical-chemical technologies that would facilitate a "renaissance of metals."

8 Giovanni Boccaccio, *Poesie nach der Pest: Der Anfang des Decameron – Italienisch/Deutsch*, trans. and commentary Kurt Flasch (Mainz: Dieterich'sche Verlagsbuchhandlung, 1992).

9 Friedrich Schleiermacher, *On Religion: Speeches to Its Cultured Despisers*, trans. Richard Crouter (Cambridge University Press, 1996): 52.

10 Ibid., 52.

11 Ibid., 23.

12 Hegel affirms this thesis when, in his *Lectures on the Philosophy of Religion*, he characterized the *religio* of the Romans as a "religion of expediency," in which "all gods of all peoples" stand side by side and thus mutually annul each other. In the "religion of utility," the One God is only good as an esoteric trophy. Once Roman religious pluralism entered the imperial era, it proved to be an effective preliminary practice for the cult of Caesar, which in turn served as a preparatory school for monotheism.

13 Schleiermacher, *On Religion*: 50.

14 Niklas Luhmann, "4. Die Ausdifferenzierung der Religion," in *Gesellschaftsstruktur und Semantik: Studien zur Wissenssoziologie der modernen Gesellschaft,* Vol. III (Frankfurt: Suhrkamp, 1989): 273.

15 In the twentieth century, the literary and cultural historian René Girard

(1923–2015) developed a third technique of apology, after the one against the heretics within and the one against the pagans without: he defended the ethically and culturally dynamic truth-content of the Christian religion by describing the execution of Jesus as an archetypal act in which an innocent victim is killed for the sake of the internal purification of a society poisoned by plagues of rivalry, along the schematic lines of expelling a scapegoat.

Girard's analysis shows features of a gnosis without transcendence, insofar as it grants priority to knowledge over faith. The crucial discovery – that the victim of "purifying" violence is innocent – belongs to the realm of knowledge that can be reached by means of reason. What is called Christian "revelation" implies the anticipation of a demystifying general theory of culture and morals. One might connect this to drafts of a general cultural semiotics as per Yuri Lotman, and a general narrative theory as per Albrecht Korschorke.

16 From which it follows that practical understanding from an internal perspective, and theoretical understanding from an external perspective, can never be congruent. Theology as a reflection theory of faith cannot emerge from an internal perspective, whereas theopoetics, as part of ethno-semiotics, general cultural theory, and ego technics, allows for maximal external convergence toward an existence bound in symbols and myths.

17 Socrates' last words – "Crito, we ought to offer a cock to Asclepius. See to it, and don't forget" (*Phaedo* 118a) – are only to be understood in an ironic mode. It would be in keeping with Plato's approach to the figure of Socrates if Plato – in his "true lies" manner – had also invented it. It represents the compromise between idealist philosophy and popular religion; formulated on the threshold between esoteric and exoteric, it signifies that those who know should remain conscious of their distance from the many. In this way, Plato suggests a Greek path to a double religion. See Jan Assmann, *Religio Duplex: How the Enlightenment Reinvented Egyptian Religion*, trans. Robert Savage (Cambridge: Polity, 2014).

18 Heinz-Theo Homann, *Das funktionale Argument: Konzepte und Kritik funktionslogischer Religionsbegründung* (Paderborn: Schöningh, 1997).

19 Peter Schäfer, *The Jewish Jesus: How Judaism and Christianity Shaped Each Other* (Princeton University Press, 2012).

20 On the connection between conscious productions of trauma and "memoactive fitness" in traumatized people, see Heiner Mühlmann, *Die Natur des Christentums* (Paderborn: Wilhelm Fink, 2017). In the same work, Adolf Holl's thesis points to the nexus of unconscious trauma and the desire for redemption, which is characteristic of complex cultures: "Without a fundamental disturbance, religion would be superfluous," cited from *Wie gründe ich eine Religion* (St. Pölten and Salzburg: Residenz Verlag, 2009): 77.

9 Revelation whence?

1 The *locus classicus* of the distinction between the four manifestations of benevolent "mania" – in the areas of prophecy, healing arts,

poetry, and erotic rapture – can be found in Socrates' second speech in Plato's *Phaedrus*. The fourth mania is elevated by Socrates as an affective preliminary stage of love for wisdom: from it (given requisite reflection!) there ensues a transition from affection for beautiful bodies to love for beauty as such, which the soul illuminates as the splendor of the good and the true. Philosophy thus constituted itself as the fifth mania: a prosaic enthusiasm through participation in the independent life of the idea.

2 In the thirteenth century and thereafter, there circulated rumors of a "Treatise of the Three Impostors," a supposed book holding that Jews, Christians, and Muslims had been deliberately misled by Moses, Jesus, and Muhammad. See Wolfgang Gericke, *Das Buch "De tribus impostoribus": Ausgewählte Texte aus der Geschichte der christlichen Kirche* (Berlin: Evangelische Verlagsanstalt, 1982).

3 Exodus 3:14.

4 See ch. 6, "The Reciprocity of Giving," in Walter Burkert, *Creation of the Sacred: Tracks of Biology in Early Religions* (Cambridge, MA: Harvard University Press, 1998): 129–55.

5 See ch. 7, "The Validation of Signs: A Cosmos of Sense," in Burkert, *Creation of the Sacred*: 156–76. Advocates of Christian *Vestigia Trinitatis* theology occasionally differentiate between signs that speak to heathens, and miracles that will open up to believers.

6 Kurt Flasch, *Warum ich kein Christ bin: Bericht und Argumentation* (Munich: C. H. Beck, 2013): 131.

7 Carsten Colpe, *Griechen – Byzantiner – Semiten – Muslime. Hellenistische Religionen und west-östliche Enthellenisierung* (Tübingen: Mohr Siebeck, 2008).

10 The death of the gods

1 Nicholas Evans, *Dying Words: Endangered Languages and What They Have to Tell Us* (Malden, MA: Wiley-Blackwell, 2010): xviii. There currently exist about 2,700 complete or partial translations of the New Testament, including quite a few in cultures without written languages, for which the New Testament is the first book – and probably also the last.

2 Hugo Ball, *Flight out of Time: A Dada Diary*, trans. Ann Raimes, ed. John Elderfield (Berkeley: University of California Press, 1974): 12.

3 Ibid., 108.

4 In his interpretation of new French theory, *The Possessed Individual: Technology and Postmodernity* (London: Palgrave Macmillan, 1992), Arthur Kroker develops the thesis that the modern media environment constitutes not so much an object world, as an ensemble of psychologically invasive agencies that generate alternative obsessions that have ceased any longer to be spiritual. In the terminology used here, we might say that personal and technical mediumism merge with one another. Demons become persuaders. The influencer phenomenon, propagated in the years after 2001, attests to the ways in which obsessive media consumption fosters a massive susceptibility for vague obsessions through vapid agents of seduction.

11 "Religion is unbelief": Karl Barth's intervention

1 See Book IV.4 in Aurelius Augustinus, *City of God*, Vol. II: *Books 4–7*, trans. William Green (Cambridge, MA: Harvard University Press, 1963): 16–17.

2 Karl Barth, *Eine Schweizer Stimme: 1938–1945* (Zürich: Zollikon, 1945): 113.

3 See §17 of Karl Barth, *Church Dogmatics, I.2: The Doctrine of the Word of God*, trans. G. T. Thomson and Harold Knight (London: T&T Clark, 2004): 297–300.

4 Karl Barth, *The Epistle to the Romans: Sixth Edition*, trans. Edwyn C. Hoskyns (Oxford University Press, 1968): 298.

5 [Translator's note] "Music for a Guest: A Radio Broadcast," in Karl Barth, *Final Testimonies*, trans. Geoffrey W. Bromiley, ed. Eberhard Busch (Grand Rapids: Eerdmans, 1977): 24.

6 Galatians 2:20; John 15:4. The figure of reciprocal embedding in a common spiritual sphere can also be found in the Gospel of Truth, a Gnostic homily probably written around 150 CE and, in Coptic translation, collected in Codex I of the Nag Hammadi library: "They were joyful in this discovery, and he found them within himself and they found him within themselves" [Translator's note: *The Nag Hammadi Scriptures: The International Edition*, ed. Marvin Meyer (New York: HarperCollins, 2008): 37].

7 [Translator's note] Galatians 2:19.

8 Barth, *Church Dogmatics, I.2*: 302.

9 Friedrich Nietzsche, "Twilight of the Idols, or, How One Philosophizes with a Hammer," in *The Portable Nietzsche*, trans. and ed. Walter Kaufmann (New York: Penguin Books, 1982): 483.

10 See page 151 of the standard pagination in Johann Gottlieb Fichte, *Attempt at a Critique of All Revelation*, trans. Garrett Green, ed. Allen Wood (Cambridge University Press, 2010): 125.

11 *Adolf Bastian and His Universal Archive of Humanity: The Origins of German Anthropology*, ed. Manuela Fischer, Peter Bolz, and Susan Kamel (Hildesheim and New York: G. Olms Verlag, 2007).

12 "The Antichrist," §16 in Nietzsche, *The Portable Nietzsche*: 582.

13 [Translator's note] Book Three §258 in Friedrich Nietzsche, *The Gay Science*, trans. Walter Kaufmann (New York: Vintage Books, 1974): 217.

14 Barth, *The Epistle to the Romans: Sixth Edition*: 296.

15 In the "Preface to the First Edition" of his *Epistle to the Romans*, Barth professed that he was "bound to labour with Paul," and could not remain an unmoved spectator in his presence (1) – which shows that he did not in every case bow to theology's characteristic saying-too-much, for which his book provided a most extreme example (together with Ernst Bloch's *Spirit of Utopia* and Franz Rosenzweig's *Star of Redemption*): Barth was just as capable of stylistic understatement right from the start.

16 Early evidence is found in 1 John 3:16: "We know love by this, that he laid down his life for us – and we ought to lay down our lives for one another."

17 The second edition of the *Epistle to the Romans*, from 1922, already described itself as a self-criticism of the first.
18 [Translator's note] Cf. Nietzsche's account of the history of *Zarathustra*: "this highest formula of affirmation that is at all attainable ... was penned on a sheet, with the notation underneath '6000 feet beyond man and time.'" See *Ecce Homo* in Friedrich Nietzsche, *Basic Writings of Nietzsche*, trans. and ed. Walter Kaufmann (New York: Modern Library, 1968): 751: 6,000 feet is the elevation of the village of Sils Maria, where Nietzsche lived at the time.
19 [Translator's note] See "The Antichrist," §19 in Nietzsche, *The Portable Nietzsche*: 586.
20 Linus Hauser's *Kritik der neomythischen Vernunft* has been published in three volumes: Vol. I: *Menschen als Götter der Erde, 1800–1945* (Paderborn: Schöningh, 2005); Vol. II: *Neomythen der beruhigten Endlichkeit, Die Zeit ab 1945* (Paderborn: Schöningh, 2009); Vol. III: *Die Fiktionen der Science auf dem Wege ins 21. Jahrhundert* (Paderborn: Schöningh, 2016).
21 See "Selbstfesselungskünstler zwischen Gottsucherbanden und Unterhaltungsidioten. Für eine Kultur diesseits des Ernstfalls und jenseits von Macht, Geld und Unsterblichkeit," in Bazon Brock, *Die Re-Dekade: Kunst und Kultur der 80er Jahre* (Munich: Klinkhardt und Biermann, 1990): 127ff.
22 See "Towards a Critique of Hegel's *Philosophy of Right*: Introduction," in Karl Marx, *Selected Writings*, ed. David McLellan (Oxford University Press, 1977): 63–74.
23 In an unpublished fragment from autumn 1881, Nietzsche relates criticism "exercised against everything" to a magical-thinking "willingness to harm" that in modern times is seen as a tendency at work in the competition and struggles of parties, merchants, and states. "Criticism ... is a final expression of power by those without influence – a continuation of witchcraft." See *Nachgelassene Fragmente 1880–1882*, in Friedrich Nietzsche, *Sämtliche Werke: Kritische Studienausgabe*, Vol. IX, ed. Giorgio Colli and Mazzino Montinari (Berlin: Walter de Gruyter, 1988): 516.

12 In the garden of infallibility: Denzinger's world

1 The church writer Tertullian (*c.* 155–*c.* 220 CE), who was born in Carthage and became a founder of Latin theology, popularized the translation of *anathema* by *damnatio*. The accursing exclusion, by means of the formula *anathema esto*, was also practiced by Paul the Apostle, for example in his Epistle to the Galatians 1:8–9.
2 For example, as related to buildings of the Ottonian period or to Cistercian architecture, in contrast to the *stylus sumptuosus*.
3 See §222 in Heinrich Denzinger, *Enchiridion symbolorum: Definitionum et declarationum de rebus fidei et morum, Compendium of Creeds, Definitions, and Declarations on Matters of Faith and Morals*, Latin–English, ed. Peter Hünermann, Robert Fastiggi and Anne Englund Nash, 43rd edn. (San Francisco: Ignatius Press, 2012): 82.

Medieval theologians were moved by the question of how much time had passed from the creation of Adam and Eve to their expulsion from Eden; the orthodox answer was seven hours. Curious questions about the whether and how of paradisiacal sexual intercourse thus should have been made irrelevant by the brevity of their abidance; in practice, however, there was lively debate about this. See Kurt Flasch, *Eva und Adam: Wandlungen eines Mythos* (Munich: Verlag C. H Beck, 2017): 72–80.

4　This doctrine helped to bring into existence the bizarre instrument of the baptismal enema after 1310, with which fetuses who died *in utero* could be given the consecrated water of baptism *per vaginam* by Catholic midwives; the rite was in evidence in remote localities in Austria up to the early twentieth century. The baptismal syringe belonged in the professional bag of all midwives even after 1800. If Lenin had lectured that "the truth is always concrete," the empirical evidence of religious history responds: delirium is even more concrete.

5　Denzinger, *Enchiridion symbolorum*, §286, p. 103.

6　Ibid., §377, p. 136.

7　Ibid., §748, p. 245.

8　Ibid., §762, p. 249. The question of castration among the clergy had already been addressed at the First Council of Nicaea in 325 CE, which promulgated as the epitome of canon 1 that "If anyone has been castrated by physicians during an illness or by barbarians, he may remain in the clergy. But if anyone is healthy and castrates himself, it is appropriate that he be excluded from the clergy" (cf. Denzinger, *Enchiridion symbolorum*, §128a, p. 52). The problem of voluntary castration was perceived as disturbing in Nicaea not least because the dictates of the God of heaven – whom one typically addressed as *hypsistos* or *altissimus*, the Most High – were meeting traces of resistance from older earth-bound fertility religions in many areas of Magna Graecia. In Asia Minor and Anatolia, the cult of the mother goddess Cybele remained alive for centuries through its castrated priests (*galloi*).

9　Denzinger, *Enchiridion symbolorum*, §1341, p. 346. The Valentinian thesis contained a theological heresy in its gynecological formulation, insofar as it contradicted the established two-factor doctrine, according to which, at the incarnation of Jesus, the immaterial sperm of the male Logos had to be united with the real human corporeality of the mother, whereas the Valentinian water-conduit theory precluded any female contribution. The prevailing doctrine of the time certainly assumed that the child was formed *in utero* from the mother's clotting blood (an inference from the suspension of menstruation). In the case of Jesus, it could not have happened that real male sperm defiled the maternal blood – the blood of Mary, after all, remained the "Most Chaste."

10　Ibid., §1346 and §1347, pp. 346–7.

11　Ibid., §3400, p. 689.

12　See Aurelius Augustinus, *City of God*, Vol. III: *Books 8–11*, trans. David S. Wiesen (Cambridge, MA: Harvard University Press, 1968).

13　(Deutero-) Isaiah 44:19.

14　Denzinger, *Enchiridion symbolorum*, §3546, p. 711.

15 Barth detested the term from the beginning.

16 *Propheten in deutscher Krise: Das Wunderbare oder die Verzauberten: Eine Sammlung*, ed. Rudolf Olden (Berlin: Rowohlt, 1932).

17 See Ralf Frisch, *Alles gut: Warum Karl Barths Theologie ihre beste Zeit noch vor sich hat* (Zürich: Theologischer Verlag, 2018). The thesis of this work is that Karl Barth's teachings should have a promising future if one reads his *Church Dogmatics* as an aesthetic manifesto, comparable to Tolkien's fictions. According to the author, Barth's opus should be read as belles-lettres or fine literature, beginning with "Revelation-Dadaism," then planing progressively over the waters of Apollonian epic.

13 Fictive belonging together

1 The approach to this can be found in the Latinization of philosophy by Cicero: in his *Tusculan Disputations* (Book II, 10–13), he coined the expression *cultura animi* (the cultivation of the soul), from which *cultura* as such emerges after the genitive object is dropped.

2 See Karl Eibl, *Karl Eibl, Animal poeta: Bausteine der biologischen Kultur- und Literaturtheorie* (Paderborn: Mentis Verlag, 2004).

3 See "Letter on Humanism," in Martin Heidegger, *Pathmarks*, ed. William McNeill (Cambridge University Press, 1998): 269–71. For Nietzsche's "eternally the same house of being is built," see "The Convalescent," §2 from Friedrich Nietzsche, *Thus Spoke Zarathustra*, in *The Portable Nietzsche*, trans. and ed. Walter Kaufmann (New York: Penguin Books, 1982): 329.

4 Plato's early dialogue *Protagoras* reveals at least this much concerning theorems advanced by the thinker from Abera: he believed in the teachability of virtue, and most particularly in the art of living together in the *polis* – something that must be taught and learned because it cannot rely on innate knowledge.

5 [Translator's note] Cf. Plato's *Protagoras*, in *The Collected Dialogues of Plato*, ed. Edith Hamilton and Huntington Cairns (Princeton University Press, 1963): 322d. Plato's text, in its English translation by W. K. C. Guthrie, renders the second virtue, *aidos* in Plato's Greek, as "respect for one's fellows," whereas Sloterdijk's text gives the second virtue as *Götterfurcht*, "fear of the gods." Later in this chapter, Sloterdijk also associates "fear of the gods" with the Greek term *eusebeia*, which generally refers to the proper ways to reverence the gods.

6 [Translator's note] See §27 in Martin Heidegger, *Being and Time*, trans. Joan Stambaugh (Albany: State University of New York Press, 2010): 124.

7 Jörg Rüpke, *Pantheon: A New History of Roman Religion*, trans. David M. B. Richardson (Princeton University Press, 2018): 382.

Carsten Colpe's opus distinguishes among different types of dealings with the gods: cultic, cultless, cultivated, speculative, and critical. See Carsten Colpe, *Griechen – Byzantiner – Semiten – Muslime. Hellenistische Religionen und west-östliche Enthellenisierung* (Tübingen: Mohr Siebeck, 2008): 43–154.

8 The American cultural anthropologist Paul Stoller offers a case of extreme ambiguity in the role of the ethnologist; between 1976 and 1984, Stoller had been initiated into the magic of the Songhai people in Niger and Mali. See Paul Stoller and Cheryl Olkes, *In Sorcery's Shadow: A Memoir of Apprenticeship among the Songhay of Niger* (University of Chicago Press, 1987).

9 See Friedrich Nietzsche, *The Birth of Tragedy out of the Spirit of Music*, §15, in *Basic Writings of Nietzsche*, trans. and ed. Walter Kaufmann (New York: Modern Library, 1968): 98.

10 Kurt Flasch, *Kampfplätze der Philosophie: Große Kontroversen von Augustin bis Voltaire* (Frankfurt am Main: Vittorio Klostermann, 2008).

11 Plato, *Laws*, Book I, in *The Collected Dialogues of Plato*, ed. Hamilton and Cairns: 626a.

12 Called Lacedaemonians in the text of Plato's *Laws*.

13 Plato, *Laws*, Book X, in *The Collected Dialogues of Plato*, ed. Hamilton and Cairns: 909a–d.

14 In this case, the kinship logic presumes a matrilineal or bilinear protocol.

15 Cf. Erik Peterson, *Monotheismus als politisches Problem: Ein Beitrag zur Geschichte der politischen Theologie im Imperium Romanum* (Leipzig: Hegner, 1935).

16 See the ninth section of Jacob Burckhardt, *The Age of Constantine the Great*, trans. Moses Hadas (Berkeley: University of California Press, 1983): 292–335.

17 The Statue of Liberty in New York Harbor, inaugurated as a gift from the French people to the United States and dedicated in October 1886, bears the seven-pointed radiate crown of the Roman Christian cult.

18 G. W. F. Hegel, *Aesthetics: Lectures on Fine Art*, Vol. II, trans. T. M. Knox (Oxford University Press, 1998): 887.

19 [Translator's note] Winning at least 5 percent of the vote is an electoral threshold in a number of European countries (including Germany) – so, typically, necessary for a party's representation in the legislature, unless certain other conditions are met. A "5 percent party" would thus be a minor party, but still at least minimally successful enough for voice and visibility.

20 In 390 CE, Gothic troops carried out a massacre in the hippodrome of Thessaloniki, in which 7,000 citizens were reportedly killed; Theodosius I had ordered this retaliatory action after incensed partisans of a locally popular charioteer had murdered his master of troops, the Gothic General Butheric. On account of the massacre, Ambrose denied Theodosius I access to the cathedral of Milan and compelled the emperor to an act of penance.

21 Dante Alighieri, *Divine Comedy: Paradiso*, Canto 32, lines 31–6.

14 Twilight of the gods and sociophany

1 Voltaire's dictum "Écrasez l'infâme!" – "Let us crush the infamy!" – referred to the repressive institutions of his time that came to light

in the alliance of state and church (Roman Catholicism first and foremost).

2 [Translator's note] See the end of the "Introduction" to Karl Marx, *Grundrisse: Foundations of the Critique of Political Economy*, trans. Martin Nicolaus (New York: Penguin Books, 1973): 111.

3 Hermann Cohen, *Religion of Reason: Out of the Sources of Judaism*, trans. Simon Kaplan (Atlanta: Scholars Press, 1995). See also Mark Lilla, *The Stillborn God: Religion, Politics, and the Modern West* (New York: Vintage Books, 2007).

4 François-René de Chateaubriand, *The Genius of Christianity, or The Spirit and Beauty of the Christian Religion*, trans. Charles I. White (Baltimore: John Murphy & Co., 1856): 49.

5 In his study *God is Beautiful: The Aesthetic Experience of the Quran*, trans. Tony Crawford (Cambridge: Polity, 2018), Navid Kermani continues the program of aesthetic apologetics from a Muslim point of view, and brings forth evidence that reception of the Quran was inherently in the aesthetic element from an early stage, if not from the beginning.

6 See §822, in Friedrich Nietzsche, *The Will to Power*, trans. Walter Kaufmann and R. J. Hollingdale (New York: Vintage, 1968): 435.

7 See the essay "Twilight of the Gods," in Peter Sloterdijk, *After God*, trans. Ian Alexander Moore (Cambridge: Polity, 2020): 1–16.

8 See "Seele und Maschine," in Gotthard Günther, *Beiträge zur Grundlegung einer operationsfähigen Dialektik, Erster Band* (Hamburg: Meiner, 1976): 79.

9 See Pierre Legendre, *Leçons IV: L'inestimable objet de la transmission* (Paris: Fayard, 1985). On the complexity of so-called "secularization," see *Säkularisierung: Grundlagentexte zur Theoriegeschichte*, ed. Christiane Frey, Uwe Hebekus, and David Martyn (Berlin: Suhrkamp, 2020).

10 Nietzsche already interpreted the emergence of collectivist ideologies (as compensatory forms for the traditional "proclivity for the herd") as proceeding from discontent with the impositions of individuality: "In general, the tendency of socialism, like that of nationalism, is a reaction against becoming individual. One has difficulties with the ego, the half-mature crazy ego, and wishes to put it back under the bell cover." Friedrich Nietzsche, *Nachgelassene Fragmente 1880–1882*, KSA 9: 515.

11 Rudolf Pfeiffer, *Die Klassische Philologie von Petrarca bis Mommsen* (Munich: C. H. Beck, 1982).

12 *The Linguistic Turn: Essays in Philosophical Method*, ed. Richard Rorty (University of Chicago Press, 1967).

13 See "How Is Society Possible?" in Georg Simmel, *On Individuality and Social Forms*, ed. Donald N. Levine (University of Chicago Press, 1971): 6–22; Niklas Luhmann, *Theory of Society* (Stanford University Press, 2012).

Günter Dux's work *Historisch-genetische Theorie der Kultur: Instabile Welten – Zur prozessualen Logik im kulturellen Wandel* (Wiesbaden: Springer VS, 2017), which has so far not received the appreciation it deserves, must be named as a worthy, sometimes superior, alternative to Luhmann's system-theoretical proposals.

14 [Translator's note] See §1038, in Nietzsche, *The Will to Power*, trans. Kaufmann and Hollingdale: 534.

15 In their studies on *German Ideology* (1845), Marx and Engels made explicit the idea that communist intellectuals are authorized to represent the true needs of working "humanity." The fact that they must assume office in the mode of a self-appointment proceeds from the advantage of their concrete and generally true theory over the abstract and particular social criticism of the Young Hegelians. On this, see Johannes Weiss, *Handeln und handeln lassen. Über Stellvertretung* (Opladen: Westdeutscher Verlag, 1998): 153–73.

16 Jan Assmann, *Achsenzeit: Eine Archäologie der Moderne* (Munich: Verlag C. H. Beck, 2018).

17 Title of a polemic by Celsus, the second-century Platonist, arguing against the doctrines of Christianity, drafted around 178 CE.

18 Posthumously edited, 1983.

19 Armin Nassehi, *Muster: Theorie der digitalen Gesellschaft* (Munich: C. H. Beck, 2019).

20 Friedrich Gogarten, "Zwischen den Zeiten," in *Die Christliche Welt* 24 (1920): 374–8. The regressive simplicity of Gogarten's utterance is evident when contrasted with Nietzsche's appeal: "We children of the future, how could we be at home in this today? We feel disfavor for all ideals that might lead one to feel at home even in this fragile, broken time of transition." See Book Five §377 in Friedrich Nietzsche, *The Gay Science*, trans. Walter Kaufmann (New York: Vintage Books, 1974): 338.

15 Glory: poems of praise

1 [Translator's note] See "Remembrance," in Friedrich Hölderlin, *Poems and Fragments*, 4th Bilingual edn., trans. Michael Hamburger (London: Anvil Press Poetry, 2004): 578–9.

2 Surah 26:224. What is meant are the old Arabic poets who, more than anything else in their works, bore witness to a pre-Islamic belief in fate.

3 [Translator's note] For the original context and the classic, nineteenth-century rendering of the line as "All that is solid melts into air …," see Karl Marx and Friedrich Engels, *The Communist Manifesto*, trans. Samuel Moore (London: Penguin Books, 2002): 223.

4 Book Three §125 in Friedrich Nietzsche, *The Gay Science*, trans. Walter Kaufmann (New York: Vintage Books, 1974): 181.

5 See Thomas Macho and Peter Sloterdijk, *Weltrevolution der Seele: Ein Lese- und Arbeitsbuch zur Gnosis* (Munich: Artemis & Winkler, 1994).

6 Heinrich Niehues-Pröbsting, *Der Kynismus des Diogenes und der Begriff des Zynismus* (Frankfurt am Main: Fink, 1988).

7 Cf. the exclamation of Adam in Friedrich Gotthold Klopstock's 1759 hymn "The Spring Festival": "Here I stand. Everything around me is All-mighty! Everything a miracle!"

8 See "Third Part: Before Sunrise" §4 from Friedrich Nietzsche, *Thus Spoke Zarathustra*, in *The Portable Nietzsche*, trans. and ed. Walter Kaufmann (New York: Penguin Books, 1982): 278.

9 See Macho and Sloterdijk, *Weltrevolution der Seele*.

10 The scene of Alexander's conception, from the oft-copied *Alexander Romance*, inspired Raphael's student Giulio Romano (1499–1546) to produce a work of explicit theopornography in the Sala della Psiche of the Palazzo Te in suburban Mantua. There, one can see a bearded male dragon, depicting Zeus, with a considerable erection, moments before the act of penetration with the future bearer of god and king, who is herself naked, or clad only in something like a bikini top.

11 For established monarchies, systemic changes in religious cult represent a moment of crisis, because during the transition period the alliance between throne and cult appears to be endangered. After strong initial success, the religious founder Mani failed in his attempt to establish a new synthesis of Buddhism, Zoroastrianism, and Christianity with the Persian kings, because the Sasanian monarchy decided to maintain its alliance with the Zoroastrian priests; by the same token, in the Roman Empire, cult change found success because of Constantine's sponsorship on behalf of the new theopolitical propriety.

12 The differentiation between the exalting and detracting speeches (*laudationes* and *vituperationes*) that prefigures modern "critique" is laid out in ancient and classical practices. Before the onset of the imperial era, the diatribe evolved into a veritable art of insult in Rome, not least in the polemics of *populares* and *optimates*. Catullus mocked Caesar and his friend Mamurra as queer diseased twins who shared one sofa; Sallust accused Cicero of corruption and self-deification.

The art of invective reached the peak of its development among the early Doctors of the Church, with whom raging against non-Christians produced the successful polemical genres of the *adversus Judaeos* and *adversus haereticos*. Among them, Jerome of Stridon (*c.* 347–420 CE) holds a distinguished place. One gets the basic impression of his manners when he called heretics "two-legged thistle-eating donkeys" and qualified dissident Christians as "beasts for the slaughter headed for hell." He excused his own rants as expression of his "Dalmatian temperament."

13 Karlheinz Stierle, *Petrarca: Ein Intellektueller im Europa des 14. Jahrhunderts* (Munich: Carl Hanser Verlag, 2004).

14 Six years after the coronation of Petrarch, the ingenious populist Cola di Rienzo seized power in Rome thanks to analogous neo-republican acclamation mechanisms. But because of his megalomaniacal attitudes – he allowed himself to be escorted through the city in constant triumph as the "candidate of the Holy Spirit" with power of salvation – he was deposed, after six months as "tribune," in the final months of 1347.

15 Book 3, ch. 7 in Marcus Fabius Quintilian, *The Orator's Education: Books 3–5*, trans. Donald A. Russell (Cambridge, MA: Harvard University Press, 2002): 104–11.

16 In his *Histories* (VI.53), which is devoted to the constitution of the Roman Republic, Polybius mentions an old Roman funeral custom among the illustrious families of the *nobiles*, of having a son or relative recite a *laudatio funebris* in the forum, with the body of the deceased generally propped upright on the rostrum, as if sitting and listening in.

17 It can be no coincidence that only John the Evangelist, of Greek origin, cites the formula "It is finished" (*tetelestai*) as Jesus' last words on the

Cross (John 19:30). A contemporary translation would render it as "Mission accomplished." On the expression *amechania*, see Thomas Buchheim, *Die Sophistik als Avantgarde normalen Lebens* (Hamburg: F. Meiner, 1986).

18 *The Arabian Nights*, trans. Husain Haddawy, ed. Muhsin Mahdi (New York: W. W. Norton, 1990): 3.

16 Poetry of patient endurance

1 Takayoshi Oshima, *Babylonian Poems of Pious Sufferers: Ludlul Bēl Nēmeqi and the Babylonian Theodicy* (Tübingen: Mohr Sieback, 2014): 31.

2 2 Corinthians 3:3. In Romans 2:14–15, when Gentiles, who do not "possess" the law, instinctively do what the law requires, they show that what the law requires is "written on their hearts."

3 The Quran also claims that its pre-existing original is inscribed on a tablet in heaven.

4 Oshima, *Babylonian Poems of Pious Sufferers*: 42.

5 The main proponent of Jewish neo-Kantianism, Hermann Cohen (1842–1918), confessed that he could love God only as the avenger of the poor.

6 Not to be confused with Nebuchadnezzar II, who ruled 605–562 BCE and who deported Israel's elite to Babylon in 597.

7 Aside from Psalm 109, which performs a magical anathema and prays that death be turned upon those making wicked accusations, and aside from the final verse of Psalm 137 ("Happy shall they be who take your little ones [of Babylon] and dash them against the rock!"), Psalm 58:8 is particularly important for understanding the lamentation of Job as an introversion of aggression: "Let them be like the snail that dissolves into slime; like the untimely birth that never sees the sun." See, later in the present chapter, the discussion of Job's lamentation.

8 Oshima, *Babylonian Poems of Pious Sufferers*: 79.

9 Peter Schäfer, *Two Gods in Heaven: Jewish Concepts of God in Antiquity*, trans. Allison Brown (Princeton University Press, 2020): 122.

10 Friedrich Nietzsche, "Origin of Sin" §135, in *The Gay Science*, trans. Walter Kaufmann (New York: Vintage Books, 1974): 187–8.

11 Proverbs 13:24.

12 Friedrich Nietzsche, "New Struggles" §108, in *The Gay Science*, trans. Kaufmann: 167. Among those of the first generations who dared to indicate a shadow proper to God, philosophers of history played a leading role. Deliberating on Leibniz's theodicy (i.e., on the tribunal that human reason had instituted against God, on the charge of permitting evil), Odo Marquard said that it had ended in the acquittal of God "on the basis of proven non-existence," thus in an atheism *ad maiorem Dei gloriam*, by dint of which the custodians of godless humanity recommended themselves as ersatz gods.

[Translator's note] See "Entlastungen: Theodizeemotive in der neuzeitlichen Philosophie," in Odo Marquard, *Apologie des Zufälligen* (Stuttgart: Reclam Verlag, 1986): 13–29.

13 Oshima, *Babylonian Poems of Pious Sufferers*: 132.
14 Psalms 18:24–5.
15 Job 3:3, 11, 16.
16 Job 10:18–19.
17 Cf. the basic questions of gnosis handed down by Clement of Alexandria: Who were we? What have we become? Where were we before we came into this world? What have we been thrown into? Whither do we hasten? From what are we redeemed? What is birth? What is rebirth?
18 Job 38:4, 8–11, 32–3.
19 Job 39:26–7.
20 Job 40:4.
21 Philippe Nemo, *Job et l'excès du mal* (1978) (Paris: A. Michel, 2001).
22 See "The Reciprocity of Giving," in Walter Burkert, *Creation of the Sacred: Tracks of Biology in Early Religions* (Cambridge, MA: Harvard University Press, 1998): 129–55.
23 As, under the influence of Emmanuel Levinas, Philippe Nemo did in *Job et l'excès du mal*.

17 Poetry of exaggeration: religious virtuosos and their excesses

1 See Book IV, ch. 18, in John Locke, *An Essay Concerning Human Understanding*, ed. Roger Woolhouse (London: Penguin, 1997): 607–13.
2 Giordano Bruno conceptualized a general theory of active and passive fascinations in his erotomagic work *De vinculis in genere* (1591), in which the world is described as a field of attractors and their effects on whatever is susceptible to attraction. One key sentence reads: "The one who is bound encounters the bonding agent through all the senses, up to the point that a perfect bond has been made such that the former is totally immersed, and desires to be totally immersed, in the latter" (155). The bonding agent enters into the one to be bound through the gate of the imagination as the *vinculum vinculorum*. The art of bonding consists above all in recognizing the desires of the person to be bound. See "A General Account of Bonding," trans. Richard Blackwell, in Giordano Bruno, *Cause, Principle and Unity: Essays on Magic* (Cambridge University Press, 1998): 143–76.
3 Philippe Nemo, *Job et l'excès du mal* (1978) (Paris, 2001).
4 Latin *fascinatio*: bewitchment, enchantment. Cf. Galatians 3:1 – *Quis vos fascinavit?*: "Who has bewitched you?"
5 *Anthropologie der Artikulation: Begriffliche Grundlage und transdisziplinäre Perspektiven*, ed. Magnus Schlette and Matthias Jung (Würzburg: Königshausen–Neumann, 2005); Dieter Claessens, "Heraustreten aus der Masse als Kulturarbeit: Zur Theorie einer Handlungsklasse," in *Klassenlage, Lebensstil und kulturelle Praxis: Beiträge zur Auseinandersetzung mit Pierre Bourdieus Klassentheorie*, ed. Klaus Eder (Frankfurt am Main: Suhrkamp, 1989): 303–40.
6 The Damascus event, taken as historical, dates to around the year 35 CE; scholars have generally dated the writing of the *Actus apostolorum* around the years 80–90 CE. A tension persists between tendencies toward an earlier dating (around 62 CE) and a later dating (up to

120 CE); a later dating would preclude the possibility of an identical author having written the Gospel of Luke as well as Acts.

7 The Austrian Hindu monk and Sanskrit scholar Agehananda Bharati (1923–91) remarks that one of the masters of his order, Sri Ramakrishna Paramahamsa (1836–86), practiced enraptured states with ease, as if he were a Mozart of *samadhi*, perfect enstatic meditation.

8 2 Corinthians 12:1–10. The Pauline speech of the "third heaven," which refers to his vision of paradise, testifies to the numerical ambiguity of the concept of "heaven." The heaven to which Jesus ascends 40 days after Easter is not marked by an ordinal number. The authors of the Gospels may well have known that, according to the Aristotelian cosmology of the heavens, there were a certain number of concentric celestial spheres, the last of which formed the boundary with nothingness. The idiomatic expression describing lovers as being "in seventh heaven" is premodern. With Dante, the ascent in *Paradiso* takes place up to a ninth heaven, which is called the crystal heaven.

9 On Paul as the founder of a "doulocracy" (government by slaves) see Stathis Gourgouris, "Paul's Greek," in *Paul and the Philosophers*, ed. Ward Blanton and Hent de Vries (Fordham University Press, 2013): 346–7.

10 See the 1896 lecture, "The Will to Believe, Lecture to the Philosophical Clubs of Yale University, New Haven, Connecticut, and Brown University, Providence, Rhode Island," in William James, *Writings 1878–1899*, ed. Gerald Myers (New York: Library of America, 1992): 447–704.

11 [Translator's note] Ibid., 466.

12 See Book VIII, ch. 6 of Quintilian, *The Orator's Education: Books 6–8*, trans. Donald Russell (Cambridge, MA: Harvard University Press, 2001): 464–5.

13 Ibid., 468–9.

14 Rudolf Bultmann, *The History of the Synoptic Tradition*, trans. John Marsh (New York: Harper & Row, 1963): 167.

15 Thomas Macho, *Todesmetaphern: Zur Logik der Grenzerfahrung* (Frankfurt am Main: Suhrkamp, 1995).

16 [Translator's note] Compare Sloterdijk's German original, *Vorlaufen in den eigenen Tod*, with Heidegger's *Vorlaufen zum Tode*, which is variously translated as "anticipation of death" or "running toward death," a sort of turning toward death in anticipation and facing it resolutely.

17 Joseph de Maistre referred to this method in his infamous apology praising the executioner in the first of his *St Petersburg Dialogues* (1821). Only half a century before de Maistre's terror-friendly excursus, the Protestant Jean Calas had been publicly executed in Toulouse in March 1762, using an alternative method of the wheel (he was strapped backwards onto the wheel and turned for hours in increasing extremity of pain). The event became known across Europe through Voltaire's intervention, in particular his *Treatise on Tolerance* (1763), which led the Parisian courts, in 1764, to annul the Toulouse court's decision and, in 1765, to posthumously exonerate Jean Calas.

18 Surah 4:55–6: "Hell is a sufficient Inferno. Those who reject Our

revelations – We will scorch them in a Fire. Every time their skins are cooked, We will replace them with other skins, so they will experience the suffering. God is Most Powerful, Most Wise."

19 Jacques Le Goff, *The Birth of Purgatory*, trans. Arthur Goldhammer (University of Chicago Press, 1984).

20 Apart from this, the Vatican has long responded to any attempt to relativize the dogma of hell by retreating to the ontologically weighted topological argument that hell is the state of remoteness from God – something that begins here [in the life of the damned] and continues post mortem ad infinitum. With regard to the schema of transposing the designations of life and death in Christian rhetoric, see the discussion later in this chapter.

21 See *On the Genealogy of Morals*, "Second Essay: 'Guilt,' 'Bad Conscience,' and the Like," §22, in Friedrich Nietzsche, *Basic Writings of Nietzsche*, trans. and ed. Walter Kaufmann (New York: Modern Library, 1968): 529.

22 Hugo Ball, *Byzantinisches Christentum: Drei Heiligenleben* (Munich: Duncker & Humblot, 1923).

23 Ibid., 25.

24 See Book VI in Aurelius Augustinus, *City of God*, Vol. II: *Books 4–7*, trans. William Green (Cambridge, MA: Harvard University Press, 1963): 364–5: *Nulla quippe maior et peior est mors, quam ubi non moritur mors.*

25 In his autobiographical novel *A Portrait of the Artist as a Young Man* (London: Penguin Books, 2003), James Joyce portrays the extremes in Catholic poetry that revels in the infernal. In its pages, the post-mortem condition of those cast down is depicted as the epitome of darkness, stench, noise, self-hatred, the torment of fire, and despair in the face of infinity. The greatest agony lies in the idea of eternity as such, according to which, even after millions of years in the glowing mire, one has scarcely crossed the threshold to never-ending damnation; the priestly imagination does not neglect to emphasize that the penitents never get accustomed to their wretchedness in the blazing fire – they experience it forever as if just this moment they had plunged with vivid senses into the unbearable: "At the end of all those billions and trillions of years eternity would have scarcely begun" (142). And yet each individual moment, because of its intense unbearability, is itself like an eternity, thus creating an eternity from the unbearable perspective of its eternal immutability. Finally, the priest appeals to his young listeners (who are at that point having their first experiences with solitary unchastity), with the remark that he hopes there will not be any among them who will have the grievous experience that inevitably results from unrepented sin.

26 Thomas Macho, "Et exspecto," in *Das Leben ist ungerecht* (St. Pölten and Salzburg: Residenz Verlag, 2010): 65–88.

27 Adolf Harnack, *Militia Christi: The Christian Religion and the Military in the First Three Centuries*, trans. David McInnes Gracie (Philadelphia: Fortress Press, 1981): 55.

28 Ball, *Byzantinisches Christentum*: 17.

29 Ephrem the Syrian, *Des Heiligen Ephräm des Syrers ausgewählte*

Schriften, trans. and ed. Adolf Rücker and Otto Bardenhewer (Kempten: Verlag der Jos. Kösel, 1919): 96–100. On the pelican myth, see Louis Charbonneau-Lassey, *The Bestiary of Christ*, trans. and abridged D. M. Dooling (New York: Penguin, 1992): 258–66. The more than 1,000-page French original of the *Bestiaire du Christ: La mystérieuse emblématique de Jésus-Christ* was published by Desclée De Brouwer & Cie. in 1940.

30 Throughout his life, Karl Barth challenged infant baptism as a relapse of church ritual into mere custom (ultimately into heathen magic) and a prelude to ethno-religious enchantment. He did not forget: on the fronts of the First World War, the subject-objects of childhood baptism almost always shot at each other.

31 Ball, *Byzantinisches Christentum*: 18. The anchorites, on the other hand, are called "the athletes of despair."

32 For those suspected of heresy whose guilt was deemed probable, the Spanish Inquisition established its procedures on the principle that the suspect should never be informed of the precise nature of the accusation. The interrogations fostered a pseudo-intimate atmosphere in which delinquents would find it easier to remember sins and blasphemous remarks, whether or not they had really transgressed as they reported. If the state of the inquiry remained unsatisfactory, torture was applied. Those who summarily admitted everything under torture could gain nothing because the inquisitors were required to bring precise admissions to light. They applied the ordeal as a distressing investigation into the heretics' most hidden thoughts. Even after the ordeal, many of them still did not know what they should have said. During the interrogation, the inquisitors, sometimes well-trained psychologists, stood close behind the outstretched delinquents and fostered a mood favorable to confession with suggestive questions posed in a mild tone. If those who did not confess were condemned to death, they were given the opportunity, before the pyre was lit, to say what they had withheld. If they acknowledged and repented their heresy at the last minute (or if they correctly guessed what they were expected to confess), they received absolution; in which case, they were strangled, then burned, but with the assurance that they might avoid the eternal fires.

33 Aurelius Augustinus, *De vera religione. Über die wahre Religion*, ed. Wilhelm Thimme (Stuttgart: Reclam, 1983): 123.

34 See §36 of Martin Heidegger, *Being and Time*, trans. Joan Stambaugh (Albany: State University of New York Press, 2010): 166.

35 Matthias C. Müller, *Selbst und Raum: Eine raumtheoretische Grundlegung der Subjektivität* (Bielefeld: Transcript Verlag, 2017).

36 [Translator's note] Friedrich Nietzsche, *On the Genealogy of Morals*, "Third Essay: What Is the Meaning of Ascetic Ideals?" §11, in *Basic Writings of Nietzsche*, trans. and ed. Kaufmann: 553.

37 Hans Peter Duerr, *Die dunkle Nacht der Seele: Nahtod-Erfahrungen und Jenseitsreisen* (Berlin: Suhrkamp, 2015).

38 Arnold Gehlen, *Man: His Nature and Place in the World*, trans. Clare McMillan and Karl Pillemer (New York: Columbia University Press, 1987): 54–64. "Relief" as a figure of thought (suggesting an effort to spare oneself some effort, or as a release for spiritual or intellectual

activity) already underlay Ortega y Gasset's 1933 meditation on technology. See "Man the Technician," collected in José Ortega y Gasset, *History as a System and Other Essays toward a Philosophy of History*, trans. Helene Weyl (New York: W. W. Norton & Company, 1962): 87–164.

39 Jörg Traeger, *Renaissance und Religion: Die Kunst des Glaubens im Zeitalter Raphaels* (Munich: C. H. Beck, 1997).

40 Ariel Glucklich, *Sacred Pain: Hurting the Body for the Sake of the Soul* (Oxford University Press, 2001). Glucklich contests the thesis advanced by Elaine Scarry, in her well-known book *The Body in Pain: The Making and Unmaking of the World* (Oxford University Press, 1987). Scarry argues that those who are flooded by pain are delivered over to the self-referentiality of pain and become thereby "worldless." Glucklich grants that this description may indeed apply to examples from the experience of torture and war that Scarry favors. Glucklich, however, examines cases from the spiritual sphere to show that suffering can also be transitive: as a suffering-for and as an exemplary experience of pain – indeed, as a performance of higher agency or quality. In fact, experiences of pain in a spiritual and artistic context quite often bestow subjective states that provoke one's capacity for articulation; one might justifiably refer to pain as an unpredictable "semio-somatic force."

41 After an "inhabited" statue of Buddha, probably of Chinese origin, was examined in 2015 by CT scans and endoscopy in a clinic in Amersfoort, Netherlands, reports of "living Buddhas" can no longer be dismissed as legendary. In the given case, one is probably dealing not with a *sokushinbutsu* mummy, but with the approximately 1,000-year-old post-mortem mummification of a scholar, presumably made by his admirers.

42 René Fülöp-Miller, *The Mind and Face of Bolshevism: An Examination of Cultural Life in Soviet Russia* (New York: Harper & Row, 1965): 191.

18 Kerygma, propaganda, supply-side offense, or, when fiction is not to be trifled with

1 Giacomo Leopardi, "Dialogue between Fashion and Death," in *Essays and Dialogues of Giacomo Leopardi*, trans. Charles Edwardes (Boston: J. R. Osgood & Co., 1882): 22–3.

2 [Translator's note] Romans 13:14; Colossians 3:8–10. N.B. Paul was a tentmaker by trade.

3 Heiner Mühlmann, *Die Natur des Christentums* (Paderborn: Wilhelm Fink Verlag, 2017): 97; Heiner Mühlmann, "Die Ökonomiemaschine," in *5 Codes: Architektur, Paranoia und Risiko in Zeiten des Terrors*, ed. Igmade (Basel, Boston, and Berlin: Birkhäuser Verlag, 2006): 227.

4 1 Peter 5:8.

5 Reinhold Merkelbach, *Isis regina – Zeus Sarapis: Die griechisch-ägyptische Religion nach den Quellen dargestellt* (Stuttgart and Leipzig: Teubner Verlag, 1995).

6 In his book *Im Anfang war Johannes: Datierung und Theologie des vierten Evangeliums* (Stuttgart: Quell, 1997), the Heidelberg theologian Klaus Berger departs from the consensus to argue for the plausibility of

an earlier dating of John in 69 CE, not least because the evangelist made no mention of the siege of Jerusalem in August of 70 by the future emperor Titus (whereas in the Gospel of Mark one finds the allusion that not one stone of the temple will be left upon another – all will be thrown down). Berger's position would suggest that John wrote his spiritually demanding account, riven with anti-Jewish sentiment, in the midst of the First Jewish–Roman War – which seems unlikely, though not impossible of course (an author like Franz Rosenzweig, after all, could commit his *Star of Redemption* to paper, starting in August 1918, while serving on the Balkan front of the First World War). John's non-mention of the siege of Jerusalem might equally argue in favor of a later dating: by around the year 100 or 110 CE, the events of the First Jewish–Roman War could have become simply uninteresting for the pneumatic, anti-Jewish Hellenistic Christians of Alexandria, among whom the evangelist may have lived.

7 Matthew 26:36–45.
8 Hans Küng, *Christianity: Essence, History, and Future*, trans. John Bowden (New York: Continuum, 1995). Küng distinguished six historical "paradigm shifts" of Christianity, and these form the framework of orthopoetic activities conditioned by time and space. Anyone who falls into one of the aforementioned paradigms during their lifetime becomes an apprentice, journeyman, or master of the craft of being Christian in the context of their time.
9 For comparison: the population of ethnic and cultural Jews currently numbers at least 14.2 million people.
10 See Hermann Detering, "The Fabricated Paul: Early Christianity in the Twilight," trans. Darrell Doughty, in *The Journal of Higher Criticism* 10.2 (2003): 2–199.
11 John 1:11.
12 Galatians 3:28. Since being Greek, *eo ipso*, implied not being circumcised, Paul's addressees in his Epistle to the Galatians required a special explanation of why baptized Greeks did not need circumcision – and why, indeed, in borrowing this ritual, they would lapse from Christian freedom into slavery under the law. Slaves of the freedom under Christ are no longer in need of Jewish moral practice.

Paul subverted Greek usage by appropriating the word *ekklesia* – which means the popular assembly of the *polis* – for the Christian community and declaring it, in a decidedly political-antipolitical way, as the epitome of the community in the "house of God" (*oikos tou theou*). The differences between slaves and free, Greeks and Jews, women and men are not only voided by the brevity of the time remaining, they are also rescinded as a result of the egalitarian incorporation of all the baptized into the suggestively–subversively redefined *ekklesia*: "Church" constitutes the epitome of "free slaves" (*douloi*) under God's house rule. This also remains in effect because, with baptism, the adoption of the subject as a child of God takes place. The *ekklesia*, as an assembly of the slaves of Christ and the children of God, can only have been composed as theocratic and as subject to the master of the house.

In the twentieth century, anti-liberal, anti-pluralist, anti-modernist theologians (e.g., Dietrich Bonhoeffer, Emanuel Hirsch) make recourse to intuitions of this tendency, when they want to assign to the church the special role of a primordial community, a *sanctorum communio* effected by the spirit.

13 1 Corinthians 7:31.

14 Stalin's remarks on linguistics appeared as replies to questions that had been posed to him by Soviet students; they were published in the *Pravda* newspaper in 1950: Joseph Stalin, *Marxism and Problems of Linguistics* (Honolulu, Hawaii: University Press of the Pacific, 2002).

15 Adolf Harnack, *Militia Christi: The Christian Religion and the Military in the First Three Centuries*, trans. David McInnes Gracie (Philadelphia: Fortress Press, 1981).

16 Bart D. Ehrman broaches some of these in his popular book *Misquoting Jesus: The Story Behind Who Changed the Bible and Why* (New York: HarperCollins, 2005), an *opusculum* that enjoyed many weeks on the *New York Times* bestseller list.

17 Christoph Luxenberg, *The Syro-Aramaic Reading of the Koran: A Contribution to the Decoding of the Language of the Koran* (Berlin: Verlag Hans Schiler, 2007).

18 The emphasis on subsequent generations applies all the more pertinently to the twentieth century, in which statistical Islam experienced an eightfold growth in its adherents due to its extreme natural increase (from around 150 million to over a billion – and, a decade and a half into the twenty-first century, up to more than 1.5 billion) – a development that can be better grasped with demographic and geopolitical analysis, social psychology, and feminist criticism than with theological arguments. Apart from that, the predominance of statistical Christianity in the world today is likewise also largely a demography-driven effect: between 1910 and 2010, the number of Christians increased from 600 million to 2.2 billion – without this being primarily attributable to the activity of Christian missions. New Muslims and Christians are everywhere more likely to emerge in birthing beds than in missionary tents.

Be that as it may, the efficacy of the missions should not be minimized either. In Sub-Saharan Africa, the number of Christians rose from 10 million in 1900 to 350 million at the turn of the twenty-first century. The alliance of bed and school in the present era has been less well studied – by far – than the alliance of throne and altar in the period from the early Middle Ages to the First World War.

When Florence Nightingale (1820–1910) went to school in Hampshire, when she wasn't being homeschooled by her father, she found joy in solving word problems like this in her math exercise books: suppose there are 600 million pagans in the world, how many missionaries does it take if 1 missionary is needed for 20,000 pagans?

19 Ruth A. Tucker, *From Jerusalem to Irian Jaya: A Biographical History of Christian Missions*, 2nd edn. (Grand Rapids: Zondervan, 2004): 25.

20 In his short dialogue from 1774, "Conversation of a Philosopher with the Maréchale de —," Denis Diderot's philosopher reported a conversation with a pious and principled lady who said that it was out of deference to fashion or custom that she allowed her beautiful bust to excite the admiration of men other than her husband – "as

if," the philosopher commented to the maréchale, "nothing was more customary than to call oneself Christian and yet not to be so."

21 Matthew 23:8–9.

22 Formulated with exemplary ambiguity in Paul's Epistle to the Ephesians 6:14–17: "Stand therefore, and fasten the belt of truth around your waist, and put on the breastplate of righteousness. As shoes for your feet put on whatever will make you ready to proclaim the gospel of peace. With all of these, take the shield of faith, with which you will be able to quench all the flaming arrows of the evil one. Take the helmet of salvation, and the sword of the Spirit, which is the word of God."

23 [Translator's note] Religions of supply: where the terms of what is on offer (the revelation of God) are dictated by church authorities or by sources still higher, rather than conforming to the demands of the common people in the manner of the modern marketplace. See Peter Sloterdijk, *You Must Change Your Life: On Anthropotechnics*, trans. Wieland Hoban (Cambridge: Polity, 2013): 84–5.

24 This was not, one might observe, a matter of senile gloom: Augustine was 43 years old when he formulated his merciless theology of mercy in 397 CE. See "Miscellany of Questions in Response to Simplician," in Augustine of Hippo, *Responses to Miscellaneous Questions*, trans. and ed. Boniface Ramsey (Hyde Park: New City Press, 2008): 169–231.

25 John 15:22 and 15:24.

26 Matthew 12:31–2.

27 Gilles Deleuze, "Nietzsche and Saint Paul, Lawrence and John of Patmos," in *Paul and the Philosophers*, ed. Ward Blanton and Hent de Vries (Fordham University Press, 2013): 381–94.

28 The Book of Mormon was published in 1830.

29 Romans 10:13–15.

30 See Niklas Luhmann, "4. Die Ausdifferenzierung der Religion," in *Gesellschaftsstruktur und Semantik: Studien zur Wissenssoziologie der modernen Gesellschaft*, Vol. III (Frankfurt: Suhrkamp, 1989).

31 The most explicit transfer of non-Christians to the Christian hell is found with Lactantius (c. 250–c. 325), a North African convert of Berber origin, who in the last years of his life was a client of Constantine the Great, who from 317 onward entrusted him as tutor to his son Crispus. In Lactantius's work *De mortibus persecutorum* (On the Deaths of the Persecutors), which was widely read in the Middle Ages, the author fantasized with palpable pleasure on the theme of the everlasting fire to which the anti-Christian Caesars were committed after their deaths. His compatriot Tertullian had already urged the postulate of eternal fire around 200 CE.

It is not hard to explain why, by the sixth century at the latest, the great majority of bishops accepted the theologically and psychopolitically founded systemic indispensability of eternal hell. When the Second Council of Constantinople, in 553 CE, finally anathemized the doctrine attributed to Origen on the restoration of all things with God (*apokatastasis panton*), this expressed a defense of hell against the subversive metaphysics of the happy end of all things. This doctrine was effectively subversive insofar as it infringed upon the phobocratic foundations of ecclesiastical authority over souls and the legal safeguarding of oaths.

32 Hence the Apocalypse of Peter, discovered in 1887 in Akhmim, Egypt; cf. also *The Passion of Saints Perpetua and Felicity*, edited in Carthage sometime after 203 CE.

33 Tertullian's *Apologeticus* (197 CE) hints at this when, in §32, the author claims that Christians, far from being a threat to public order, in fact prayed for the emperors, for the peace of the empire, and for the postponement of the impending end (*pro mora finis*).

34 Quoted from Michel de Certeau, *The Mystical Fable*, Vol. I: *The Sixteenth and Seventeenth Centuries*, trans. Michael B. Smith (University of Chicago Press, 1995): 166.

35 Ryan S. Schellenberg, "Danger in the Wilderness, Danger at Sea: Paul and the Perils of Travel," in *Travel and Religion in Antiquity*, ed. Philip A. Harland (Waterloo, Ont.: Wilfred Laurier University Press, 2011): 141–61.

36 Gunnar Heinsohn, *Söhne und Weltmacht. Terror im Aufstieg und Fall der Nationen* (Zurich: Orell Füssli Verlag, 2003).

37 Francis Xavier's arm is also discussed above, in Chapter 3.

38 "A Fond Note on Myth," in Paul Valéry, *The Outlook for Intelligence*, trans. Denise Folliot and Jackson Mathews (Princeton University Press, 1989): 44.

39 Edward Bernays, *Propaganda* (Brooklyn: Ig Publishing, 2005).

40 Cotton Mather, *Magnalia Christi Americana or The Ecclesiastical History of New-England, from its First Planting in the Year 1620, unto the Year of Our Lord 1698* (London, 1702). The 1820 edition was preceded by the quasi-Virgilian motto, *Tanti Molis erat, per CHRISTO condere gentem*: So much labor did it cost to establish a people for Christ. Mather's ecclesiastical history of New England reads like a modern replica of the history books of the Hebrew Bible, in which God continually makes history through those who belong to him. Nothing happens on the soil of the new colonies that cannot be read as a sign of "His gracious presence" over the American people as the second Israel.

41 Romans 10:15.

42 Karl Jaspers, *The Question of German Guilt*, trans. E. B. Ashton (Fordham University Press, 2001): 26.

19 On the prose and poetry of the search

1 See Tertullian, "On the Veiling of Virgins," in *The Ante-Nicene Fathers: The Writings of the Fathers Down to A.D. 325*, Vol. IV, ed. Alexander Roberts and James Donaldson (New York: Charles Scribner's Sons, 1926): 27.

2 "A Fond Note on Myth," in Paul Valéry, *The Outlook for Intelligence*, trans. Denise Folliot and Jackson Mathews (Princeton University Press, 1989): 44.

3 See ch. 14 in Samuel Taylor Coleridge, *Biographia literaria*, ed. James Engell and W. Jackson Bate (Princeton University Press, 1983).

4 The expression "the pooling runoff of peoples" (*colluvies gentium*) goes back to the German researcher C. F. P. von Martius, who toured South America between 1817 and 1820. He used it to designate new tribal

formations through fortuitous amalgamations of small migrant groups in Brazil. The term was taken up by Wilhelm E. Mühlmann in his investigations into mechanisms of the "emergence of peoples from their refuges" with heterogeneous ethnic sources. See "Colluvies gentium: Volksentstehung aus Asylen," in Wilhelm Emil Mühlmann, *Homo Creator: Abhandlungen zur Soziologie, Anthropologie und Ethnologie* (Wiesbaden: Otto Harrassowitz, 1962): 303–10.

5 Hans G. Helms, *Die Ideologie der anonymen Gesellschaft: Max Stirners "Einziger" und der Fortschritt des demokratischen Selbstbewußtseins vom Vormärz bis zur Bundesrepublik* (Cologne: Verlag Du Mont Schauberg, 1966).

6 Pew Research Center, "The Changing Global Religious Landscape" (April 5, 2017): 8–10: https://assets.pewresearch.org/wpcontent/uploads/sites/11/2017/04/07092755/FULL-REPORT-WITH-APPENDIXES-A-AND-B-APRIL-3.pdf.

7 See Chapter 16 above.

8 That the concept of purgatorial fires was just about to reach its prime years – from the point of view of the visual arts at least – is argued and elaborated in Christine Göttler, *Die Kunst des Fegefeuers nach der Reformatio: Kirchliche Schenkungen, Ablaß und Almosen in Antwerpen und Bologna um 1600* (Mainz: Verlag Philipp von Zabern, 1996).

9 Raymond Schwab, *La renaissance orientale* (Paris: Payot, 1950).

10 [Translator's note] Martin Buber, *Ecstatic Confessions: The Heart of Mysticism*, trans. Esther Cameron, ed. Paul Mendes-Flohr (San Francisco: Harper & Row, 1985): 11. In 1993, Peter Sloterdijk was himself the editor of a German edition of this collection.

11 Joseph Campbell, *The Hero with a Thousand Faces*, 3rd edn. (Novato, CA: New World Library, 2008); for the legend "The Four Signs," see 46–8.

12 In this way, it also forms the individual equivalent to Christian historical time, which is defined by the tension of Judgment ever postponed, and the ever growing distension of the zone of the next-to-last.

13 Philip A. Harland, "Journeys in Pursuit of Divine Wisdom: Thessalos and Other Seekers," in *Travel and Religion in Antiquity*, ed. Philip A. Harland (Waterloo, Ont.: Wilfred Laurier University Press, 2011): 123–40.

14 On ambiguities of the Actaeon myth in classical and modern literature, see Wolfgang Cziesla, *Aktaion Polyprágmon: Variationen eines antiken Themas in der europäischen Renaissance* (Frankfurt am Main: Peter Lang Verlag, 1990); for discussion of Giordano Bruno, see especially 89–111.

15 Walker Percy, *The Moviegoer* (New York: Vintage International, 1998): 145–6.

20 Freedom of religion

1 Jean-Paul Sartre, "A New Mystic: On Bataille's *Inner Experience*," in *We Have Only This Life to Live: The Selected Essays of Jean-Paul Sartre, 1939–1975*, ed. Ronald Aronson and Adrian Van den Hoven (New York Review Books, 2013): 55.

2 Paul Alsberg, *In Quest of Man: A Biological Approach to the Problem of Man's Place in Nature* (Oxford: Pergamon, 1970).

3 It follows from this that, in 2001, Greece should not have been admitted to the Economic and Monetary Union of the European Union (due to its unsatisfactory budget situation, which was concealed with the intention of fraud), but, more than this, also not to the European Economic Community in 1981 because of its constitution's confused religious law.

4 Robert N. Bellah formulated the exception in this problem area by applying Rousseau's term "civil religion" to the situation in the United States – to our knowledge, the only country in which the expression "civil religion" had a constructive meaning, insofar as it articulated the pre-political consent of participants in a new covenant, a new federation, of metanational construction.

Some 250 years after its founding, the United States finds itself in a state of regression into a quasi-primary (white, Anglo-Saxon) nationality (notwithstanding continuing metanational surpluses) and also civil-religious decline (in the face of evangelical-fascist escalations).

5 In the papal encyclical *Quanta cura* (1864), Pope Pius IX condemned both the idea of religious freedom and the separation of Church and State, and recalled that his predecessor, Pope Gregory XVI (in office from 1831 to 1846), had dismissed the idea of religious freedom as an "insanity." Pius IX deplored modern attacks on the fellowship between Church and State, which, he said, had ever proved itself propitious and salutary, and he condemned the "machinations" of "naturalism," as well as the heresies of those who impugn the divinity of Christ with such "wicked pertinacity."

6 Hans Ulrich Gumbrecht, *Crowds: The Stadium as a Ritual of Intensity*, trans. Emily Goodling (Stanford University Press, 2021).

7 Yann-Pierre Montelle, *Paleoperformance: The Emergence of Theatricality as Social Practice* (London: Seagull Books, 2009).

In lieu of an afterword

1 [Translator's note] Friedrich Nietzsche, "Preludes of Science" §300, in *The Gay Science*, trans. Walter Kaufmann (New York: Vintage Books, 1974): 240.

2 [Translator's note] Ibid., 240–1.

3 [Translator's note] Franz Kafka, "Prometheus," trans. Willa and Edwin Muir, in *Collected Stories*, ed. Gabriel Josipovici (New York: Alfred A. Knopf, 1993): 399–400.

.